This absorbing new book by Melissa Everett is a real page-turner—full of noble excitement. It tells us stories we need to hear for our sanity and self-esteem and solidarity as a people. It reminds us that there are quiet, dogged heroes in our time and in our midst, who put the collective good above personal gain, and that you don't have to be a superman or a saint to do that.

—*Joanna Macy*

Among today's unsung heroes are those few courageous persons who, deeply embedded in the military-industrial complex, have succeeded in breaking out of their thralldoms. Their stories, skillfully edited, vividly presented, and enriched by a thoughtful and illuminating commentary, provide inspiring examples that will encourage others to contribute in their own ways toward diverting the world from its suicidal course. I wish that all those actively or passively participating in humanity's race toward nuclear destruction would read this book.

—*Jerome Frank*

To Steven Ross McMillin
1947–1986
presente

BREAKING RANKS

Melissa Everett

NEW SOCIETY PUBLISHERS

Philadelphia, PA   Santa Cruz, CA

Inquiries regarding requests to reprint all or part of *Breaking Ranks* should be
addressed to:

New Society Publishers
4527 Springfield Avenue
Philadelphia, PA 19143

ISBN 0-86571-134-8 Hardcover
0-86571-135-6 Paperback

Printed in the United States of America on partially recycled paper

Cover design by Brian Prendergast
Book design by Tina Birky

To order directly from the publisher, add $1.75 to the price for the first copy, 50¢
each additional. Send check or money order to:

New Society Publishers
PO Box 582
Santa Cruz, CA 95061

New Society Publishers is a project of the New Society Educational Foundation, a
nonprofit, tax-exempt, public foundation. Opinions expressed in this book do not
necessarily represent positions of the New Society Educational Foundation.

ACKNOWLEDGMENTS

This book would not exist without the generous support of many friends, sources, funders, and critics. First and most heartfelt thanks go to the subjects who were willing to dredge up difficult memories, wrestle anew with some of the hardest questions of their lives, and do so under the gaze of a supportive but not always relaxing interviewer. Those whose stories were selected for publication deserve added thanks for their willingness to make their private conflicts public. The many others who shared their stories also live in these pages, by way of their contribution to my understanding of issues to be addressed and questions to be asked.

I found a few of these subjects through typical channels, such as author's queries and reading the news. But most of them came into my life through phone calls or clippings from friends and strangers who had heard of this project. The structure and content likewise benefited greatly from the interest of colleagues and friends who reviewed sections, suggested references, and at times conveyed through their eloquent silences that I hadn't quite "gotten it" yet. Valuable feedback and moral support came from Jerome Frank, Rachel Findley, Richard Fogg, Bill Torcaso, Glenn Morrow, Josephine Stein, Joanne Sunshower, Ruth Linden, Walter Carrington, Rebecca King, Eleanor Matthews, Pam Walker, Deborah Rosenthal, Robin Knowlton, Steve Bentley, Marie Cantlon, Sandra Diener, and my family. Glenn Morrow deserves special thanks for coming up with the title.

The tedious yet creative work of transcribing taped interviews—many of them less than perfect in sound quality—was done expertly by Elizabeth McClenahan, Blaise Lupo, Gladys Everett, and Katie Garate.

My interviews with Lou Raymond were supplemented by transcripts generously shared by Lou Buttino, whose National Public Radio documentary, "Choices of the Heart," also probes the conscience struggles of weapons workers. Excerpts from *Deadly Deceits* by Ralph McGehee are reprinted here courtesy of Sheridan Square Publications, Inc.

While this project was an idea in search of a sponsor, a number of private supporters and foundations kept it—and the writer—alive: the Cambridge Institute for Societal Learning, the Interreligious Foundation for Community Organization, Eddie Frazer, Carol and William Ferry, John Lamperti, Brian and Nancy Emond, Nancy Moorehead, Reverend Lucius Walker, Michael Kurjan, Paul and Selma Seto, Myra Schwartz, Barry Feldman, Steven Kropper, Stephen Woolley and Rebecca Stockdale-Woolley, Lynn McWhood, Phil O'Neil, Patti Lanich, and Melissa Wenig. Stony Point Center in Stony Point, New York generously housed, fed, and encouraged me during the early months of research.

T.L. Hill, my editor at New Society Publishers, has perfected the combination of carrots and sticks necessary to keep the prose flowing and the relationship friendly. His belief in this effort from the beginning has kept my enthusiasm high.

It is customary for authors to thank the purveyors of the comforts and vices which have kept them functioning in the manner to which they have rightly or wrongly become accustomed. In that spirit I thank the staff of the Crescent Wench bakery and cafe for letting me loiter at the window table for half-day stretches and for saying nice things when I came in frazzled.

My greatest and most personal thanks go to the friends and family who have put up with my messianic excesses during the research and writing of this book. You know who you are.

When I was twelve, in 1965, I entered an American Legion essay contest. The topic was "America's Role in Preserving the Peace." I wrote about all the little countries the United States was helping to resist communism by our military backing: Brazil, the Dominican Republic, the Philippines, Vietnam. I wrote about the boatloads of rice and seeds and schoolbooks we sent abroad so the people of the developing world could be stronger and could create strong democratic institutions. I wrote about the atomic bomb and the way it protected our allies from being pushed around.

I cribbed it all out of the encyclopedia, with a little help from my father.

I won second prize and got to read the essay at an awards banquet.

When I was thirteen, my best friend passed me a note in the hallway between English and gym. On it was a free verse poem, lettered very carefully in turquoise ink.

The poem was written in the voice of a child in Vietnam who had just seen her parents killed by napalm.

The napalm came from the Americans.

I said, "What's Vietnam?" Whatever I had learned the year before had been washed away by hormones and diet cola. But my awareness of the larger world was restored, and my curiosity awakened, by a voice of moral outrage coming from someone I knew and trusted.

I started protesting against the Vietnam War in high school on the basis of lessons that began when I read that poem. Most of the years since then, I have been involved in some campaign or other against abuses of power. I demonstrated and took part in educational programs against the nuclear reactor in Seabrook, New Hampshire, an hour's drive from my home. When draft registration was reinstated in 1980, I was on the picket lines and also studied to become a volunteer draft counselor. When the current generation of nuclear missiles was placed in Europe in the early 1980s, I sat in and spoke out because, like many, I was concerned about the first-strike potential of Pershing and cruise missiles. When friends began coming back from Central America sun-tanned and fired up about the differences between the Nicaraguan revolution they saw and the one portrayed by the Reagan administration, I went to see for myself and published *Bearing Witness, Building Bridges: Interviews with North Americans Living and Working in Nicaragua*.

The closer I got, the more complex the issues seemed. But while many of my activist friends were pulling back from involvement in these movements because they found the complexity daunting, I was drawn in. I left my first career as a computer programmer in 1979 and have spent the years since then writing. I have tried to develop a blend of journalism and oral history that brings questions of peace and justice alive for the nonspecialist by approaching them through individual human stories.

Along the way, I have had to rethink, refine, and defend my own positions, moderate the ideological rigidity I can now look back on with embarrassment, and realize that "the other side" is made up of human beings too. For years, I assumed that to protest government programs and to hold some genuinely "counterculture" values—such as the idea that it's okay not to get rich—meant to live as an outsider, to be misunderstood, to be angry a lot. Then I began to hear very "mainstream" voices—retired NATO generals, respected scientists—stating, in the most patriotic of terms, that our overreliance on military might was no better for us than it was for the global balance. They gave me a sense of legitimacy and helped me break free of the myth that defending the status quo equals "objectivity" while challenging it means "bias."

The stories in these pages are about people who believe, as I do, that the United States has strayed from the Jeffersonian ideal because our international relations are based too much on projection of power and too little on visions of common security. They are about folks who see this situation as possible only when we, the people, have not done our homework (or have cribbed it from the encyclopedia). They are about people's discovery that they—all of us—have great, unrecognized power, and can enhance our own lives and security by exercising it.

CONTENTS

War will exist until that distant day when the conscientious objector enjoys the same reputation and prestige that the warrior does today.
—John F. Kennedy

INTRODUCTION

> The challenge to humans in our time is whether they can become
> aroused not just over small but over large dangers, whether they can
> perceive universal problems as well as personal ones, whether they
> can become as concerned over their survival as a species as they are
> over their jobs.
> —Norman Cousins, *Human Options*

> What do you mean, do I know why there were Nazis? I don't even
> know what's wrong with the can opener.
> —Woody Allen, *Hannah and Her Sisters*

This book is about heroes, although most of them would protest to
hear themselves so described. They are people who have become so
concerned over global issues that they have quit jobs, challenged
employers, given up high honors, jeopardized personal security and
family relations, burned bridges, and risked ridicule. They are squeaky
wheels and misfits in the noblest American tradition, and they have
devoted themselves to fighting another American tradition: our zeal,
often denied but more often demonstrated, to go to war. These people
have emerged from careers in the military, the weapons industries, the
intelligence community, and elsewhere in the foreign policy
establishment to challenge government actions and policies—including
the nuclear arms race, intervention in developing countries, the use of
covert operations to carry out politically unpopular policies, and the
unchecked power of the military and the industries that support it—
which they think make us less secure and less respected in the
international community. Their views vary, but they each ground their
challenges in the deeper values—democracy, justice, tolerance, love
of peace—in which we as a nation say we believe.

1

Bill Perry joined the staff of Lawrence Livermore National Laboratory in 1980 as director of public relations, thinking he was promoting a great hall of science. He resigned a year later over the lab's role in nuclear weapons research and soon emerged as chair of the Marin County Nuclear Freeze Campaign.

Charlie Liteky, as a Catholic chaplain, won the Congressional Medal of Honor for bravery in Vietnam. With obvious sorrow, he renounced the medal in 1986 to protest "another Vietnam" in Central America and went on to risk his life by fasting for forty-seven days to galvanize the movement against military intervention in Central America.

Thomas Grissom, a physicist described by his boss at Sandia National Laboratory as "the most promising I've ever hired," resigned in protest from his $75,000-a-year job running a group which designs nuclear weapons triggers. Now, for half the pay but twice the satisfaction, he teaches science at an experimental college that stresses human values and broad vision. He does so with the hope of helping the next generation of scientists turn their talents away from technologies of violence.

David MacMichael, a CIA analyst, challenged the Reagan administration's portrait of Nicaragua as an exporter of revolution and found himself unemployed as a result. After considerable private struggle, he went public with his challenge in the New York Times in 1984. He went on to testify on behalf of Nicaragua in its lawsuit against the United States at the International Court of Justice, and to devote himself to exposing the deceptions and illegalities behind the contra support network.

Daniel Cobos, an airborne translator for the Strategic Air Command, says he flew regular reconnaissance missions in support of the contras in violation of the Boland amendment. In 1987, he won an extended battle with the air force by receiving an honorable discharge as a conscientious objector.

David Parnas, a computer scientist and long-time consultant to the Naval Research Laboratory who was a member of a blue-ribbon advisory panel for the Star Wars program, resigned to protest what he believed was "a fraud" by scientists interested only in research funds. Parnas went on to address, in speeches and articles, the technical and political problems of space-based defense and the deeper issues of reliance on technical fixes to human conflicts.

Jerry Genesio, a proud cold warrior in the 1950s Marine Corps, changed his views after his brother's death in Vietnam and his own visit to Central America. In 1985, he helped to found and direct a visionary new organization called Veterans for Peace.

Ralph McGehee was recruited by the CIA in 1952 to participate in what he saw as a holy war against world communism. But in the course of twenty-five years of service in Southeast Asia and Langley, Virginia, he came to believe he was working for no less than "the covert action arm of the presidency." Now in retirement, he works full time for the abolition of CIA covert operations.

Lou Raymond was supervisor of the salvage yard at General Dynamics' Quonset Point, Rhode Island plant. Looking into the hull of the massive Trident II submarine, the company's main product, Raymond felt the first tensions between his Catholic faith and his source of income. After several years of struggle, he quit in protest and went into business building houses. He also helped start an interfaith group called Exodus, which provides support for workers in weapons industries who are experiencing ethical conflict.

As a foreign service officer, John Graham was a self-described "soldier of fortune." He participated in the CORDS counterinsurgency program in Vietnam and in NATO planning sessions for deployment of the neutron bomb in Europe. Pushed to clarify his values during a near-death experience on a burning cruise ship, he now runs the Giraffe Project to empower people to "stick their necks out" for the common good.

While their journeys, backgrounds, and conclusions about US foreign policy are very different, these men share important common ground. Each was a cold warrior who worked in support of nuclear deterrence and interventionist policies in the Third World, and each now believes those strategies and the worldviews underlying them are mistaken, counterproductive, and dangerous. In their initial career choices, these men were motivated by a combination of grand ideals and everyday self-interest. They lived apparently coherent, often comfortable lives and found satisfaction in their work. But under the surface, something came unglued. Along paths characterized by many stumbles and a few transformational moments, they have searched for new ways to live—and lead others—in harmony with their new values.

A few have become principled pacifists, but most simply have taken stands against what they see as excessive or misapplied force, inhumane or ineffective tactics, ill-informed or dangerous policies, to restore integrity to a system of military defense they still see as legitimate. They all have taken personally what Sir Hartley Shawcross said at Nuremberg: "There comes a point where a man [*sic*] must refuse to answer to his leader if he is also to answer to his conscience." By decisively ending their own contributions to the problems they perceived and by finding coherent ways to work toward alternatives, they have honored that voice of conscience. They have found the courage to be self-critical, to abandon familiar positions, and to make changes in the ways they live, not only when the payoff is clear, but also in those more common situations when nothing is clear except the need for change.

These people struggled, often in isolation, with a vague but mounting awareness that their beliefs didn't really explain the world they lived in. They wanted very much to keep believing in the institutions on which they relied for paychecks, self-esteem, and self-definition. But questions kept arising, and ultimately they had to choose between loyalty to the received wisdom and commitment to the truth as they saw it.

Following the truth they perceived led these men to question the institutions they came of age in, worked for, and trusted. That in itself is difficult enough. But in turn those questions led to deeper ones—"How did I get here in the first place? What is motivating me to stay? How do I handle changes in my life?"—whose answers are connected to what it means to be a man in the United States. Men constitute more than 99 percent of the top echelons of the armed services, weapons industries, intelligence agencies, and executive branch of government. "Wars will cease when men refuse to fight—and women refuse to approve," Jessie Wallace Hughan, founder of the War Resisters League, said half a century ago.[1] And so, although women are closer now to the fighting role, this book is about men. It is about the ways in which their upbringing and expectations have influenced both their initial choices of profession and their ability to question and change.

The quintessential historical example of this kind of turnabout is that of Major General Smedley Darlington Butler, one of only four two-time recipient of the Congressional Medal of Honor. A crusty veteran who led military operations in Latin America and the Caribbean in the early twentieth century, Butler astonished the audience at an American Legion dinner held in his honor in 1931 by saying, "I was a racketeer for Wall Street. I made Mexico, and especially Tampico, safe for the oil companies . . . I helped purify Nicaragua for the international banking house of Brown Brothers . . . I could have taught Al Capone a few lessons. He ran rackets in three cities. But the Marine Corps operates on three continents."[2]

Butler was not antimilitary and could not be called soft on much of anything, but he concluded from his experiences on the battlefield and with his superiors that "we must give up the Prussian ideal—carrying on offensive warfare and imposing our wills upon other people in distant places. Such doctrine is un-American and vicious . . . There must be no more reactionary and destructive intelligence work. The true domestic enemies of our nation—hunger, injustice and exploitation—should concern the military intelligence, not the subversive shadows of their own creation . . . "[3]

Butler is such an appealing historic figure because his zest for combat was tied to a zest for living and a reverence for life. These made him a soldier who was willing to avoid an ill-conceived battle for the same reasons he was eager to fight a just one. In this, he was far from unique. Most of the blunders the United States has made since Butler's time have given rise to similar dissident voices, still alive and ringing with urgency, warning us against repeating their mistakes. Bill Gandall, who as a young marine participated in the US invasion of Nicaragua in 1928, travels around the country at the age of 92 with the message that today's Sandinistas are as entrenched, and in his view as legitimate, as the original Sandino. George Zabelka, the chaplain who blessed the Enola Gay's crew before the first atomic bombing, crisscrosses the country to describe his horror at laying eyes on the wounded children of Hiroshima. Phillip Roettinger, who as a marine and CIA officer helped coordinate the CIA-backed coup against Guatemala in 1954, now lobbies full time against CIA covert operations as ineffective and despicable.

The premise of this book is that Smedley Butler was right, and that his modern counterparts are a source of great untapped wisdom about the factors which predispose the post–World War II United States to address its problems militarily, and about what it will take to reverse that trend. Of course, social change is much more complicated than the individual changes of heart and mind that contribute to it. But the actions of dissenters like these have been major catalysts for the peace movement. Among the most sensational modern examples are the role of antiwar veterans and Daniel Ellsberg's release of the Pentagon Papers in bringing the Vietnam War to a halt. But there are many others.

—Former weapons scientists have been a driving force behind the *Bulletin of Atomic Scientists,* the Federation of American Scientists, the Union of Concerned Scientists, and numerous other lobbies and publications opposed to the nuclear arms race. In recent years, a pledge not to accept Star Wars research funds was signed by over twelve thousand scientists and engineers and became a major vehicle for organizing opposition to the Strategic Defense Initiative.

—Former air force pilot Howard Morland's article, "The H-Bomb Secret," in *The Progressive* and his subsequent book, *The Secret That Exploded,* challenged the cult of secrecy around nuclear weapons by showing that the real keys to their manufacture are easy to find in publicly available sources.

—Dr. Charles Clements, a Vietnam-era pilot turned doctor who spent many months practicing medicine in a guerilla-controlled zone in El Salvador, brought back eyewitness information on that country which contradicted the Reagan administration's claims that democracy was blooming. Through the book and Academy Award–winning film *Witness to War*, his was one of the first voices of concern on Central America to reach a mass audience.

—Bob Aldridge, an engineer at Lockheed, figured out from design considerations that the submarine-launched ballistic missiles he was developing could be targeted so precisely that they must be meant for hardened missile silos. His book *First Strike!* and subsequent testimonies and articles helped to demonstrate that nuclear war planners have been pushing for first-strike capability since the late 1970s.

—The operations of the CIA in Southeast Asia, Angola, Latin America, and the United States have been copiously documented by former agents and analysts who came forward, sometimes at the cost of income and years of legal battles. Examples include Philip Agee and Victor Marchetti, whose numerous books analyze patterns of deception and illegality by the CIA; John Stockwell, whose *In Search of Enemies* documents the agency's involvement in Angola; Frank Snepp, whose less radical but still informative *Decent Interval* focuses on agency and military activities in the waning days of the Vietnam War; Phillip Roettinger, who was involved in the CIA's orchestration of the Guatemalan coup in 1954 and who draws parallels between that operation and the current contra war; and Ralph McGehee and David MacMichael, whose stories are told in these pages.

The inside perspective of such dissenters gives them two strengths: credibility and a subtle understanding of these institutions and the people who work in them. And these insights are far from uniformly negative. When the more strident voices in the peace movement vilify their former colleagues, they are in a unique position to remind us that weapons are made and wars are fought by three-dimensional human beings who love and worry and grow. They also remind us that while the military-industrial complex is far from passive in its courting of economic opportunity, it ultimately keeps growing because we all keep feeding it. Their insights and the strategies they develop as activists are illuminating for anyone else who wants to make a difference.

To make a difference. In some respects, these are stories of people who gave up status and influence, who became downwardly mobile. Many handed over security clearances, said goodbye to secretaries and travel budgets, sacrificed titles and prestige. But they did so because they decided that their sense of power on the inside was illusory. They looked for and found empowerment in unorthodox, creative ways: either working directly for social change, or choosing work such as teaching or counseling that can help build the world they want to live in.

The changes undergone by these men are different from, and deeper than, the mood swings from hawk to dove that many of us go through as we and circumstances evolve. Many of them started out as self-described conservatives; in the course of their realignments on issues of war and peace, some have found a deeper, more authentic conservatism, an affirmation of something in this nation and culture that they care about conserving with integrity.

These changes involve thinking differently—in different modes, not just having different ideas. They do not mean abandoning one side's propaganda only to adopt another's. They mean learning to think critically and to live deliberately, even when doing so challenges accepted authority. These people do not look for trouble, but they do cope with it when it results from thinking for themselves.

And trouble does come to many of them, as it does to others who question authority. Dr. Donald Soeken is a psychiatric social worker specializing in the treatment of "whistleblowers"—people who expose offenses like cost overruns, illegal waste dumping, or sexual harassment in government and industry. He surveyed ninety-eight whistleblowers and concluded that they get "pummelled" psychologically and economically. Every survey respondent who had worked in the private sector had been fired, and many in government had had to fight to keep their jobs. The pay for their risk taking included harassment by peers and supervisors, sleep loss, weight gain, depression, and anxiety. Many were shocked that the friendly, apparently caring people they worked with day after day could not even begin to appreciate the ethical basis of their actions. But despite the trauma, a vast majority of these whistleblowers said they would do the same thing again. Their actions made them feel better about themselves and often helped to correct the patterns of abuse they had reported.[4]

The men in this book did not merely challenge the methods employed in getting the job done; they ended up challenging the premises of the job itself. They too were pummelled, but they survived—and more. They are what Gail Sheehy calls "pathfinders," people who have weathered major crises and emerged stronger, who have managed to find in their crises a source of greater understanding and richer lives.

There is much debate in social science research about how one gathers a "true" life story. Is it better to stand back, treating the story as fixed and independent, or to interact with the storyteller to pull on the threads of memory, tease out new connections, suggest new interpretations? This book is very much based on the latter philosophy, known by sociologists as the "life history" method, which as Gelya Frank writes, "blends together the consciousness of the investigator and the subject, perhaps to the point where it is not possible to disentangle them."[5]

These studies are based primarily on the subjects' own memories, with all the rich self-reflection and all the danger of bias which that implies. The purpose here is to learn how these individuals see events unfolding, how they chart the evolution of their critical perspectives, what turning points stand out in their memories. My interviews with these men were sometimes confrontational but mostly informational and evocative: "How did you decide what to believe? Were you angry? What made you pay attention to that new wrinkle? What about this criticism of your work? How does your life feel different as a result of these new changes?"

Even when the life in question is relatively free of controversy, the approach is emotionally charged. When the topic touches some of the major controversies of the era, the question of method looms even larger. This book is an exercise in what Robert Jay Lifton calls "advocacy research," an activist's inquiry into the lives and testimonies of a particularly interesting group of dissidents who have had to struggle to be heard and who arguably still have not received the hearing which their claims and experiences merit. My goal in these pages has been to maintain what Lifton calls "disciplined subjectivity."[6] The reader who is still struggling for a place to stand on these issues will find the chapter notes a useful source of historical context and opposing points of view—of which there are many.

"There are really two different kinds of public figures," antiwar activist David Harris says in the film *Carry It On.*[7] "There are idols and there are heroes. An idol is something that exists beyond the people, that shows people what they can't be. In a sense, it exists as a negation of the people who worship it." Rambo and Luke Skywalker and the rest of the spectrum of pop warriors are idols in this sense. Watching them may be cathartic, but it is not inspiring.

"But the other kind of public figure," Harris goes on, "is a hero, and a hero is somebody who teaches people what they can be. A hero is really an available model." In the United States at the end of the twentieth century, we need heroes and we need hope and we need to let ourselves admit that. There is an element of inevitability in the way most of us regard the wars now fought in our names, the corruption of science, the legitimacy of "national security" secrets, the tendency to regard protesters as troublemakers if not traitors. There is an element of inevitability in the way most of us regard the war that would really end all wars. But as Paul Loeb writes in his study of the peace movement,

Hope in Hard Times, "Perhaps present hope can best be found in the fact that individuals have changed, and in turn nourished further changes in others."[8] The stories which follow are about people who have learned to think for themselves and to act in behalf of the future, and who in doing so have caught a glimmer of that hope.

1 THE BLOOD OF THE POOR
JERRY GENESIO

The airport in Tegucigalpa, Honduras is a point of entry for many from the United States who are players in, or who seek to understand, the geopolitics of Central America. Usually the most difficult thing about landing in Tegucigalpa is remaining calm while the plane descends between two jagged mountains. But a recent delegation of sixteen US military veterans found that the mountains were just the beginning of the obstacles they would face.

The sixteen—representing eight states, three wars, and every branch of the military—wore T-shirts and baseball caps identifying them as Veterans for Peace (VFP). They were a few days into a fact-finding tour through Guatemala, Honduras and Nicaragua. They turned in their passports as required at customs, and they waited, without explanation.

Jerry Genesio, the president of Veterans for Peace, paced and smoked. The quintessential redneck, with bulky body and baggy jeans, he is not a man who deals well with uncertainty. After twenty minutes, he marched up to a customs official.

"I asked, 'What's the problem?' He pointed to my hat. I said, 'Come on. You're for peace too, aren't you? Isn't everybody?'

"He said, 'Communists don't understand peace.'

"I said, 'I don't understand why "for peace" is such a controversial idea. You'd think we were called Veterans for Unconditional Surrender.' "

The encounter was typical for the scrappy, intense ex-Marine whose life has increasingly become that of the crusader. Something in Genesio's manner suggests a tanker full of nitroglycerin in the hands of a skilled driver who is well aware of the nature of his task and enjoys the skill it demands of him. He is self-contained and speaks precisely, but underneath the controlled exterior is an obvious and visceral anger. And still deeper, below the anger, is grace. When his emotional armor drops to show that quality, it seems to drop all at once, revealing a thoughtful man who is angry, primarily, because he wants the world to be a kinder place.

"One of my earliest memories is sitting on my father's shoulders in Milford, Massachusetts, across the street from the drugstore, watching the V-J Day parade and being glad the boys were coming home safe from World War II," he recalls. Now a high-tech suburb, Milford was still a small town when he came of age, bursting with energy and tempered by Catholicism, shaped by the dual authority of twelve years of parochial school and a father who was always willing to black and blue the hides of kids who didn't measure up. There was no perceived contradiction between the Catholicism of the era and the use of violence in defense of a just cause; sometimes the church actively encouraged it. Genesio remembers seeing his older brother, Red, bloodying the nose of a kid on the playground and being marched to the principal's office by a nun—who accompanied him to defend him because "the other kid was wising off." As a teenager, decked out in a Marlon Brando leather jacket, he could hold his own in drinking and fighting. But he also contained the seeds of today's seriousness and can say unpretentiously, "I would have died for my faith."

When their father passed away in 1950, Red Genesio became "the man" of the family and an authority figure as well as a role model for Jerry, three years younger. He remembers, "There was a lot of sibling rivalry. My mother would say, 'You'll have to ask Red if that's okay' or 'Red will handle that.' " Their brotherly relationship was one of passionate affection and frequent blowups. In junior high, Jerry almost drowned while trying to keep up with Red's friends on a swimming expedition in a local abandoned quarry. When he first received his driver's license, the two boys locked themselves in the garage to duke it out over who got the car on Saturday night; a lucky punch that bloodied Red's eyebrow heralded a new, more egalitarian relationship. "Red said to me, 'We aren't going to fight anymore, because if you ever do anything like this to me again I'm going to kill you.' "

What really pushed Jerry Genesio into adulthood was the military, and his brother pushed him into the military. With three high school friends, Jerry fantasized about joining the Marine Corps after graduation. He remembers, "I happened to mention that idea in front of Red. He went into hysterics and said, 'You'll never make it through boot camp.' At that point, I had to go in the marines." He went, foremost, "to become a man. It was a rite of passage: boot camp, surviving boot camp, not cutting and running. I was going in for the right to wear the marine uniform. And in the process I was going to show my brother that we weren't going to go through life with him always being the man and me always being the child."

Secondary but often on his mind was the broader mission of the era. In the Catholic education of the 1940s and 1950s, communism's threat to the faith was a dominant theme. When Genesio got on the bus for boot camp at Parris Island in 1956, at the peak of the Hungarian uprising, it was with the expectation that "we were being primed to go over and help the Hungarians crawl out from under the big black boot."

The United States never went into Hungary. Genesio did prosaic things in the marines—drove trucks, typed—but he did them in exotic places like Okinawa and the Philippines. In the Philippines, during maneuvers called Operation Strong Back, he jumped out of a chopper just as it was being lifted by an updraft. He broke enough leg and foot bones to be unfit for duty as a grunt, and spent the next few years in the environs of Great Lakes Naval Hospital—part of that time on a team whose job was tracking down deserters—until he was discharged for medical reasons.

He looks back on his six years in the marines as simple and fulfilling. "I was proud of the service, I was proud of myself. I had gotten some raw deals, but they were from individuals." What he didn't get was combat experience, a fact he sees as crucial in making him a strong supporter of the Vietnam War. "As a peacetime marine I was even more invested in standing up for the honor of the military, living by the standards I learned there, believing in whatever the US was fighting for, because I hadn't proved myself in battle."

He settled in North Carolina near Camp LeJeune and worked heavy construction. He met and two weeks later married a woman with a child and no husband, delighting in the role of provider. His geopolitical views were still simple. When the Cuban missile crisis erupted, "I wanted to nuke 'em. I supported Kennedy one hundred percent." He was a cold war optimist: secure, militant, cocky. The future seemed to be unfolding with a certain predictability. As he puts it, "The people I was drinking beer with were America's number-one rednecks. I never had any exposure to any other ideology. I never thought much about it. I did my job. I raised my family. I was making good money. I drank a lot of beer. I don't know when I started to grow in terms of thinking beyond what I had to do today to survive." The marriage, which was rocky from day one, occupied much of his energy; work and union politics took up the rest.

What began the erosion of his old views was the bullet that killed his hero, John Kennedy, and continued with the other political assassinations of the 1960s. His cosmology had been based on the assumption that somewhere, somebody was in charge. To see several of the strongest leaders shot dead gave him, for the first time, a sense of living on unsteady ground. He reacted with a new combativeness, an instinct to fight back whenever a clear battle presented itself.

One such battle came to a head on the job in the late 1960s. When an engineering screw-up cost the company dearly, the engineer Genesio worked for blamed a foreman who was fired as a result. But Genesio, who had seen the engineering drawings, went to the union. His disclosures led to a strike and the boss's lasting enmity. A while later, a second strike erupted, this time over what he saw as a ridiculous technicality. He refused to walk, made more enemies, convinced some co-workers that it would be a good idea to form an independent union, and soon found himself standing on the bed of a pickup whipping up enthusiasm for the new union.

One day he was a local hero. The next day he was summoned to a meeting with the president of the established union. "He came with four or five henchmen, and they all had weapons. The nominal leaders of our group were called into the president's motel room, with him and the guys with the guns. He never raised his voice. He just said, 'Look, there isn't going to be an independent union here. We have people on this job who will bust your heads.' I said okay. The next morning, I quit that job." He found work as a pharmaceutical sales representative and put his remaining energy into saving his marriage.

Genesio's world unraveled further in 1969 when he got a phone call from his stepfather, who said with no preamble, "Red is dead." Red had become a paratroop instructor and made the army his career. When the men he trained began running into conditions in Vietnam he could not fathom and so could not prepare them for, Red volunteered for a tour there himself. Their mother protested, as did his wife, the rest of the family, and the community. Only Jerry, who shared Red's belief that communism had to be stopped in Asia so it wouldn't need to be fought on our own soil, said, "Hey, give him a break. I understand where he's coming from. He has to make a decision he can live with."

Red's letters home spoke of cowboy-style exploits, like his practice of strapping himself by the legs into a helicopter in order to lean out and aim a machine gun downward. When the phone call came only seven weeks after the brothers said goodbye, Genesio loaded his family into the car, drove all night, got badly lost on the way, and finally walked into his mother's house to find her numbed by sedatives and half-bald from tearing out her hair. "For the second time," he understood, "she had lost the most important man in her life."

The army's official version of Red's death was that the ammo carried by the helicopter had been rigged with explosives by a saboteur. But a member of the team that recovered the body said Red had been killed from below, apparently by a booby trap rigged by the Vietcong with an unexploded US 500-pound bomb.

When the coffin came back to Maine, Genesio was talked out of looking at the body by an army escort who warned him that it would be decomposed, yellowed by quinine, and badly mutilated. "You'll never remember your brother any other way," said the officer. In Genesio's mind, he chickened out. As a result, for the rest of the war, he was haunted by his brother's face in every POW on the news and steeped in guilt for not identifying the body positively. Unraveling the conflicting versions of his brother's death became a crusade, both for the sake of his mother, who remained a "basket case," and for himself.

This was one of many battles that, finally, would be won for their own sake. Ever since his brother had told him he wouldn't survive boot camp, Jerry Genesio has been a man who cannot bear to be told "you can't." After years of struggle and with the aid of his congressman, he finally saw the autopsy report. It turned out that Red had died of traumatic amputation of his leg, strapped characteristically into the chopper when it was destroyed by a bomb from below. But there was more: Red had been killed in Cambodia, where the Nixon administration had never admitted sending troops.

In those years, the antiwar movement was a maddening presence. When disaffected veterans of the era read aloud the names of war dead from the steps of the Capitol, Genesio remembers vividly, "I wanted to be there, just to stand there, when they read my brother's name— because I wanted to personally kill the sons of bitches who would politicize his death that way."

By that time also, it was obvious that his marriage was over. A divorce was imminent and custody battles were raging, but the Catholic church of the era simply did not acknowledge divorce as an option. "When I most needed my church, when I just needed someone to talk to, it wasn't there for me," he remembers bitterly. He found a new job in pharmaceutical sales near Red's widow and three children in Maine, bought land and moved into a mobile home, and attempted to get some perspective on his life.

At first Genesio struggled. He spent his first months in Maine "getting so drunk I wouldn't know where I was." What brought him back to steadier ground was a friendship that soon became a romance. Judy Lothrop, his boss's new secretary, arrived from California and her own broken marriage the week Genesio was assigned to teach all the secretaries how to use the company's new phone system. The two were at zero points in their lives, but they noticed right away that they could communicate with each other. It became a healing relationship for them both. While his first courtship had lasted two weeks, this one took two years while each tied up loose ends. In 1972, they married and built a modest dream house in Sweden, Maine for his two sons and her three children.

Judy Genesio is an unpretentious and straightforward woman. Her thick grey hair is pulled back with barettes like a teenager's, and she has an appealing dimpled face. She moves back and forth between the roles of homemaker—getting pizza for the visiting journalist and apologizing for the disarray of the house—and participant in the discussion as a sharp-minded, sensitive partner. She is aware that their relationship is special, and says, "We've cut each other down to nothing and built each other back up again, and we've each recognized potential in the other that we haven't been able to see in ourselves." He calls her "my best friend," adding, "Judy and I have spent hundreds of hours—hell, we've spent years on end—just talking. It's contributed to my knowledge of who I am, and I've learned what a thinker she is."

During the early 1970s, Genesio continued to react to the turmoil in his life and to a growing sense of injustice by effectively declaring, "This is it. Nobody messes with me." He established himself in home and career conspicuously enough that he was soon invited into local politics by way of appointment to the town appeals board. He was its chairman in 1975, when Central Maine Power moved in unannounced and cleared a huge swath of woodland through the town for a power line. Everybody grumbled, but few were inclined to fight it. Genesio said, "See you in court."

He first took part as chair of the appeals board. When the editor of the local newspaper told him the issue wasn't being covered because there simply weren't reporters available, he quit the appeals board and began filing news copy, which was duly published. Ultimately, the utility settled out of court and replanted sixty thousand trees.[1]

Over the next seven years, Genesio continued to string for two local papers, the *Bridgton News* and the *Lewiston Sun,* covering local stories like the selectmen's meetings that were closed to the public, and the community church run exclusively for summer people and padlocked every September. "I developed a real passion for exposing violations of the public trust. I was questioning all authority." Initially, the questions were unfocused, angry, and reactive, as was his public image. But lessons emerged. "When the utility backed down, it was because they were very upset about the bad publicity. My articles attracted the *Portland Press-Herald* and the television stations. I was beginning to discover that individuals have power, that we can empower ourselves, that it's a state of mind."

One source of empowerment for Genesio was the discovery that he could write, and he spent many a weekend cloistered in his attic, tinkering with fiction and poetry. His wife remembers, "He would work until five in the morning sometimes. When I got up, there would always be a new installment to read with my coffee. It was wonderful." *Yankee* magazine published his account of Red's heroism in saving the life of a paratroop trainee.[2] And it was through fiction, unexpectedly, that Genesio first expressed a new viewpoint about Vietnam and US power that had been taking shape in his mind.

When I asked him about the first signs of that change, he sat quietly. Judy, close by, said, "It started with that short story you wrote, the one about the trucker."

"I haven't thought about that for years," he said, "but you're right. A lot of my feelings that I couldn't consciously get to ended up in that story. I disguised myself by creating a character, this trucker who was alone a lot. There was something happening inside me that made me feel very lonely, that I was the only person this was happening to.

"Judy just hit a trigger. I've never talked about this in this way before. I was very much alone because people were not wanting to listen to the problems I sensed, and to a large degree I wasn't even sure what they were myself. I was just beginning to put on the brakes. I was just stopping and preparing to turn around. I was awful, uptight. The trucker story was a release, just like opening a steam valve. I talked in it about going through a process of cleaning the attic, looking at all the things that had been stored in the attic, and individually deciding which things could stay and which ones could be thrown out. I must have written it in 1976 or 1977."

As he spoke, Judy ducked out, then returned with a manuscript saying, "Here it is. I found it the other day when I was filing. Do you remember what you called it? 'Of Trust, Truckers, and Tragedy.' "

The story is a bleak one, about an independent truck driver with responsibilities to his family and strong ideas about earning one's own way in the world. He is a hard-working family man who defies the truckers' strike of 1974 and is killed as a result. But the trucker is also a veteran, and much of the story is devoted to describing his disillusionment with the war he had fought.

> Hank was a patriot, though this patriotism blazed much more feverishly within him thirty years ago than it did of late, for many reasons. Then, it was all he had. Through it he believed he would become a man, quickly and unquestionably . . . Then, he was a vacuum, sucking in any and all information that was allowed to filter down to him. He was hungry for it, seeking it, believing it and believing the source. Didn't he pledge allegiance to it each morning for years? . . .
>
> Lately the vacuum was outside of himself and even the few sorted bits of information he wanted to retain seemed to be sucked back out every time he turned on the tube, where the vacuum really was. His mind, like the attic, had seen many spring cleanings come and go.

Some beliefs, like so many boxes of old magazines, were discarded without a second thought. Others were passed along like Grandma's Bible. It was the ejection of stronger faiths that scarred his soul and shook his confidence. His belief that a lone radical had assassinated John Kennedy was one of the first of these. The bits of facts that he wanted to retain had been sucked out and replaced with images of evil conspirators. His belief in Vietnam's just cause was another. Every flag-draped coffin that came back sucked something out of him, but probably not as much as those who returned still able to talk about it. Hank had always been skeptical about local political shenanigans, but he had believed that the White House was the symbol of integrity and incorruptibility. Even that had been destroyed by Watergate . . .

Gradually he began to wonder . . . What of the medals he had won? Did he earn them killing patriots who were brainwashed and blind? Or was he?

Genesio just stared at the sheaf of papers. "I wrote this in 1974! That indicates to me that I was having very serious reservations about my brother's sacrifice a lot earlier than I thought. I must have been questioning what they sent him off to die for."

To question authority at all was fundamentally at odds with his background. "Remember," he says, "I grew up in a world where old Dr. Carroll never made a mistake. The teachers were always right, the nuns were always right, the priests were always right. You never questioned these things. If you read something in a textbook, why would anyone question it? If it's written, that's the way it is."

Watergate brought his questioning to a conscious level, and with it came a real sense of betrayal. "That's why we both became so angry. I had trusted them. I had been lied to. I believed everything they told me. If the White House could lie about this, how many lies had I been told about my brother's death and what he died for?" More and more, the energy that he had been pouring into reconciling Red's death and into local battles began to draw him into a broader arena. He read Vietnam history, political philosophy, economics. The couple decided to go back to college—together, as they were doing most things by that point—and took classes at the University of Southern Maine in the evenings.

At the same time, Genesio's social situation had become quite sticky. His reputation as an agitator had gotten him blackballed from the town historical society, despite the fact that he was acknowledged as the most active researcher in local history for miles around. The battle to keep the church open year-round had made more enemies. He came to regard the problem as small-town elitism. "I didn't have a college degree, so I couldn't play in the same league with the people who did. It was that simple." As a result, in those years, he became interested not only in winning the battles he took on but in vindicating himself as a working-class, self-taught individual. He read and wrote tirelessly.

Those years also cemented an important friendship, with the closest thing to an older brother since Red's death. Reverend Willard Bickett, who had "retired" to the area and promptly returned to active ministry, took an interest in the changes Genesio was navigating through. Bickett provided conversation during endless scrabble and bridge games, books, opportunities to learn public speaking as a guest preacher, and a key piece of advice: "Decide which battles you're going to fight, boy. You can't take 'em all on. You're all over the place."

Genesio continued to be a crusader, but in early 1979 the battleground changed and the stakes were raised. While the implications of his findings were international, the object of his wrath was his own employer. He had risen from salesman to sales manager in a major company marketing blood and blood products. He won frequent awards and free trips, had the reputation of being able to sell ice cubes to Eskimos, and took great satisfaction honing his human relations skills. While attending a cocktail party with a group of executives during a sales seminar in San Francisco, Genesio heard a troubling remark. It was "an offhand comment to the effect that if the rebels in Nicaragua won this revolution, we would have to start looking for another blood supply. The company had given up a large part of the domestic blood market because they could buy it so cheaply in Latin America: Nicaragua, Colombia, El Salvador."

At the time, Nicaragua was second only to Haiti as the poorest country in the hemisphere, with an average yearly income of $300 and extremes of human misery deepened by the earthquake of 1972, forty years of dictatorship, and a revolution.[3] A primary source of income for many destitute Nicaraguans was donating blood to the blood banks owned by the Somoza family and nicknamed "Casa de Vampires." Donors received $1 per liter for donations of plasma that sold for $26 to $30 per liter in the United States. They could come back as often as every three days if their strength held up. The blood operation was a major scandal in prerevolutionary Nicaragua, according to Dutch journalist Piet Hagen, who writes in *Blood: Gift or Merchandise?*:

> According to Nestor Duque Arango, a Nicaraguan refugee, the plasma center in Managua not only exploited poor and undernourished people who donated of their own "free" will, but also political prisoners of Somoza's National Guard. In November 1977, the liberal newspaper *La Prensa* reported that at least one donor died because of too-frequent plasmapheresis. Other reports say that at least ten donors died.[4]

"My antennas went out," says Genesio, "because I had no idea that a significant fraction of the blood was coming from outside the country.

Nothing had ever required me to think about it. I had been in the business long enough to know that plasma from Third World nations was not considered to be of high quality because paid donors in these countries, invariably the very poor, subsist on inadequate diets that are usually very low in protein. Ironically, this blood was being imported specifically for plasma proteins. I also knew that the southern half of the Western Hemisphere was and still is an area where hepatitis B and hepatitis non-A, non-B, two very virulent strains of the disease, are endemic. The established screening test for hepatitis B is only seventy percent effective. There is no screening test for hepatitis non-A, non-B.

"All this technical stuff about the blood industry has a very real, human consequence: tens of thousands of people a year in the US get hepatitis from blood plasma, and many die. These patients die not from their disease but from the treatment. And now, with the AIDS epidemic, I have more than a little curiosity about whether there's a connection to those or similar blood operations, since a major source of the company's imported blood was Haiti."

This was the blood Genesio was selling for a living. Imports from Nicaragua did indeed stop a few months before the Sandinista triumph, when angry mobs destroyed the "Casa de Vampires." Programs with other Third World countries have been gradually cut back since the advent of AIDS. But when he made the discovery, the practice of importing blood from Third World countries was still common, and Genesio became obsessed with finding out just what he was contributing to as he drew his otherwise satisfying paycheck.

He began yet another compulsive research effort. He sent endless Freedom of Information Act requests to the Food and Drug Administration. Told at first that there was very little on record about the import of blood plasma, he kept pushing and eventually accumulated cartons of documents. The piles of paper that had been littering his office for years now crept out into the living room, kitchen, bedroom. He read about the blood business, multinational economics, Latin American history and politics. Judy, at the time, found him "obsessive" and "irrational." For a couple of years, she recalls, "He couldn't talk about anything else, and he hadn't learned yet that you couldn't get people to agree with you by badgering. If you didn't see things his way, you were crazy."

His discoveries were potent fuel for that obsessiveness. "Tons of blood plasma had been imported from Latin American nations during the 1960s and 1970s, with the heaviest import flow coinciding with the period of greatest US bloodshed during the Vietnam War. Much, if not most, of this plasma was being sold to the US government for use in treating war casualties." Connection to Vietnam, of course, was connection to Red, so it was with personal horror and rage that he concluded, "the US government was reluctant to ask the American people to participate in a blood drive necessitated by an undeclared war they did not support. The plasma importation scheme made this unnecessary and resulted in huge, windfall profits for the US commercial blood industry. The only losers were our boys who were receiving this plasma on the battlefields of Vietnam, and the Latin American peasant classes." He became single-minded and inaccessible, spending every spare moment up in his study. Sometimes he worked on what eventually became a screenplay and a nonfiction account of the scandal. Other times he just sat, smoking and looking out the window, getting used to the new landscape of his mind.

With Jerry hooked on Central America, Judy Genesio faced a decision. For the first ten years of the marriage, she had been content to let him tilt at windmills on his own time. But when he stopped being able to talk about anything but the blood of the poor and the responsibility of the well-off, their worlds became too separate and too much at odds. I sat with Judy in what used to be her kitchen and now looks more like the Veterans for Peace situation room, with a small television set tuned to the Iran-contra hearings, a twelve-cup coffeepot nearly full, and newspapers and legal pads everywhere. While her husband inspected his vegetable garden, she picked up the story from her own perspective.

"If anybody had asked me when we met in 1969, I would have described myself as a Republican. But a year before that, I had voted for Robert Kennedy in the California primary. I liked him. I went home to watch the returns and saw him shot. I don't have any idea why I liked him, because I thought I was a conservative at that time. I certainly thought the government was right as far as Vietnam went, and that the kids in Berkeley who were raising hell were wrong.

"I was twenty-five, maybe twenty-six. I had three babies, and that's all I did. I read the newspaper every day and listened to the news, but obviously I did no analyzing. I don't think I knew Robert Kennedy was working for social justice, or that the Democrats were any different from the Republicans. They were just people. You voted for the person you liked. Until maybe four or five years ago, my sense of social issues and how they related to politics just didn't exist.

"I understand why people can't just come over to your side when you tell them about Nicaragua. It's such a painful process to relearn everything you've ever learned. Everything you've ever done in your life is connected to what you believe. I don't know if I ever thought there was a question I should ask. Until I was in my thirties, I thought I knew it all."

For her, too, Watergate was a catalyst. "Nixon," she says, "had a lot to do with my asking questions." And Jerry's preoccupation with Central America led her to be concerned. But for the first year or two after he began the blood research, the couple's communication deteriorated badly. "He was reading *The Nation*. I was reading *Reader's Digest*. We would just sort of look at each other across this big void," she recalls. His style was abrasive and at times frightening. "I remember being in the car together on a business trip. It was four or five hours. He started on Nicaragua and the revolution. I thought, 'You sound like a communist.' I got really scared. I had no idea what a communist was, except that communists were people who criticized our way of life." For quite a while she fought back by tuning him out.

She also fought back by creating a niche for herself. "Around that time I got into making dolls, at first for the kids, but actually turning it into a business, and moving it out of the house. The marketing, the manufacturing, everything—it was something I had claimed for myself. I had to say, 'If you're gonna write and do all this stuff, then, damn it, I'm going to have mine.' It was just a period that, I think, any marriage has to go through that succeeds today and has a give-and-take and a successful relationship beyond just the house and the kids, especially in our generation. We were completely role-oriented, just went right down the chute after high school and did exactly what we were expected to."

Then, in 1983, the couple won a Caribbean cruise in recognition of Jerry's sales performance. As she relates, "We landed in Jamaica, the Grand Cayman Islands, Cozumel in Mexico and a couple of other little islands, all supported by the US and supposedly great places. All I could see when we got off that ship every day was horrible, horrible poverty, people begging . . . I'd read about these things, and had seen a few similar things in the South, but I hadn't ever seen it quite like this. Maybe Jerry had talked enough by then about Nicaragua, and things were starting to work in my head. Hearing what was going on after a revolution, and then seeing what conditions these people lived under, I started wanting to see if things really were different in Nicaragua. Jerry had told me an enormous amount of stuff, but I suppose I'm a person who can't just be told things. I have to see for myself."

In 1984, Jerry Genesio contacted Witness for Peace, a church-based group which sends short- and long-term delegations to the Nicaraguan war zone to observe and report on conditions firsthand, and by their presence, they hope, deter contra attacks on civilian targets. Such a trip was a serious proposition, and the orientations stressed that no one's safety was guaranteed. Jerry assumed he would go on his own, but Judy, who by then was curious in her own right and saw the trip as an event that would save or sink the marriage, said, "Sign me up."

Ocotal, Nicaragua is a dusty little town with unpaved streets in the middle of the war zone. It had just suffered a fierce contra attack that had demolished several agricultural cooperatives when the Witness for Peace delegation arrived. Yet they were received not as citizens of an enemy nation, but as potential friends. Judy remembers, "What really firmed up my position was comparing this place to Caribbean countries we had visited on our cruise, countries that were supposedly doing it right the US way. In Mexico and the Cayman Islands, there were such misery and poverty and begging, and an attitude toward Americans that said, 'You've got everything and we want some.' In Nicaragua, people might have been just as poor, but they didn't beg. They weren't after what we had. They were proud. They had won something. I guess I felt this must have been the way it was in our own country when things were brand new."

The Genesios concluded from their two weeks in Ocotal that the threat perceived by most Nicaraguans in the war zone was not from the Sandinistas but from the contras. That conclusion was formed during time spent with Benjamin and Dona Alamen and their son, Julio, daily sharing rice and beans and not much else, and hearing the gunfire every night. It was there, for the first time in all those unsettled years, that Genesio found some kind of reconciliation of Red's death, Vietnam, and his imperfections as husband and father and brother.

"I had gone through years and years with my arms just flailing about in struggle with something, trying to find answers: Why were all these people killed in Vietnam? Could a God allow us to drop bombs on Hiroshima and Nagasaki? Why are all these kids starving in Africa? I was beating on the heads of everybody I could reach, trying to find those answers. But in Ocotal, I realized that I was looking for answers that might not exist. All I could do was decide what was right, and do it, and not look for any greater gratification than that.

"Judy likes to say that I live in a black-and-white world. Something is right or it's wrong. I think that's been true, but I'm beginning to see shades of gray. To do that, I had to get rid of my anger. I used to push my way through cement walls, wear myself out shoveling shit against the tide. But I left all that behind in Ocotal, seeing the kids, seeing Judy sitting in the Alamens' dining room with little Julio climbing on her lap and crying, all of us crying. At that time, my son Louis was in the marines and her son Mark was in the army, and I realized that if the US were to invade Nicaragua, these were quite literally the people our sons would be sent to kill. It was too much."

At the park in Ocotal, the Witness for Peace group stood in a vigil with the community, a crowd of five hundred. As visitors and

Nicaraguans took turns at the podium saying why they had come and what they had observed, Genesio was unable to keep silent. He walked to the front of the crowd, found a translator, and hesitantly began to tell the story of his brother's death and his own years of reconciliation. "For the first time," he says, "I understood the people who had stood on the steps of the Capitol in the Vietnam era and read my brother's name. It came over me like a flash. I remember telling that story and crying, having a hard time getting it all out. For the first time in fifteen years, I felt whole."

Jerry Genesio has always spoken his mind to whatever degree he has known it, but he was brought up with typical attitudes toward letting feelings like pain show. "Even at my brother's funeral, I was too macho to cry," he recalls. But this, too, has changed. "Vietnam took away forever the illusion that men didn't cry. We saw them on TV all the time, crying out in pain, crying when their buddies were killed. I learned from that," he reflects. "But I guess learning that it was really okay for a man who's on the burly side and makes his living by his strength to cry without feeling ashamed, that was another gift I got from Nicaragua."

It is almost a cliché among those who have visited Nicaragua with groups such as Witness for Peace that returning to the United States is in many ways harder than the time spent side by side with peasants, although the latter involves taking greater physical risks. The trip made concrete the impressions that had until then been tentative. The Genesios returned to Maine burning to tell their story, and were soon visiting local schools and churches with a slide show. Back at home, they were "the town communists." But in spite of the skepticism and fear in some audiences, Genesio noticed an opening. "When I mentioned that I was a veteran, people perked up. It gave me credibility."

Unlike many veterans he knew, who had worked hard to leave behind their memories of war and their identities as veterans, Genesio decided to take advantage of his. The couple formed Veterans for Peace in 1985 with Ken Perkins, a Korean War medic who is now a pharmacist at the local Veterans Administration hospital; Doug Rawlings, a Vietnam veteran and poet who teaches at the University of Maine; and Willard Bickett.

Veterans for Peace opposes nuclear weapons, military intervention in Central America, economic support for apartheid, and the premise that more weapons mean more security. Its founding principles are derived from the Atlantic Charter, signed by Roosevelt and Churchill after World War II, which affirms the right of every country, satellite or superpower, to self-determination, and calls on nations to work seriously at resolving their conflicts by methods other than war. By drawing on such an eminent and noncontroversial document, these activists are making the point that, unlike their most conspicuous predecessors in the 1960s, they think they fit into this country's historical mainstream. It is the post–World War II reliance on military might which they see as the dangerously radical position.

In their most optimistic moments, Genesio and his cohorts figured that they might create a statewide organization that would turn a few heads. But they had hit upon something potent. In two years and advertising only by word of mouth, the group grew to include nine hundred members in forty states. VFP aims to create both a mass political base and a network of local groups working creatively on projects of their own—including educational campaigns against war toys, debates with contra spokespersons, and nonviolent efforts to block weapon shipments to Central America.

Some of VFP's most visible members are retired officers such as Colonel Jim Burkholder, whose thirty-three years in the army included working as an aide to General William Westmorland in Vietnam, and Colonel John Barr, a former nuclear war planner now dividing his time between Veterans for Peace and Beyond War. At the same time, VFP attracts enlisted men and women who, like Genesio, need to make peace with their identities and experiences as veterans. For them, the healing process involves telling their own war stories and simply being heard.

Genesio is modest in his assessment of what Veterans for Peace—or any organization—can accomplish. "People who think we're going to have instant victory are fighting for the wrong reasons. Humanity has been mean and greedy since we came down from the trees. All we can do is hold the line. But if it weren't for Veterans for Peace, and Witness for Peace, and the rest of the groups, tens of thousands more Nicaraguans would already be dead, because the United States would already have invaded. I believe that."

From the group's birth, the Genesio home became a command post. He set up a computerized mailing list, printed brochures, and talked endlessly on the phone to veterans from around the country who heard about the organization from friends. Many called to ask, "How can I see for myself?" Needing little provocation, Genesio put together the May 1987 trip that included the altercation at the Tegucigalpa airport. While his first Central America trip had been about emotional resolution, this one was concerned with deepening his analysis and lining up hard documentation. The veterans met with more than fifty church, human rights, labor, press, opposition, and government spokespersons in the three countries.

Adding to the official meetings were unofficial adventures. In Guatemala, one former marine went to a clinic for an eye problem just after a body had been dropped off by a gang in an unmarked van. In Honduras, a visit to Palmerola Air Base revealed overwhelming parallels to Vietnam, from the "temporary" hooches and concrete-reinforced airstrips to the poverty and prostitution and noisy appeals to Yankees for money in neighboring Comayagua. While embassy and military officials claimed there had been only four US military casualties since the beginning of maneuvers in Honduras, the veterans ran into a Honduran reporter who showed them a detailed list of forty-five. "They're playing with the numbers again. It's déjà vu. We have learned nothing," Genesio concluded.

During the trip, Genesio willed himself to stay cool and analytical, but at several points his temper flared. In a Nicaraguan refugee camp in Honduras, a filmmaker asked him, "Why are all these people here if Nicaragua is such a benign place?" Genesio shot back, "Because we're funding the contras."⁵ Later, in Nicaragua, meeting with a spokesman for the Conservative Party, one of the losers to the Sandinistas in the 1984 election, he was shocked to hear the candidate say he lost fair and square. "I thought sure he of all people would claim the election was rigged. But no. He said the Sandinistas won it, which indeed most international observers also say. He added that, if anybody was trying to tip the scales of that election, it was the US embassy and the Catholic church. Well, my country and my church are two institutions I grew up expecting better of. And while, a few years ago, I would have reacted with blind anger, now I came home not just angry but absolutely determined not to let them get away with it."

Genesio certainly is not alone in his anger. It would be naive to expect that the rage and unhealed psychological wounds of many veterans could be overcome simply by the organization's commitment to nonviolence. While generally one of well-disciplined and orderly action, VFP's history features some spectacular blowups. Most noteworthy was the Easter 1987 demonstration outside Ronald Reagan's California retreat, which was marred by a brawl between a handful of veterans and a carload of Secret Service men. But many members testify that they are drawn to Veterans for Peace precisely because it has them, as it has helped Genesio, begin to heal their anger.

Genesio's initial trip to Nicaragua provided great emotional fuel for his work with Veterans for Peace, and a subsequent tragedy added to his drive. Although their children by each previous marriage were adults and out of the nest, the Genesios remained a close family. One of Jerry's fondest relationships had been with his first wife's son, Tony, whom he had adopted and who had spent much of his time in Maine. In the spring of 1986, Tony was killed in a highway accident. That loss became a symbol and focal point for Jerry, who gave Veterans for

Peace the energy of his grief as well as his experience. "Now I had lost a father, a brother, and a son," he says. "I could understand what those losses felt like, and I could feel all the more rage for the mothers in Nicaragua who have lost so many of their kids so unnecessarily."

Genesio's turnaround was really several. One set of changes has revolved around the military's influence on his view of world events and his role in them. In the 1950s, he was a marine who saw a strong global role for the US military as essential in keeping the peace. Now, in the 1980s, he sees that projection of power as part of the problem. "I believe in a strong national defense," he says. "But maintaining large numbers of troops outside our borders isn't defense. It's adventurism." He hasn't given up the conviction that real-world conflicts may require military solutions, but he sees those solutions as a last resort that is too often used uncritically.

Another set of changes continues, in his relationship to his corporate employer and his view of the relative merits of resigning in protest or using his income as a base from which to build Veterans for Peace. Unlike the men whose stories follow, Genesio was saved from the brutal dilemma about the ethics of living literally on "blood money" from the Third World by the natural self-destruction of the programs that had awakened his concern. He finally quit his job in early 1988, after eighteen years, when Veterans for Peace had grown large enough to pay him a stipend.

But the deeper changes in Jerry Genesio are not just in his views on foreign policy and not just in his career path. Where once his worldview was black and white, he has slowly admitted shades of gray and complexity of motives. Sometimes he succeeds better than others. The anger he once turned against the communist menace is still visible, now pointed toward what he sees as the excesses of his own country. But it is tempered with sorrow, a desire to understand rather than to judge, and a commitment to using his human relations skills to "sell" others on the discoveries that have so changed his life.

Once Genesio defined himself largely by the role he had been taught as a Catholic, working-class man. He still brings the history of his faith and class and gender to bear on experience, but these factors no longer rigidly dictate his choices. He has learned to think for himself. He has accepted enough of his own strengths and foibles that there is much less left to prove. His turnaround took on perfect symmetry on Memorial Day, 1988, nearly twenty years after his time of rage against the antiwar veterans who "politicized" his brothers death. That day, he led a group of Maine veterans on a march to the vacation home of Vice President George Bush, displaying crosses which bore the names of US service personnel—seventy by that time, according to his latest research project—killed in Central America. More than a newsworthy

Memorial Day angle, the demonstration was an effort to bring the issues home in terms of both self-interest and global justice, to show the connection between the two in bad policies that come home to roost. Genesio today has been tempered by his own losses to be capable of tenderness—to other veterans, to the victims of policies he opposes, and even to their perpetrators. As Willard Bickett says, "When I first met Jerry, he was the militant marine. He was armored. Well, he's still militant. But the armor has finally fallen away."

2   THE TIN MAN
CHARLIE LITEKY

> Son, I'd rather have one of these babies than be president.
> —Lyndon Johnson, awarding the Congressional Medal
> of Honor to Charlie Liteky for bravery in Vietnam,
> Washington, DC, 1968

> It is with great sadness that I renounce the Congressional Medal of
> Honor, but compassion for the victims of US intervention in Central
> America says I must . . . My renunciation in no way represents
> disrespect for the medal itself or for the recipients of medals of valor
> throughout history. My action is directed toward the inhumane
> foreign policies of my government, policies that cast shadows of shame
> over the heritage of this country . . . I find it ironic that conscience
> calls me to renounce the Congressional Medal of Honor for the same
> basic reason I received it—trying to save lives.
> —Charlie Liteky at the Vietnam Veterans Memorial,
> Washington, DC, 1986

Charlie Liteky was awarded the Congressional Medal of Honor in 1968 while a Catholic chaplain in Vietnam. In 1986, he became the first person ever to have the audacity and conviction to give that medal back. Eighteen years older and with his army crewcut softened a bit, Liteky knelt at the Vietnam Veterans Memorial, "The Wall," in Washington, DC. He wore a baggy white linen jacket and an uncomfortable-looking necktie. In his hand was an envelope labeled, "Contents: 1 Congressional Medal of Honor." Solemnly, amid clicking press cameras, milling tourists, and a circle of applauding friends, he laid the envelope down. Liteky's action was not merely symbolic; it also involved the considerable personal sacrifice of a $250 monthly stipend, which had been a significant source of income since he left the priesthood and army. And while Liteky does not attach enough value to material goods to regard his actions as sacrificial, this was only the beginning of his sacrifice. A few weeks after he renounced the medal, Liteky and three other veterans risked their lives in a 47-day, water-only fast on the steps of the Capitol—the first of two—in an effort to galvanize the movement against US intervention in Central America.

The renunciation was not simply a quiet personal gesture, but a carefully conceived public protest. "My action," he said, "is directed toward the inhumane foreign policies of my government, policies that cast shadows of shame over the heritage of this country and place the United States outside the company of civilized nations, nations that respect international law and universally accepted norms of morality . . . The United States has responded to the needs of oppressed people in El Salvador by supporting their oppressors . . . In Nicaragua, the US government response to the oppressed is the creation, direction, and support of a counterrevolutionary army . . . We have become a nation that arrogates to itself the right to impose its way of life on any country too weak to defend its independence."

Park police picked up the medal, as they do everything left at the memorial, and consigned it with perfect poetic irony to the lost-and-found department. But Liteky was in the process of finding something—a lost side of himself, a renewed sense of mission. This man and his quest—for a viable approach to nonviolence in the Reagan-era United States and for a coherent but politically committed life—have inspired some in the peace movement, outraged others, and left still others with the nagging question, "Isn't there a better way?"

A *Washington Post* article in the summer of 1986 compared Liteky to Major General John Singlaub, who was relieved of his command in 1977 for insubordination and went on to create the World Anti-Communist League. Crusty and stubborn veterans of the same war, Singlaub and Liteky each live embattled lives and see their crusades in stark moral terms. Each is considered eccentric, or worse, by opponents. How did Charlie Liteky—ex-priest, small-time football star, recipient of the Medal of Honor, raised in a military family—end up devoting his life to convincing the US government that military might has been used indiscriminately and to our detriment in international relations in general and toward Central America in particular?

I met Liteky a few months before he renounced his medal. He still had a certain military look: football shoulders, narrow hips, a plain gray T-shirt tucked neatly into belted jeans, very white socks. He invited me into the office he then occupied at Americans for Peace in the Americas, a small education and lobbying group in Washington led by veterans. On one wall was a spectacular poster portraying former

Air Force Commandant David Shoup, another Medal of Honor winner, crewcut and stern. The caption was Shoup's 1966 statement:

> I believe that if we had and would keep our dirty, bloody, dollar-soaked fingers out of the business of these nations so full of depressed, exploited people, they will arrive at a solution of their own . . . and if unfortunately their revolution must be of the violent type, because the "haves" refuse to share with the "have-nots" by any peaceful method, at least what they get will be their own, and not the American style, which they don't want and above all don't want crammed down their throats by Americans.

Modest and serious, but equally impassioned, Liteky told his story.

He was a navy brat who grew up in housing projects—Newport, Jacksonville, San Francisco—running with a pack of neighborhood rowdies who divided their time between football and small-time juvenile delinquency. His father, a strong-willed World War II navy man known at home as "the chief," by varying accounts either taught his three sons to fight at an early age or actually battered them. Liteky's pathway into the priesthood was shaped by that authoritarian environment; by the family's brand of Catholicism, which tacitly equated virtue with prominence in the church; and by an unusual, mystical strain of spirituality so deep in him that it was "no big deal" when he found prayer pouring out of him in alien tongues. What he came to call his "prayer life" became so consuming that it essentially railroaded him into seminary.

Liteky identifies one specific turning point which led him to the priesthood. Just home to Florida from World War II, "the chief" lost his temper with his bicycle-stealing, hooky-playing son and gave 13-year-old Charlie a "shape up or ship out" order. After a blowup that ended with the boy cornered in the bathroom and his father banging his head against the shower tiles, Charlie stole $30 from his mother's purse and shipped out for two glorious, nomadic weeks. When his parents caught up with him—holed up in the old housing project in Virginia where his best buddies still lived—his father lured him home with the fiction that his mother was on her deathbed.

"Something changed when I walked back into that house," Charlie Liteky reflects. "I began to live for approval, especially my father's. I went from not giving a damn, or from getting attention by doing what people disapproved of, to just the opposite. Even the noble quest of becoming a priest, of giving up everything, that fit right in with my need for approval. I tried to be pleasing and acceptable to God. So I lived a pretty straight life, and I did a lot of good things, but somehow the motivation wasn't love. It was seeking approbation."

He spent nine years at the Seminary of the Missionary Servants of the Most Holy Trinity, in the outback of Alabama, studying Latin and systematic theology and church history, leaving behind his given name for the priestly "Father Angelo." Since novices were not allowed to pick up a newspaper or listen to the radio, "the only source of information about the outside world was our instructors, and they weren't always the most knowledgeable. One instructor told us Korean War stories, about taking land one hill at a time. But mostly the 1950s exist in my mind as a big empty period as far as the outside world goes."

Liteky threw himself into his vocation with the drive of one who can't face the thought of failure. Paul Hendrickson, who spent his own youth at Holy Trinity and is now a staff writer for the *Washington Post*, writes movingly about Liteky and others he met there in *Seminary: A Search.*

> I met him when I was twenty, in 1964, the same summer I reported to the novitiate. I had gone down to the northern neck of Virginia, where Charlie was stationed in a rural parish, to help out in his summertime Bible program. Charlie had been a priest for four years then, and it was going downhill faster for him every year. What I chiefly remember about him that summer is the way he could mesmerize those rural Virginia kids, probably without half knowing. Father Angelo wore black knit sport shirts and black stovepipe pants and seemed to float instead of walk . . . He was in his mid-thirties and wore funny wire-rim glasses, and in an ascetic way, I suppose, he was a kind of John Wayne of the priesthood. He looked studious and wasn't. I remember that he prayed a lot."[1]

As a priest he was popular, respected, effective, and miserable. He had virtue; he wanted romance. The more he tried to suppress his sexuality, the more he had to suppress all that made him human. His misery showed.

"Why don't you join the army, maybe go to Vietnam, get your mind off your own problems?" his superior suggested, and in the patriotic fervor of the early Vietnam years, he enlisted. In those days, Singlaub and Liteky would likely have hit it off. Both enlisted because they saw in the war a chance to serve and perhaps to exercise a flair for drama. Both believed that the United States had its hands tied unnecessarily by the wimps in Congress and the crazies in the streets.

As chaplain for the 199th Light Infantry, Liteky was responsible for leading religious services, counseling troops, and comforting those who were wounded, whether by bullets or "Dear John" letters. Often he went along on combat missions. US Army archives contain remarkable film footage of him giving communion to the troops.[2] In white robes and a brocade sash, standing above the green-fatigued youths, he exhibits the larger-than-life quality that remains part of his public persona to this day. He moves with the grace and power of a football player, which indeed he was in seminary, and when he speaks there is an effortless fullness to it. In his face is something frightening, an eery cheer that seems jarringly out of place in the war zone. He is heard praying, "Give us the strength to do your will," and in hindsight these words speak not only to the soldiers' fighting strength but also to the priest's own spiritual crisis.

He went to Vietnam as a priest who needed a change of scene and to do his part in a war which he had never had the slightest occasion to question or even think much about. "When we trained for Vietnam as chaplains, we learned about the kinds of emotional and spiritual concerns the troops would have. We learned about Buddhism and Vietnamese culture on a very simple level: what they ate, what their houses were made of, that kind of stuff. But none of the training classes we had ever went into any detail about the history of our involvement, the French presence, who Ho Chi Minh was, what the treaties had been . . . "

Not long after his company had been airlifted into an area near Bien Hoa, he went out with a platoon on a routine mission to search out an enemy mortar site. They had no idea that they had just been dropped into the middle of a major North Vietnamese staging area for the Tet offensive. Spotting three figures in the jungle, they gave chase automatically. He says, "We thought we were chasing three Vietcong. They had never done us much harm. They would maybe set a booby trap or fire on you from a distance, to harass you a little. But we didn't think much about chasing them into the woods. We just did it . . . We ran into the side of a battalion-sized camp of the North Vietnamese Army."

The scene shifted suddenly from stealthy patrol to open combat, and Liteky went on autopilot. He crawled right into the line of fire and, using his body as a stretcher, maneuvered a wounded man back to safety. His fellow soldiers at first thought he had lost his mind. Sometimes crawling and sometimes running upright as though protected by a bulletproof bubble, and with shrapnel wounds in the neck and foot, he pulled out over twenty men during the four-hour battle. He gave first aid to some and last rites to others. The *Congressional Record* pulls out the stops in describing his valor: "Through his indomitable inspiration and heroic actions, Chaplain Liteky saved the lives of a number of his comrades and enabled the company to repulse the enemy. Chaplain Liteky's actions reflect great credit upon himself and were in keeping with the highest traditions of the U.S. Army."[3]

It was his first time under fire. Sometimes he is cavalier about it. "I wasn't doing anything else at the time," he has said to a number of interviewers. He wasn't scared, he insists, but only because he didn't have time to be. A similar battle scene a few days later, in the thick

of Tet, put him into such a fit of trembling that he could barely
function and set him on a course that continues to this day. "Fear is
such a debilitating emotion," he says. "I feel fear a lot—felt it in
battle, feel it these days when I have to make a speech—but somewhere
along the line I've made a vow that it's not going to get the better of me."

During four and a half years as a military chaplain, including two
Vietnam tours, Liteky always believed that the war was at least just
and maybe even noble. The worst US wrongdoing he knew of was a
soldier who killed a civilian and came to confession in agony about it.
"The My Lai massacre and stuff like that just weren't happening where
I was," he says. He came home thinking that "we weren't allowed to
win."

Liteky's memories of the movement against the Vietnam War were
sparse and mostly bitter. When Jane Fonda went to Hanoi, he and
his men felt utterly betrayed. "I thought she was a flake from Hollywood
who probably got a lot of publicity out of it. The war was difficult
enough. We needed the support. I really regarded her as some kind
of traitor," he recalls. "But Daniel Berrigan. There's a guy who was a
lot harder to ignore." When the Berrigan brothers and the rest of the
Catonsville Nine, acting explicitly on the basis of their Catholic faith,
poured blood on draft files, Liteky whispered "W-o-w." This was a
felony, a risk of years in jail. Daniel Berrigan in particular spoke about
it with a raging prophetic fire. But most of the Catholics in Liteky's
circle were down on the Berrigans. "The other priests were saying
things like, 'I hope they hang the son of a bitch. He was a rebel even
back in seminary.' So eventually I dropped the subject."

It wasn't just changing times that transformed the Congressional
Medal of Honor from a treasure into a burden, from a symbol of the
good fight to a sorry thing. The "inhumane policies" in Central America
that so outraged him were not, in his mind, much different from the
ones he had willingly supported in Southeast Asia. "Central America,"
he has said many times, "isn't just in danger of becoming another
Vietnam. It already is one."

Ask Charlie Liteky to tell you how his politics changed between his
participation in the Vietnam War and his opposition to the one he
saw as parallel in Central America, and he will probably tell you about
his sex life. "My greatest change," he says, "was not in what I thought
about foreign policy or anything so grand. It was in my relationship
to the celibate priesthood and my decision to get married." As a "very
straight" priest, Liteky agonized for years over the "sin" of lust before
he began accepting it in himself. Once while home on leave, he spent
an evening making out with the sister of a friend and returned to
Vietnam consumed with an excruciating mixture of longing and guilt,
which he attempted to resolve in the confessional. But the other priest,

choking back giggles, could only say, "I'm sorry, Charlie. I can't deal with this. I'm on my way home to marry a nun." Discovering, in the late 1960s, the inordinate number of Catholic religious who had made their own separate peace with the celibacy question, Liteky felt like the last kid on the block to be let in on a very important secret.

The notoriety afforded by the medal only tightened the screws of his isolation and guilt. "People would come up to me and say, 'God, you're a hero,' at the time when I was feeling the worst about myself." Eventually, watching soldiers crawl each night under the barbed wire to visit the local whorehouses, Liteky did likewise and lost his virginity with a Saigon prostitute at the age of 38. "The sex was nothing. Five minutes. But the guilt. That's what changed my life. I had always thought of myself as set apart, somehow. That helped me accept my own humanness," he says.

He began courting the notion that he was human and that the proper spiritual path for him involved acknowledging, not sabotaging, that humanity. In doing so, Liteky stood up to the church, the military, and the lifelong indoctrination that manhood requires an iron will. "I couldn't be a really loving person until I learned to think for myself, and that was when I left the priesthood," he says.

With the culmination of his service in Vietnam, Liteky's spiritual crisis came to a head. He applied for release from his vows three times and twice withdrew his application in panic. Finally he was cut loose at the age of 45, an ex-priest looking for love in San Diego. Once he had set out to discover women, he notes, "the information came in pretty easily."

Establishing an identity apart from the church and the army was more of a long-term proposition. Liteky drifted for some years, supplementing his pension with day labor. He spent a few years holed up in various cottages and cabins working on a novel. Eventually, during a period when his mother was dying and he needed expensive dental work, he took a job as a counselor with the Veterans Administration (VA) in San Francisco.

Working with drugged-out, bitter, alienated, and adrift participants in the war he had tried to forget, Liteky was compelled to deal with his own history and status as a veteran. At the same time, he saw case after case in which the VA dealt with vets more as a public relations problem than as desperate and damaged human beings. Until then, Liteky had thought of society's dominant institutions as being on his side. But here, through the simple process of trying to help his peers, he was plunged back into the underdog status that had been his as a housing-project kid.

While a priest, he had often taken the initiative to start social programs, from helping to bring Vietnamese war orphans to the States for adoption to founding drug rehabilitation centers for veterans upon his return. Still finding ministry a natural way to spend his life, Liteky participated in a small-scale mutiny against the VA by helping a group of veterans start an independent, live-in community for counseling and drug rehabilitation.

In San Francisco, too, he found a life partner. Three women had refused his marriage proposals, and he had said no to three others when he met Judy Balch, an ex-nun and antinuclear activist who was testing the waters of courtship at just the right time. They were married in 1983 in a big church wedding with Pachelbel's Canon playing.

The sequence of events that led Liteky to become involved with the Central America issue began soon after that. He and Judy were just settling in together and beginning to shop around for a house. He was taking sailing lessons and, at 55, discovering fun. But he was also rediscovering the suffering of those around him. His parish was one of many in 1984 considering a declaration of sanctuary for Central American refugees, and it was not a debate he could stay out of. He remembers, "One evening, Judy said, 'Hey, how about going over to the church to hear some refugees who are speaking?' That night changed my life."

Liteky went to the lecture without any particular expectations. What he heard was a typical horror story, which is not a contradiction in terms when it comes to El Salvador. The refugee was a 16-year-old girl who had been cornered by soldiers on her campus in San Salvador during the tense period just before the university was closed by government order. For no apparent reason, she had been shot in the stomach and left for dead. Her intestines were literally hanging out of her body when she staggered up and looked for help. The only aid available to her was an underground doctor. Licensed physicians there are required to report all bullet wounds to the police, and in the unique logic of El Salvador's *anticommunismo,* this constitutes a virtual invitation for a visit by the local death squad. Liteky listened in disgust and fascination as the girl told of the doctor's arrest, the paramilitary dragnet that later went after her, and the arrest and torture of her father as the police closed in on her. By a combination of minor miracles, both father and daughter had escaped alive and found each other in San Francisco.

"It's like something out of the Middle Ages, and our country has a responsibility," Liteky said, his voice trailing off. "I usually truncate this story here when I tell it, because it is so macabre," he went on after a pause. "But what really curdled my blood, what made me absolutely clear that I had to take a stand, was the father's testimony that, while he was being tortured, he heard the voice of a gringo giving instructions."[4]

Liteky forced himself to go and hear other refugees' stories and was chilled by their consistency. With other veterans he met through his job, he began taking a stand locally, writing letters to newspapers, speaking to church forums, picketing showings of *Rambo*. It was a partial success. "The media took a great interest in the fact that we were expressing these sentiments about manhood and war, as veterans. But when we talked about Central America, they didn't want to hear it. It got to the point where we'd try to say the words 'Central America' in every sentence so they couldn't cut it out, but they still found ways."

Through that activity, he was invited to join a fact-finding delegation to the region composed of Vietnam veterans. On the trip, Liteky was struck not only by the extent of the misery but by the disparities he saw between the US government's official pronouncements and his own observations. The delegation's first stop was El Salvador, one of the Reagan administration's model democracies.

"We saw the cathedral in downtown San Salvador where four hundred fifty people were crammed in and trying to live. The stench of cooking smoke and sweat was so heavy I couldn't wait to get out. Some of those people had been cooped up in there for over four years. Then we met with the Mothers of the Disappeared, who risk their lives to try to get some word about their relatives in prisons. We saw the books they're given to go through in the police stations, with pictures of mutilated bodies, to try to identify their loved ones.

"By the time we got to Nicaragua, it was like a breath of fresh air. Here was a nation trying to rebuild itself. Where were all the oppressors that I'd heard about?" The climax of the trip was a visit to a military hospital in northern Nicaragua. He walked into a ward as he had walked into the Salvadoran refugee's lecture, without any particular expectations, but he ran out sickened. This, more than anything else on the trip, was Vietnam revisited. "I was practically shaking as I stood outside that ward in Nicaragua, because as a chaplain, I had had to go around through the same kinds of wards and give these young men some kind of consolation—men with their legs and arms and even their testicles blown off, men who were paralyzed, men who would never know the love of a woman again . . . "

Even after leaving the priesthood, Liteky had remained a charismatic Christian and continued to take his spiritual life very seriously. But he came home from Central America depressed, angry, stunned, knowing his life had changed though having no idea what to do now. He landed in Miami, where his wife waited to begin a joint vacation. "She came all excited, and here I was on the edge of depression. I said, 'Judy, I'm sorry, but I've got to have a few days by myself to decompress.'" He holed up in a friend's condo, stalked the beaches, tried to write or just think straight, got nowhere. "Finally, as I was packing up and was about to put the typewriter back into the case, I said, 'No, I've got to give it one more try. I am going to write something.' So I sat down and put my fingers on the keys, and the words came out: *Are you willing to be led?* I said, 'Jesus! Is that all? I guess so . . .' "

Getting in touch with feelings and accepting spiritual guidance have become points of honor for Charlie Liteky. To be "in your head" is for him the worst alienation possible. He seems to know the difference, even though he can't always explain it. And he says that while a few lessons from the outside world have helped—a marriage encounter workshop he once attended as a priest, for instance—he simply decided to start paying attention to his feelings during his period of self-discovery after leaving the priesthood to reconcile his spiritual and sexual selves. His philosophy echoes Stanley Keleman's observation in *The Human Ground: Sexuality, Self, and Survival*: "If you are an alive body, no one can tell you how to experience the world. And no one can tell you what the truth is, because you experience it for yourself."[5] In Central America, Liteky "just tried to feel what was coming in to me from the people who were speaking to us. And I didn't feel any phoniness from the Nicaraguans. But when I got to the US embassy, I felt like I was in the presence of a used car salesman."

As fellow seminarian Hendrickson points out, "Charlie does not have very great powers of abstraction." In fact, he has at times shown a distinct anti-intellectual bias or lack of self-confidence in that department. When he first went to Washington, it was to work at Americans for Peace in the Americas, then run by Charles Clements, an articulate and polished speaker who had led his Central America tour. Liteky remarked, "I look at Charlie Clements, and I'm very much in admiration of him. He's gifted with a lot of gray matter. But I've got to say, 'Well, this Charlie here has got to do his bit, figure out what his contribution is.' " It took him very little time to determine that his strength was spiritual, and it was on that ground that he had a chance of pushing the struggle to the limit.

During the 1986 fast, he was often questioned about the logical underpinnings of his position. "How do you know the Nicaraguan government isn't in the midst of, or isn't planning, a Stalinist purge? Shouldn't we keep the contras alive as a contingency? What about Nicaragua's censorship?" asked one Republican representative who stopped by to talk. Instead of pointing out the relationship between external destabilization and internal repression or comparing Nicaragua's human rights record with those of US client states in Central America, Liteky punted. "I'm not responsible for what the Sandinistas do. I'm only responsible for what my government does."

As he became consumed by Central America and carried out many of his protests in the company of veterans, Liteky was soon compelled to take another look at Vietnam. Reading critical documents on US foreign policy such as *The Pentagon Papers,* Blanch Wiesen Cook's *The Declassified Eisenhower,* and Noam Chomsky's *Turning the Tide,* he began to see events through Third World eyes and, with that impetus, to reinterpret the war that made him a hero. The book that really made his old conceptual frameworks tumble down was Joseph Ampter's *Vietnam Verdict: A Citizen's History,* and reading it was so painful that he remembers scribbling in the margin, "Oh, God, please don't make me go through this again." The whole war, he came to believe, was based on a lie—the Gulf of Tonkin incident—told to the nation by the very president who had pinned the Medal of Honor on his chest. "I don't know about you," he says, "but for me there is nothing more personally hurtful than being lied to."

The issue of truth engages not only Liteky's personal sense of fairness but his Christian morality. Lying is very close to the essence of evil, in his mind. Reading M. Scott Peck's *People of the Lie,* a Christian psychotherapeutic discussion of evil as that which hides the truth, Liteky had another of the moments of illumination which seem to characterize his development. "The Reagan administration," he decided, "is an administration of the lie. They hide the truth, they obfuscate the truth, they run from the truth." His lobbying efforts in Washington did not refute that point of view. He was quickly daunted by the differences between his perspective and those he saw in Congress. A legislative aide told him, "Charlie, you're sincere and you've been there but you're going at it all wrong. Washington doesn't relate to moral arguments. You have to frame it in terms of political pragmatism." Liteky hit the roof. "I don't want a Congress that doesn't respond to moral arguments representing me."

And so, the medal renunciation. Press interviews followed, and a few editorialists were emboldened to suggest a need for more such acts of courage. Liteky's few months on the east coast kept stretching, as did his phone bills, in spite of his frequent lament, "I really did leave my heart in San Francisco." The contra aid debate grew fiercer until— with the gallery packed with outraged opponents—the Democrat-controlled Senate and House passed a $100-million aid package.

On Labor Day, Liteky stood on the Capitol steps in the same unmatched clothing he had worn to give up the medal. With him were three other distinguished and stubborn veterans: George Mizo, 40, a thrice-wounded and amply decorated officer who had served in Vietnam; Brian Willson, 45, a burly lawyer from Vermont who served in air force intelligence in Vietnam; and Duncan Murphy, 63, a World

War II ambulance driver whose commitment to peace was born of his presence at the liberation of the concentration camp at Belsen. Their joint statement read in part, "We are so convinced of the immorality and illegality of this new Vietnam . . . that we offer our lives in a statement of ultimate protest . . . We choose not to be a party to crimes against humanity committed in the name of the American people. When leaders act contrary to conscience, we must act contrary to leaders. We will be praying for a change of the hearts and minds of our own people. We will patiently look for evidence that the North American people refuse to live in the silence of implied consent."

Liteky, Willson, Mizo, and Murphy were not the first activists to consider starving themselves to death. Mitch Snyder, once a stockbroker but for years an advocate for Washington's homeless, had fasted almost to the point of death several times. The 1983 "Fast for Life" on the west coast had involved several dozen well-respected veterans of industry and academia who united in a last-ditch plea to prevent deployment of the controversial new generation of "Euromissiles." The fasts of Irish Republican Army prisoners, including the death of Bobby Sands, had drawn world attention to conditions in British prisons.

Never had the biblical line about using the most humble to challenge the established order seemed so apt. A common spectacle in the early days of the fast was Charlie Liteky, pacing back and forth across the east stairway of the Capitol and holding a "Stop the Killing" sign, with some tourists cutting a wide swath to avoid him and others asking, "What's that guy, an abortion protestor?" But the Veterans' Fast for Life emerged as citizen diplomacy par excellence and superb, if death-defying, political theater. Its purpose and its strength were less in changing minds than in opening the hearts of those who already had reason to be skeptical of the administration's positions. A woman from the farm belt wrote, "I don't quite understand what you fellows are trying to do, but I think you're onto something big." Daily support vigils on the steps swelled from ten people to over two hundred. Demonstrations took place not only in Berkeley and Boston, but in Pittsburgh and Kansas City. The fast led veterans in San Francisco to build a huge, conspicuous "Central American War Memorial" and inspired a few creative community groups with pro-contra legislators to park "bloodmobiles"—for atrocity victims—in front of the offending lawmakers' offices. Several dozen veterans sent their medals to Mizo to be returned, with his own half dozen, in a ceremony on the grounds of the Lincoln Memorial. Mail grew to over one thousand pieces a day. At first inspiring not much more than an occasional National Public Radio report, the fast ultimately found its way into the national print media and even onto "The Phil Donahue Show." "Aren't you being a little messianic about this?" Donahue asked. Liteky, all bones and alternately eloquent and dazed, just shook his head no.

At first too wrenched by her husband's threatened slow suicide to leave San Francisco, Judy Liteky finally came east to help by holding signs, passing out leaflets, and briefing the increasing number of reporters who showed up as the weather became colder and the four veterans more gaunt. One day in early October, Paul Hendrickson, too, sat on the east steps of the Capitol with his old friend. Looking at the bony face of the cantankerous football player, seminarian, and hellraiser, Hendrickson felt compelled to argue with what he saw as a death wish deeper than politics and a spirit that had possibly looked too long into the depths. He also wrote a newspaper piece about his misgivings. In it is this dialogue:

> "But will it make any difference?" I said.
> "I don't know that it will," he said.
> I wanted to say, "Do you think you're Jesus Christ or something?" but instead I said, "What about Judy?" Again, I wanted to say, but didn't, "Yeah, you save Nicaragua, and you kill your wife, eh, Charlie?"
> He didn't really answer, just nodded beatifically. Prophetic disequilibrium.[6]

And when it seemed that the stated goals of the Veterans Fast for Life had arguably been achieved—a shot of adrenalin for the movement strong enough to counter the confusion, extra work, and ideological splits created by the fast—when the other three veterans were ready to reclaim their lives and go forward with less sacrificial forms of activism, Charlie Liteky deliberated for days about "going all the way."

Hendrickson concerns himself with analyzing the logic of the fast, of nonviolence, of social activism. Liteky is profoundly aware that all the logical analyses in the world can't really measure the impact of actions like his fast, and for his own spiritual reasons has concerned himself instead with letting go of the need for guarantees.

There are abundant reasons—in Liteky's psyche, in the roughness of his childhood, and in the heady but disembodied spirituality of his youth—for his absolutist approach. Some of it, certainly, lies in the psychology of the Medal of Honor, which has weighed down many a recipient with the pressure to keep doing great things. Time-Life Books' *Above and Beyond: A History of the Medal of Honor from the Civil War to Vietnam,* notes with understatement that "the Medal of Honor changes profoundly the lives of the men [sic] who earn it . . . From that moment on, they are no longer simple soldiers, but public heroes, keepers of a great trust and tradition. And their lives are never the same."[7]

For much of his life, Liteky has had an unusual emotional relationship with death. As a priest he ministered extensively to the dying. His personal losses include a kid brother, Jimmy, who drowned in a swimming accident in 1959. To a group of supporters who expressed concern about the outcome of the fast, he drew himself up from his standard thoughtful slouch and delivered a soliloquy about meeting his maker: "I expect it to be beautiful, splendid, with white light everywhere and peace . . . " Says Hendrickson, "I think Charlie wants very much to go home." After explaining the fast in an interview with seeming detachment, Liteky paused and then added, "I don't expect to live that much longer anyway. Both my parents died of heart failure in their early sixties, and I'm fifty-five." And an off-the-cuff remark on the third day of the fast revealed another rarely exposed side of the man. "You know," he said to the other veterans, "sometimes I feel it would be easier to die than to stay here and go through all the frustration it's going to take to turn this country around."

Liteky is American to the core. He denies death and defies it and flirts with it, and all sincerely in the name of life. He has hopelessly grandiose dreams, and some of them come true. He follows his heart and then figures out explanations for what he already believes. He is capable of deep compassion and harsh sacrifices. Some of his free-spiritedness no doubt comes from the fact that he rarely has had to worry about making a living. But some of it comes from his own determination to "grow in love."

Liteky makes people angry, including many who are nominally on his side. He violates the expectations we have of larger-than-life individuals: that they will not make mistakes, that they will not wear their vulnerabilities on their sleeves, and most of all, that they will not ask others to follow in their path. He has always had a ministry, and increasingly since he discovered global issues, that ministry has been about making people uncomfortable.

In the process, he functions as a powerful psychological mirror for others. "I think Charlie's story is mostly about his father—such an authoritarian man, so angry," Paul Hendrickson speculates. "But then, I've been working through a lot of father-son stuff lately."

Though his way of life is difficult, he is believable when he says he loves it. Our second interview came after he and his wife had bought a house in Washington, during a slump in his speaking invitations. The place was a modest two-story row house within walking distance of the Capitol, where he still held frequent vigils. It reflected its owners' values, with a meditation room, austere furnishings, books everywhere and a few cartoons on the refrigerator. Obviously feeling at home, he remarked, "I said to Judy last week, just to see how she'd react, 'Let's go back to San Francisco. Let's forget all this grand

planning. Let's get normal jobs. Let me go back to my sailing lessons.'
But as I said all that, the thought came into my mind, 'Let's just lie
down and die.' "

Liteky has influenced many people to deepen their commitment to
peace work precisely because he raises so many more questions than
answers. He challenges business as usual in a way that is disturbingly
biblical. In his eyes, he is looking for a way to bring practical
nonviolence into the American political culture. Sometimes he seems
realistically aware of the uphill nature of this undertaking, but only
sometimes.

One of the few people whom he considers to be genuinely on his
wavelength is Brian Willson, one of his companions in the fast.
Willson, like Liteky, grew up in a conservative and religious family
with an especially rigid paternal authority—Willson's father regularly
gathered his family around the radio during the McCarthy era to listen
to Fulton Lewis report on alleged communist sympathizers, in order
to keep an eye out for them in their small upstate New York town.
Willson enlisted in the air force and served as an intelligence officer
in Vietnam. But his turnaround was well underway in basic training,
when he confronted a dummy he was supposed to stab with a bayonet
and said, "I can't do this."

Willson, too, has become a full-time activist veteran who emphasizes
risk-taking action out of a conscious commitment to break with the
gradualist approach. Before the fast, living in a book-filled cabin in
Vermont, he said thoughtfully, "I've read Gandhi and King, not once
but over and over. I'm concerned with figuring out how to go beyond
despair, beyond the powerlessness so many of us seem to be feeling.
We create our own realities to a great extent, after all. There are a lot
of good people in this country, in this culture, but there are no
conventional political mechanisms that really work for expressing their
visions."

Willson and Liteky share an unusual physical hardiness and a seeming
indifference to their own safety. Both see themselves as "tin men" who
found their hearts through commitment to peace activism. This may
be one reason for the driven quality of their work and for their ability
to use stark images of violence while showing almost no emotion. They
are both fascinated with the South Vietnamese Buddhist monks who
immolated themselves to protest the war, and with Norman Morrison,
the Quaker who in 1963 set himself on fire in the Pentagon parking
lot underneath the window of Defense Secretary Robert McNamara.
Willson, during the fast, carried around a letter from Morrison's widow.

Most writers who examine this troubling species of activist veteran
do so from an understandable distance. It is possible and perhaps
comforting to speculate that the violence embedded in their

"nonviolence" has something to do with these protestors' own rage, at both the war and their rigidly authoritarian upbringing. By choosing these macabre sacrifices as their model of protest, are they isolating their movement unnecessarily from the political mainstream, which has no desire to contemplate such images? Both veterans have answered that question dozens if not hundreds of times. They respond that an appreciation of war's violence and its psychological toll are precisely what they are trying to bring home to a United States which has not had combat on its soil in living memory. They see themselves as turning their own war wounds into a positive force, trying to reproduce for others Liteky's awakening in the military hospital in Nicaragua and Willson's in the Nicaraguan mountains, when he lay awake night after night listening to mortar fire and thinking, "Those are my tax dollars at work."

These difficult men, with their rage, immediacy, and flair for self-sacrificial drama, represent one thread in the growing veterans' peace movement. They have carried out numerous actions in which a dedicated few create avenues for protest that galvanize many more. They have inspired countless brigades of Vietnam veterans to station themselves in Nicaragua to rebuild cooperatives and distribute humanitarian aid. At the same time, Willson was instrumental in forming "Veterans Peace Action Teams" to mount a nonviolent challenge to US military support for the contras and the Salvadoran government.

In one campaign in the summer of 1987, Willson sat on a railroad track in Clear Lake, California outside the Concord Naval Weapons Center. A train believed to be carrying an arms shipment bound for El Salvador was scheduled to pass through. Several other veterans stood on the edges of the track, carrying signs. Nearby several hundred supporters held vigil, including Willson's new wife, Holly Rauen, and her fourteen-year-old son. The train crew and weapons center personnel had been notified by mail that the activists intended to block the shipment with their bodies. Willson alone had carried that commitment to the length of seating himself on the tracks rather than standing ready to jump out of the way. He thought the train would stop. But it didn't, and he was hit and dragged partially under the engine.

As Willson lay in intensive care with both legs amputated below the knee, I phoned Liteky in Washington to see how he felt about the action. He was several days into a second fast, but lucid and unsentimental, saying only, "Brian brought the war home. The kind of violence that happened to him has happened to thousands of Central Americans, and most of the time we're able to forget that."

That incident, with Willson through his nonviolence acting as a lightning rod for almost unfathomable violence, had the same reverberations through the peace movement as did the fast: solidarity demonstrations, extensive and respectful press coverage, redoubled commitment. A massive caravan of food and other relief for Nicaragua was organized by veterans around the United States in early 1988. Additional civil disobedience actions were sparked, many calling themselves "Nuremberg actions." After he recovered and was fitted with artificial legs, Willson and supporters filed suit against the navy, claiming a willful attack. Right after the accident, the rumor briefly flew that Liteky, Mizo, and Murphy would place their own bodies on the tracks in front of the next train in a kind of nonviolent we-dare-you gesture.

I asked Liteky about that. "The last thing we heard is that the navy has discontinued those weapons shipments until the investigation is done. So, in a sense," he wound up philosophically, "Brian did stop the train."

3 THE WHITE MAN'S BURDEN
RALPH MCGEHEE

Ralph McGehee is a study in gentleness. He speaks in a feathery voice, and simply. Gray, tufty sideburns frame his face, turn-of-the-century style, and his brow furrows reflectively. He clothes his burly frame in subdued colors. His emotional range in conversation runs from moderately subdued to moderately animated. Tinkering with a personal computer in his suburban Virginia basement, he looks like—and is—somebody's grandfather.

This particular computer, however, contains more than a few recipes and games. Ralph McGehee is developing a computerized database of CIA operations worldwide since its creation in 1947. He has cataloged hundreds upon hundreds of them in detail and broken them down into ninety-nine meticulously cross-referenced and footnoted categories. He works on it a good fifty hours a week.

McGehee is not just a doting grandfather who has let a hobby get a little out of hand. He is a CIA veteran who retired in 1977 after twenty-five years, leaving a career he began as a self-described "gung-ho" cold warrior and ended in disillusion and frustration that nearly drove him to suicide. "The CIA is not now nor has it ever been a central intelligence agency," he writes in his memoir, *Deadly Deceits: My Twenty-Five Years in the CIA*. "It is the covert action arm of the president's foreign policy advisors."[1] The bitterness of his turnaround and the stress he has suffered since then make his gentle manner all the more remarkable.

A janitor's son born in 1928 on Chicago's South Side, McGehee's earliest memory is of helping his father carry loads of trash from their apartment complex after school. "Shy and diffident" by nature, he found surprising avenues, from the football field to the ostensible defense of the free world, through which to overcome that shyness and create a niche for himself. At Notre Dame, where he graduated cum laude in business administration, he played football for four undefeated seasons and admits he "got pretty used to being in the newspaper."

A devout Baptist, McGehee came of age with geopolitical views that were simple, zealous, and not at all unusual. "Anticommunism was the issue. It was imbued in us, in all my teammates. Four of us from high school went to Notre Dame together, and they were all Catholic, which at the time meant zealously anticommunist. My father was very conservative. So everything reinforced that commitment." Reading *Time* magazine and the *New York Times,* he considered himself well-informed and had no reason to doubt the wisdom of the era. Standing in formation before a football game as the national anthem played, he felt the shiver of intermingled patriotism and personal pride that would linger for much of his career. And being proud of "our side" was inseparable from willingness to take on "their side" on any playing field.

Failing a pro football tryout after graduation, McGehee floundered for a time professionally: a year of coaching, an uninspiring position with Montgomery Ward. Having just embarked with his wife Norma on a joyously romantic 1940s marriage, he felt added pressure as a young provider with no career prospects. Then, in 1951, a telegram arrived offering him an exciting though unspecified job working for the government, doing something very important for the security of the nation.

With only that vague job description and an address to report to, he boarded a train for Washington, DC with a handful of news magazines and a sandwich. He writes in *Deadly Deceits,* "I visualized myself at a sidewalk café in Paris, sipping Pernod and discussing important foreign affairs with a diplomat . . . It was obvious to me that the monolithic international communist conspiracy was attacking our way of life, our religion, and our allies overseas. Ralph W. McGehee, Jr. was proud and happy to be on his way to help his government."[2]

From the moment he began his quarter-century with the CIA, McGehee's story can only be told through the veil of the two secrecy agreements he, like every CIA employee, signed, one when he was hired and one when he retired. Classified information must be screened out, and names of agents and contacts cannot be used, on penalty of lawsuit or criminal prosecution. McGehee's memoir is spotted with deletions by agency censors and could only be published after a two-year legal battle, but the story is still clear. It is about an ambitious and principled young man, no more naive than the culture that bred him, drawn into the CIA by his sense of mission, groomed and encouraged by expertly wielded incentives from promotion and travel to the camaraderie of one of the most exclusive fellowships in the world.

At first, the environment was more glamorous than his assignments. He was one of the delighted candidates in his training class inducted into the Deputy Directorate of Plans—later to become the Deputy Directorate of Operations, the branch concerned both with intelligence gathering and with "such other functions as required by the President and the National Security Council." But his image of life as a "debonair spymaster" was quickly soiled by three months of paramilitary and survival training. After that, he and his family landed in an idyllic, agency-provided home outside Tokyo. Working with the CIA's China operations group, which oversaw far-flung activities in the Pacific and monitored goings-on in the People's Republic of China, he spent two years as a records clerk in the shadow of Mount Fuji, followed by six months of the same in the Philippines.

The first stress McGehee felt was not associated with the job itself, but with the family pressures related to its demands for secrecy, maintenance of a cover identity, and unquestioning obedience. It began the first time Norma McGehee had to lie to friends and neighbors about her husband's work, continued whenever he took off on a mission and left her with next to no information on his whereabouts, and acquired an added dimension when his four children were old enough to complain, "Daddy, we're the only kids in school who don't know what our father does for a living."

In spite of that tension, McGehee for the most part functioned contentedly through three years in Asia and returned to Washington in 1956 as chief of records for the counterintelligence unit of China operations. The work was unutterably tedious; the filing and retrieval system was not appropriate for the task of cataloging Chinese ideographs. McGehee's first jarring realization of the potential for error in intelligence gathering came during this period. An agent recruited in Saigon and turned loose on the Chinese mainland with a million-dollar budget was found to be running not an intelligence net, as he had been hired to do, but a newspaper clipping service whose leads he would rewrite, inflate, and feed to the CIA. When the fraud was discovered, McGehee's staff—already in a state of perpetual gridlock from the volume of data and the unsystematic nature of the operation— had to find a way to purge three years worth of false intelligence.

In 1957, when the Soviets launched Sputnik, McGehee's mounting frustration with the CIA's information-processing capabilities only increased his desire to be of use. He and a friend pushed for training and reassignment as case officers and were finally accepted. In that capacity, he landed in Taipei, Taiwan in 1959 as liaison to the several intelligence services operated by the Chinese nationalists.

His job consisted of training and supervising agents working in the People's Republic, debriefing captured mainland fishermen held by the Chinese nationalists on nearby islands, and attending so many "official" social functions that the partying still stands out as a primary memory of those years. In fact, his first feeling of discomfort with his role occurred in pursuit of pleasure, not intelligence. Driving home from a costume party with his wife and a carload of friends, still dressed as "wild Indians" in feathers and warpaint and sipping champagne out of crystal glasses, he passed row after row of tin shanties, their inhabitants mostly asleep. Inside one, he saw a cooking fire still smoldering, and around it in the barren room sat several Taiwanese. McGehee met the gaze of a young man in rags, and the youth stared back. At that moment, McGehee felt an unnamed, gut-level discomfort which over the years would force the question, "How are we supposed to gain intelligence about people, or to help them, when our lives are so isolated from theirs?"

McGehee's real changes began in Thailand, his next post. The newly created US Military Assistance Command, with its four thousand regular troops, was bringing large numbers of CIA officers into the northern part of the country, ostensibly to protect Thailand from the Pathet Lao insurgency next door in Laos. McGehee's roles included supervision of intelligence gathering and training of Thai secret police in the techniques of intelligence collection. On his office wall was a poster, portraying Mao Zedong and Ho Chi Minh as fanged and clawed caricatures, reaching downward from China and North Vietnam to engulf Southeast Asia. He felt grateful to be able to take part in the region's defense. "I saw it as the white man's burden, quite overtly. I considered us to be sharing the advantages of a superior culture. But as I spent more time with Thai people, inevitably I started making personal comparisons, and I realized that we weren't superior. Their religion, for example, was clearly admirable—modest, strong, and much better integrated into their lives than we usually managed with our own."

During this tour, he had his first contact with agency operations that appeared to sacrifice intelligence gathering to political goals. He was assigned to accompany a team working with the Hmong and other hill peoples on the Chinese border. McGehee tells of a three-week hike with a Thai counterinsurgency team into those hills, replete with leeches and poisonous snakes, to accomplish a varied program: to make friends with villagers, offer them medical and agricultural training, recruit some of their young men into counterinsurgency forces, and win their approval for the construction of small airstrips on their land for resupply operations.

Overall the experience was satisfying. His team arranged for several airstrips to be built and exceeded their recruitment quotas for counterinsurgents. Only later did that pride turn to sorrow: By creating the first relationships between those remote peoples and the central government, by politicizing a population that had kept completely to itself, McGehee now believes his mission and others like it opened the way for the later destruction of those peoples by the Thai government, under the guise of wiping out communist influence.

Rotated back home in mid-1964, McGehee became responsible for overseeing the programs he had worked on in Southeast Asia. In that role he had his first contacts with William Colby, later director of the CIA but then director of its Far East division. McGehee and other desk officers regularly briefed Colby, whom he describes as "an unprepossessing, mild-mannered man you would never notice in a crowd. He had straight brown, gray-flecked hair and heavy glasses. When he talked to you, he devoted his entire attention to you and his eyes always seemed to express his understanding. His manner and attitude evoked confidence and trust . . . He regarded word usage as an art form, and he was a master at it."[3]

During that period, McGehee says, he and a contingent of his fellow desk officers were called upon to prepare congressional testimony for Colby for the purpose of winning funds for expanded paramilitary operations among the Laotian hill peoples. According to McGehee, the briefing team spared no effort in trying to win the legislators' hearts and minds. He and the others were instructed to emphasize that the situation was desperate but, with adequate funding and commitment, winnable. The testimony included a map on which, at Colby's instruction, the communist forces were colored red. According to McGehee, the team devised a new system for defining platoons that, on paper at least, inflated the few dozen groups of poorly trained teenagers into the roughly one hundred platoons that Congress was being asked to fund.

Colby's briefing was successful, and McGehee was among those who cheered it as necessary in the larger anticommunist effort, even though he saw it as a case of "policy being created from the top down and then intelligence being selected or created to support it afterwards." By the time President Lyndon Johnson announced his escalated commitment of troops to Vietnam, McGehee had requested and received reassignment to Thailand.

His assignment was to direct a program, in cooperation with the Agency for International Development, to train the 50,000-member Thai national police in methods of intelligence gathering. Testing various approaches in a broad pilot program, McGehee concluded that "the traditional approach of recruiting agents did not work. It consumed too much time, resulted in reports of doubtful accuracy, and proved to be no way to understand a burgeoning communist insurgency."

Instead, he devised a systematic, in-depth process of questioning residents of villages in which there was some evidence of communist activity. Trained "survey" teams would enter a village and, with an emphasis on establishing friendly relations as well as getting information, question every villager separately, then compare the stories for inconsistencies that would point the way to people worth questioning further.

The process was not without sobering experiences, such as the suicide of a young man who was ashamed of being exposed as an underground organizer in his village. But the method brought in much information about communist activity and was humane compared to some common alternatives. He writes, "We disseminated the final report to American and Thai intelligence organizations. Praise came back immediately. The Agency's Directorate for Intelligence gave the report the highest rating in all six of its grading categories."[4] He recalls praise from the Thai government and other agency divisions that was similarly loud and clear, as well as a cable from his acting station chief saying that the method was to be implemented on a national scale and he had been chosen, pending approval from headquarters, to run it.

McGehee was therefore shocked, when his two-year tour ended in October 1967, to learn that he was not being reassigned to Thailand and the survey program was being discontinued. This moment shattered McGehee's comfortable relationship with his employer and transformed his drive to counter a foreign threat into a drive to make sense of the mixed signals he was getting from home.

Before that fateful day, McGehee's only clue that he and the agency decision makers were on a different wavelength had been one mystifying incident a few months earlier. During a visit by William Colby, still Far East division chief, McGehee reserved a good portion of Colby's day for a private session to lay out his method and "results which had been confirmed not once or twice but two thousand times." He describes giving Colby a step-by-step presentation, complete with graphics and maps. The bottom line was that the communists in Thailand, far from being an isolated, solely military force, were a mass-based movement. That movement, he went on, had won considerable loyalty among the people and was winning more because of the US and Thai reliance on brutality. At the end, he writes in *Deadly Deceits,* "Colby seemed puzzled by my presentation. I had never seen him at a loss for words before. He looked at the ground, he looked everywhere. Finally, he looked at me and said quietly, 'We always seem to be losing.' "[5]

After his tour, McGehee was reassigned to the China section at headquarters, but he continued to be concerned if not obsessed with Thailand, the scale of communist activity there, and the CIA's rejection of what seemed to him a viable plan for dealing with it. He wrote a memorandum to Colby's successor. It came back with the response that he no longer had jurisdiction in that area.

He hit upon an idea for making himself heard which, like most of his best ideas, landed him in more trouble than he could then fathom. The CIA gives internal awards for innovative suggestions that are adopted for use; McGehee submitted a formal proposal to the awards committee. It was rejected. He rewrote it, attached more documentation, and resubmitted it. He was called before the chief of the Thai desk and sharply reprimanded for doing an end run around proper channels of authority. "Your action," he was told, "could jeopardize all future promotions for you."

Acutely aware that he had "lost the battle of Thailand," he began studying Vietnam, both as a known training ground for Thai communists and as an escape from the byzantine file rooms and incomprehensible priorities of CIA headquarters. He read everything he could find—agency sources and outside materials—on communist movements in Vietnam. He strongly suspected that they had the same mass base in the rural population that he had observed in Thailand. Yet no reports he read inside the CIA suggested such a parallel. He began to worry that the United States was missing the evidence there, too.

He volunteered for a tour in Vietnam, determined to "generate enthusiasm" for his ideas, a phrase his family still teases him about. He arrived in October 1968, just after the Tet offensive, regarding Vietnam as another, possibly more receptive ground for learning about Asian communist movements: how broad their bases of support really were, where they got their extraordinary staying power, and why the CIA, with its enormous resources and well-known anticommunist zeal, wasn't doing so well at ferreting them out. With his family back home because of the war situation, he threw himself into the work.

Like many of the CIA's seven hundred employees in Vietnam in 1968, McGehee was attached to the CORDS (Civil Operations and Rural Development Support) program, the civilian-military hybrid organized to win South Vietnamese loyalty through a combination of development aid and harsh counterinsurgency strategy. Even when he became involved in operations, McGehee still saw his major role as intelligence gathering, because "all the operatives had an intelligence-reporting responsibility too. In fact, their intelligence was prized the most because it most directly supported the continuation of the operations, which is what we in the field naturally wanted."

In *The CIA and the Cult of Intelligence,* Victor Marchetti and John D. Marks provide this summary of the CIA's presence in Vietnam: "Among other activities, the agency organized guerrilla and small-boat attacks on North Vietnam, armed and controlled tens of thousands of Vietnamese soldiers in irregular units, and set up a giant intelligence and interrogation system which reached into every South Vietnamese village."[6] McGehee says he was largely unaware of that range, but he realized early that something was amiss in the intelligence-gathering process, starting with his first briefing in the CORDS program. In light of his prior reading on Asian communism, he found the discrepancy between the agency's version of events and his own research disturbingly predictable. Again, the enemy was portrayed as a few lone marauders in the mountains and jungles, despite what he had already read about the Vietnamese communist party's development of mass organizations of farmers, students, women, and others.[7]

His first assignment in the CORDS program was as officer in charge of CIA operations for Gia Dinh province, the populous and very important area around Saigon. Intelligence reports came across his desk, many frustrating in their vagueness. Military officers attached to the agency reported to him, including, he says, some whose job was quite explicitly to lead "hunter-killer teams" against alleged communist supporters. In their reports, and in weekly CORDS meetings, he formed a rapid and clear impression of the enterprise as more interested in controlling the Vietnamese by any means than in supporting their aims as a nation.

His early months in Vietnam were filled with zealous attempts to get long-timers to heed his warning. He was so fired up because he vigorously believed in the war, and believed that it could never be won without serious study of the nature of the enemy. To that end he spoke with many key people in the agency and wrote a long, detailed memorandum on his views. Amid his many experiences of rejection—from emphatic to noncommittal—one stands out. "My immediate superior in Vietnam, a very intelligent, hard-working, dedicated man, had lost a son; the boy was killed as a marine over there. My superior's experience and expertise were in European affairs. He had come over—although he wouldn't admit it—to avenge his son's death. I went to him with this analysis. I said, 'Look, we're not telling the truth about what's going on here.' You'd think here would be a man who would jump on the information and run with it. But his only response was, 'How can you be right, Ralph, and all the rest of us be wrong?' And I understood that I would have responded exactly the same way, if I hadn't already seen what I'd seen in Thailand."

After six weeks in Gia Dinh, he was assigned as liaison officer with the head of South Vietnam's special police, the equivalent of the FBI.

He continued to observe the same pattern: denial of genuine enemy strength, coupled with reliance on violence guaranteed to push neutral civilians over to the other side. He continued to challenge the accepted wisdom about what constituted significant intelligence findings but, after about six months, decided that he was unlikely to change many minds. Looking back he sees institutional barriers, but at the time he saw case after case of individual resistance, all hard to understand, but each one a little different. "I would say, 'This is what we should be reporting.' People would respond, 'We've already reported that. There's no more interest.' "

Had the discouragements been more consistent, the pattern among them might have emerged sooner, but Ralph McGehee's career is riddled with ironies. Once while he was home on leave during the worst of his Vietnam experience, McGehee was called into headquarters to receive a medal stemming from the training division's use of the very idea he was struggling to have implemented, the survey method he had developed in Thailand.

The greater the resistance he encountered, the harder he pushed, working eighty-hour weeks divided between his office and the US Information Agency library, knocking himself out at the end of the day with strong liquor and bad television. Some days he thought the CIA was mysteriously out of touch with reality; some days he thought the agency was lying; most days he had no idea what to believe.

He had landed in Vietnam skeptical but curious, feeling personally victimized by the agency's policies in Thailand but still a functioning team member. But after a few weeks in Gia Dinh, he was so alienated that he was almost incapable of functioning socially. McGehee's idealized view of both the CIA and his fellow human beings were shattered. His nerves shot, McGehee's isolation deepened. He became so obsessed and exhausted and strung out that friends stopped having dinner with him.

Where once he had looked for every conceivable avenue to report his findings and theories, now he withdrew, resigned. This resignation even kept him silent when his old boss, William Colby, now head of the CORDS program, came through to be briefed on the state of operations. Staff member after staff member spoke with the same resolute optimism. New to the post, McGehee said little. Memories of his attempt to communicate with Colby in Thailand paralyzed him, both at the briefing and later that evening, when the two men found themselves face to face at a cocktail party. McGehee chatted mechanically about home, family, and the minutiae of office operations while a voice in his mind screamed, "You dumb, blind son of a bitch." He was powerless to let the words out.[8]

In the aftermath of that episode, he hit bottom. His spirit devastated, his body hurting all over, McGehee felt utterly lonely. Of many late nights spent staring at nothing, too tired to work and too wired to sleep, he remembers one vividly. In the living room of his rented villa—with the same Nancy Sinatra tape recycling endlessly, and punctuated by the din of bombs and aircraft—he sat arm-wrestling with reality: the war was a massacre, the United States was kidding itself and his intelligence work was helping it do so, and most of the rural population in fact supported the other side, about which we knew next to nothing because we were too damned stubborn to learn. All the grotesque aspects of Vietnam—the napalmed children, the razed villages, the Yankees seemingly blind to the impact of their actions— hurt and maddened him and would not let him rest. He imagined marching upstairs, picking up his loaded gun, and blowing himself away. But, as his mind raced, he thought, "My death should serve some purpose, like those of the monks who burned themselves in downtown Saigon. Maybe if I made a huge banner saying 'THE CIA LIES' or 'FUCK THE CIA' and hung it from the roof of the agency's Duc Hotel and then jumped off . . . I hated my inaction and myself . . . "9

In the silence punctuated occasionally by the bombing outside, the former Notre Dame football hero sat and sobbed. And from that evening of despair, a resolve crystallized in his mind: to stay alive to do something, somehow, to compensate for the damage he had contributed to and to make the truth known.

While McGehee fiercely wanted to leave the CIA, he suspected strongly that he was unemployable outside the agency. Home once on leave, he circulated what little he could call a resume, made up of vague descriptions and cover identities. But nobody wanted to hire an anxious and exhausted-looking government employee who claimed that virtually all his work history was classified information. Two of his four children were in college, and the others expected to go. "If I hadn't felt family responsibilities," he says, "I'd have been on the next plane out."

Stuck in the CIA, stuck in Vietnam, and by every indication alone in thinking the enterprise had slipped completely through the looking glass, McGehee became obsessed with rising to a level of influence from which his voice would be heard. At GS-13, a midlevel bureaucrat, he had significant responsibility but not much prestige. So he drove himself and those he supervised, and the results, as he describes them, were satisfying: an enormous increase in the production of intelligence reports, frequent recognition from headquarters in the form of in-house publication of those reports, and during his second year, the roundup and conviction of forty-one enemy spies, a network that had penetrated the highest levels of the Thieu government. Though praised for that accomplishment, McGehee was furious to note that his name was not on the list when the next round of promotions came through. When he demanded to know why, he was told, "Next year."

After two years in Vietnam and with no promotion, he came home chewed up by rage, barely able to communicate with his family, devastated equally by the grand-scale tragedy of the war and by his deepening personal chaos. Peace demonstrators in the streets of Georgetown triggered an unexpected tenderness in him, though he could not bring himself to say anything to them. Consciously, though he saw the war in Vietnam as an abomination, he still accepted the geopolitical rationale given for it.

McGehee requested and received reassignment to Thailand, which was two years deeper into the war and two years further down the road it had been on when his intelligence surveys were discontinued. Old colleagues were defeated and morose. The American school, where he had once felt secure sending his children, was now surrounded by a towering fence and run down by student drug abuse and apathy. In terms of intelligence gathering, it was "the same old fantasy," and he could play the role of willing team member only with the greatest cynicism. And now that his family was able to rejoin him, he expected himself to put up one front at work and another, that of the father whose career is under control, at home.

He kept the juggling act going until another ball was added: pain, sharp and constant, in his back where a disc was in the process of self-destructing. Under the combination of physical and emotional pressure, he blew, and wrote a lengthy and angry memo about his grievances to the chief of station. He was severely dressed down and placed on professional probation, just before his wife put him on a med-evac flight to the States for surgery.

From that point on, the memo clung to him and he was too angry to care. His personnel file began to accumulate additional memoranda suggesting that he needed counseling. After the surgery, he was given a series of home-office duties which he calls "my Siberias"—an obscure research project, followed by a desk job processing incoming cable traffic and press reports. This post, which would occupy him through his last four years in the CIA, was with the International Communism branch of the Directorate of Operations' counterinsurgency staff. As if to reinforce the low status of the job, he suddenly found himself in social isolation. "When you become a dissident," he says, "the iron curtain comes down, and it comes down immediately. One day you'd be having coffee and lunch with people, and the next day they'd be fading into doorways when you walked by. It was pretty hard." He maintained, and attributes his sanity to, one friend whose career was sufficiently dead-ended that association with McGehee couldn't harm it further. "He just listened as a friend. He was pretty right-wing politically. He would curse the agency for his reasons, and I would curse the agency for my reasons, but at least I could talk to him," says McGehee.

It was in this job, with so much time on his hands and so much anger to drive him, that his broader education began. With no career to protect and a steady stream of information crossing his desk, he began studying the issues in a new, less goal-directed manner. He read everything he could find on communist movements and wrestled with the paradox he had resisted for a decade: If these people are nothing but evil incarnate, why do they seem to have so much support in developing countries? The direct stimulus for his research was a fellow malcontent whose theories McGehee mainly regarded as comic diversion—for instance, that the Sino-Soviet split was only being orchestrated for propaganda purposes. Though he alternately avoided and baited the man, McGehee couldn't help but notice that he was reading primary sources rather than distillations of communist thought by westerners.

McGehee began to do the same, and quickly discovered four gold mines of information, most of it available in the average university library but apparently ignored by the CIA: French writings on the Vietnamese revolution, State Department reports on China from the 1940s, research by American scholars and journalists with access to Chinese source material, and the widely published writings on Asian communist revolutions by those who led them.

Afterward, McGehee enlisted some degree of support from a supervisor; while not belaboring the breadth of the research he wanted to begin, he received general approval for a systematic study and collation of these bodies of information. "It was obvious from these writings, particularly what was coming out of China and Vietnam, that the communists had actually won the loyalty of the people, to the point that many were willing to give up their lives for the cause. How did they do that? They didn't do it with mirrors. They did it with actual social equity and nationalist programs. They were modern-day Robin Hoods. If I had been a person whose children were starving, I could see that communism would have appealed to me."

He concluded that Vietnam had been a no-win situation since the first days of US military involvement. His experience in Thailand began to make diabolical sense: while he had indeed come up with a method for identifying and neutralizing communist strength there, the same method, if used in Vietnam, would have shown the war to be unwinnable. Colby's remark, "We always seem to be losing," took on new significance.

A number of stunning pieces of information crossed his desk during those last four years. First, a cable crossed McGehee's desk from two case officers in Vietnam who were sidestepping proper channels to sound an alarm that the fall of the Saigon government was imminent. He watched as the officers were reprimanded for their insubordination and then, a few months later, as the Saigon government crumbled and the Yankees scrambled as if they had had no warning.

Then, in a May 1975 article in *Harper's* magazine, Samuel Adams, an analyst who had just resigned from the agency in disgust, argued that the CIA had suppressed information about North Vietnamese troop strength. Unaware of each other, Adams and McGehee had been struggling to push similar rocks up the hill. Discovering this kindred spirit, says McGehee, "was a real breakthrough because it meant I wasn't crazy."

Finally, in 1975, his emerging ideas were confirmed by the revelations of the congressional Church and Pike committees, which detailed inefficiencies and abuses of power in the CIA. The Pike report noted major world events the agency failed to predict, from the 1968 Tet offensive to the October 1973 war in the Middle East. The Church committee concluded in strong language that the CIA was not, and perhaps had never been intended as, an intelligence-gathering agency, but produced only intelligence that would support its real purpose—to be the covert action arm of the executive branch of government. McGehee, reading the report, silently nodded.

In the aftermath of those congressional reports, the CIA was forced to reduce its ranks considerably. Just after his twenty-fifth anniversary with the agency, Ralph McGehee walked into CIA headquarters in Langley, Virginia and spied a memo announcing an early-retirement option for any employee with at least twenty-five years of experience. He was cleaning out his desk by noon. With the irony that characterized his entire career, his supervisor recommended him for the Career Intelligence Medal, a significant honor, for the four years of research that had solidified his sentiments against the agency. With more of the same irony, the citation accompanying the medal praised him for service in Malaysia, a country where he had never set foot.

McGehee was not yet fifty when he retired, and his most urgent concern was to tell the world what he had been trying to tell his superiors in the CIA. Writing and publishing his story felt "like a biological necessity." Within a month of his retirement, his basement had turned into an office, books and papers were accumulating, a brief romance with golf had ended, and a manuscript was pushing out of him. "It was something I had to do," he says, "as though it would purge the evil within me."

At first, McGehee cast about for an institutional niche to work in. "This is so weird I hate to mention it, but the first thing I did was to get in touch with the Hoover Institution at Stanford. I thought of applying for a job as editor or assistant editor for their publication, *Yearbook on International Communist Affairs*." The Hoover Institution is a prestigious conservative think tank which tends to support US interventionist policies. As he learned more about its ideological perspective, an inner voice said, "This is not where you want to work, Ralph."

He warmed up to writing his book by drafting articles about the CIA's role in Vietnam—and was taken aback when told by editors, "That's old news." Only then did he discover the publications which had been a forum all through the war for voices of dissent like his own. As he began reading *The Nation, The Progressive,* and other alternative media, he found not only new information but a whole new perspective. "I considered myself very well informed. I had been reading all this top-secret stuff, all these State Department and military intelligence documents. And at home, I'd read *Newsweek* and *Time* and the *Washington Post*. I had no idea what a completely insular worldview they represented."

Not until he began the research for *Deadly Deceits,* with the combined inside education of his CIA years and outside education of the alternative press, did McGehee's mature beliefs really form. He emerged from the CIA seeing it as the covert operations arm of the presidency, responsible for an abomination in Southeast Asia. Through the book's research, he reinforced his conviction that its activities were part of a global pattern—from Africa to Latin America, not to mention in the United States itself—and that they were not an anomaly but consistent with the purposes for which the agency was founded. "You can read declassified documents about the first meeting of the CIA leadership when it was formed in 1947. What was that about? Gathering intelligence? No, it was to plot to rig the election in Italy," he points out.

He threw himself into writing *Deadly Deceits,* first focusing on Asian revolutions and only later realizing, on the advice of an editor, that the major story to be told was his own. The writing took three years. Two more were occupied struggling with the CIA, line by line, over which of his revelations violated his secrecy agreements. The book is a compelling story of McGehee's metamorphosis from a career-minded agent and young father—at one point intrepidly chasing a water buffalo from his yard in Taiwan with a broom while his family looked on—to a veteran, suddenly rejuvenated and shouting aloud in the halls of Langley when he spied the memo announcing that he could retire.

Since the book's publication, McGehee has been kept busy as an itinerant speaker. He testified before the House and Senate intelligence committees, became a frequent guest on radio talk shows and served as an expert witness at numerous political trials.

The most noteworthy of these was the case of nineteen protestors who won acquittal after blockading the CIA's recruitment activities on the University of Massachusetts campus. Beyond the "show" aspects of the trial, heavily covered in the press because its defendants included Amy Carter and Abbie Hoffman, the case was a legal landmark because the jury acquitted the defendants based on a "necessity defense"—the argument that they had broken minor trespass laws to prevent a major and imminent harm in the form of covert operations in Nicaragua and elsewhere. McGehee's testimony drew on his knowledge of a quarter-century's covert operations: the overthrow of legally elected governments in Iran and Guatemala; the fomenting of a coup in Indonesia leading to the slaughter of half a million civilians; the deception of Congress to gain funding for the war in Laos and to which he contributed; the use of torture by South Vietnamese secret police; the Phoenix program of political assassination in Southeast Asia, which even according to Colby was responsible for twenty thousand deaths; and many other similar campaigns of violence. His testimony was key in establishing the justifiability of the protestors' specific actions in disrupting the recruitment.

> *Defense Attorney Leonard Weinglass:* Mr. McGehee, are you familiar with the recent practices of the CIA with respect to its recruitment program on college campuses?
> *McGehee:* Yes, I am.
> *Weinglass:* To what element of the CIA are college students recruited today?
> *McGehee:* They are recruited for all elements, but primarily into the Directorate of Operations.
> *Weinglass:* What do you base that opinion on?
> *McGehee:* Traditionally, two-thirds of the agency's budget and probably more than that of its manpower have always been devoted to covert operations.
> *Weinglass:* Are students who are recruited informed of that fact?
> *McGehee:* Not always, no.
> *Weinglass:* Were you in fact deceived by your recruiters when you were inducted into the CIA?
> *McGehee:* Yes, I was. [10]

McGehee was able to speak so authoritatively about the scope of the CIA's activities not only because of his experience and the research behind *Deadly Deceits,* but also because of his more recent project, the database, which he credits with quadrupling his knowledge. He describes its birth with characteristic diffidence. "When I was summarizing the agency's operations in my book, I had to go all over the place to dig out the information. So I thought, 'Wouldn't it be great to have it all in one place?' I decided on a computer project, to bring it all together by subject matter, because I'm prohibited from naming names. I went to computer shows and demonstrations and stores and laid out the problem, but nobody seemed to be able to help me. Ultimately I got a Kaypro, and my wife, who works with a computer in her job, figured out a little four-line program that let me store items on the equivalent of three-by-five cards. From there, we got more sophisticated." He prints out a few pages to demonstrate. There are entries on planted "communist" weapons shipments, "black" propaganda, election operations.

Ten years after his retirement, Ralph McGehee is one of the foremost authorities in the United States on CIA operations. Supported by his government pension and his wife's secretarial job, with his children grown and a modest house paid for, he has laid the foundation for a comfortable life doing work that, finally, feels right. Though he may seem obsessive to those who have not shared his experience, McGehee views this work as his road to personal peace. He is not what one would call a lighthearted person; beneath his calm surface, intensity and anger clearly remain.

On the wall of McGehee's office, in one of the few spaces not occupied by bookshelves, is a poster expressing solidarity with Vietnam veterans. "I realize now that I am one of them," he says. "I went through the same trauma, the same readjustment processes, the same loneliness." For him the loneliness has been the hardest part. He admits, "I really still want to be a team player, but I haven't found the right team. I know, intellectually, that I am part of a much larger movement, and I get strength from that, but I wish I had something more personal." He longs for the support of an institution, a structure, but unlike his youth, he is not inclined to stray far from his chosen path in search of it. Where once the team was a psychological necessity, today he sees it as a comfort. Now he can say for the first time, "I have a lot to offer on my own."

In the fall of 1987, McGehee and a highly credentialed group of former national-security professionals announced the creation of a new organization. The Association for Responsible Dissent (ARDIS) believes that neither honorable foreign policies nor legitimate US security interests will be served until the CIA in its present form—or at least its operations directorate—is dismantled. While the group considers covert operations to be a last resort in a crisis—to avert a nuclear war or deal with an otherwise intractable terrorist threat—it opposes their current use as an institutionalized detour around the political process.

How McGehee and others like him managed to turn around so completely remains a mystery to him. He is aware that his recruitment by the CIA was based in part on a personality test, a copy of which he was able to obtain years later from the outside firm which administered it. The ideal CIA recruit is "externalized": more oriented toward doing than planning and toward trial-and-error methods than careful conceptualization. He or she is also "adaptable" in social situations: charming, outgoing, able to meet other people's expectations, a bit of a chameleon. In both these regards, McGehee fits. But for the third category, "regulated"—somewhat rigid, responding to a relatively small number of stimuli in a relatively predictable way, and good at rote learning—McGehee falls down. "I'm far too flexible for them," he believes. "If it hadn't been for the McCarthy-era hiring push, I never would have made it." What McGehee calls "flexibility" bears some resemblance to what others have called "critical consciousness," the ability to take a wide variety of factors into account in making decisions, to look at events from more than one perspective, to self-correct in midcourse. It is an ability, ironically enough, which he cultivated while trying to do his job well in the CIA.

But the Ralph McGehee who spends fifty hours a week speaking against the CIA and patiently building his database is not so different from the younger man who put in years indexing data on China and in the file rooms of Langley. "I've always been ideologically motivated," he reflects. But it's harder now to articulate his ideology except in terms of what it isn't. "I don't consider myself a communist. I don't think I've gone that far. I just think that the United States has a lot to offer to the world, but we're taking a lot instead of giving, and wouldn't it be a wonderful world if we could turn that around?" While modest about his own contribution to that process, McGehee can still say, "I feel, these days, that the pain I went through is justifying itself in my ability to speak out. That experience is a source of credibility and confidence. Oh, there are times when I think about packing it in and going to the beach. But I also feel that, if you know the threats and you don't do anything, you're worse than the perpetrators."

4   *IN SOME OTHER WORLD*
─────────── *DAVID MACMICHAEL*

The whole picture that the [Reagan] Administration has presented of Salvadoran insurgent operations being planned, directed and supplied from Nicaragua is simply not true. There has not been a successful interdiction, or a verified report, of arms moving from Nicaragua to El Salvador since 1981.

The Administration and the C.I.A. have systematically misrepresented Nicaraguan involvement in the supply of arms to Salvadoran guerrillas to justify its efforts to overthrow the Nicaraguan government.

—former CIA analyst David MacMichael,
as quoted in the *New York Times*, 11 June 1984[1]

He must be living in some other world.
—Secretary of State George Schultz referring to MacMichael,
as quoted in *Time*, 25 June 1984[2]

David MacMichael was the first employee of the Reagan-era CIA to go public—and he did so spectacularly—in opposition to the agency's intelligence claims on one of the most feverishly contested subjects of foreign policy. As the administration lobbied for increased contra funding and mounted a series of covert operations against Nicaragua's government, it justified its actions with the claim that the Sandinistas were repressing their own people and exporting revolution to El Salvador. More immediately damaging to these efforts than a thousand coffee harvesters returning from Nicaragua with an alternative viewpoint was MacMichael, with his patrician image and scholarly voice, stating in the national media that the administration's intelligence on the matter was faulty if not downright fabricated.

"His metamorphosis," said the *New York Times,* was "the sort that intelligence officials dread."[3]

Likewise his subsequent activity. He was an observer during Nicaragua's 1984 election, testified in Nicaragua's behalf in its suit against the United States at the International Court of Justice, has spoken extensively against aid to the contras, and in 1987 took a key role in a citizen campaign to prosecute the "secret teams" whose extragovernmental foreign policy operations had been exposed in the Iran-contra hearings. Most recently, he was one of the former intelligence professionals who formed the Association for Responsible Dissent, a group opposed to CIA adventurism. But he bristles at the title chosen by the group, since his "other world" is one where dissent is by its nature responsible and constructive. "I have always said, 'Let's talk about it.' I find it very difficult to work in situations where there is no dialogue. I may be wrong about Central America or anything else, but my position is ethically and intellectually absolutely correct."

MacMichael is a complex character: animated, sharp-minded, warm and candid, but with an undercurrent of restless irritability. Mixing the eloquence of an ex-historian and the earthiness of an ex-marine, he is a virtuoso storyteller despite an occasional tendency to laugh himself to tears at his own jokes.

"Back in the marines, I used to be pretty tough. Now I'm an old sweetheart. The classic story on that one is: My brother is driving down the New Jersey Turnpike, and this cop pulls him over for speeding. My brother looks a lot like me on his driver's license picture. Cop says, 'You got a brother or cousin or something named Dave?' My brother says yeah. Cop tears up the ticket right there and says, 'He was my commanding officer. He was one mean son of a bitch, but I sure learned a lot from him.' "

The story of his two years with the CIA can only be told within the restraints of his routine secrecy agreement, which requires prior clearance on former employees' public statements. MacMichael says he bases his speaking on a "magazine article" he drafted for possible future publication, and submitted to the review process—"plus the fact that, since my main objective has been to deny that they have classified information to support their claims, I don't need to refer to any."

His story begins at the end of 1980. While the CIA performed a prehiring security check on MacMichael and he filled the time with a long-distance bicycle trip, Jimmy Carter left the presidency and Ronald Reagan was inaugurated. A foundation of the new order was the premise that revolutionary Nicaragua was behind most of the instability in the region, and was the conduit for massive arms shipments from Moscow to the Farabundo Martí National Liberation Front (FMLN), the insurgents in El Salvador.

When he joined the agency, MacMichael was assigned to the National Intelligence Council, the eighteen-member senior staff group which advises the director of Central Intelligence and coordinates CIA activities with those of other offices. He was an "estimates officer" working on Latin American affairs, part of a small analytic group charged with examining international developments that might affect the United States and preparing reports on them known as national intelligence estimates. It was MacMichael's job to keep track of any information that could have an impact on the accuracy of intelligence reporting.

As MacMichael tells it, he analyzed cable traffic, debriefed field operatives, and examined in-house files; he had access to all non-nuclear information. Evidence of the arms flow from Nicaragua to El Salvador seemed to have dwindled to nearly nothing just before he came on board, coinciding with the failure of the FMLN's "final offensive" and with the Reagan administration's ultimatums to Nicaragua. He looked for information on the FMLN's supply and support networks inside and outside El Salvador, not just for evidence of Nicaragua's involvement. But "because of the idea that the insurgency was entirely supplied from the outside," he says, "there was practically no attempt to describe what the support and supply network within El Salvador was. Nor was there an attempt to look beyond Nicaragua for alternate sources of supply and support from outside the country, because the fixation was on this Moscow-Havana-Managua pipeline." Given the surveillance technology that was available to find evidence of this much-touted pipeline, and the enormous political value it would have in support of the administration's case, he concluded that if the arms flow existed, it would have been discovered, and that if it had been discovered, it would have been on the six o'clock news.

He became interested in what, in fact, was going on in Nicaragua to deserve such awful accusations, and did a study of the degree of political opposition possible in the country. Examining the non-Sandinista opposition groups in operation— unions, political parties, church organizations—he concluded that they were in no danger of elimination or overt repression. He predicted that opposition groups would be unable to mount an effective political challenge, not because of Sandinista repression, but because the *Frente* had superior personnel, organization, programs, and prestige.

He laid out his arguments in writing and submitted the paper, only to find that "it caused a firestorm. The people who were most involved in denunciation of my paper were those who had a non-evidentiary set of beliefs about the inevitability of certain things being done under a Marxist-Leninist system, that there was an inevitable progression, that appearances to the contrary were essentially tactical steps to deceive the West. I'm not a great believer in inevitability. You have to deal with what's actually happening."

He worked on other projects but was continually drawn back into the vortex of Nicaragua and El Salvador, first by the State Department's widely criticized white paper of February 1981 and then by the approval of the first $19.5 million for covert operations against Nicaragua, ostensibly to stop the very arms flow he saw as nonexistent. He restated his views when the subject was raised in meetings, and says a senior aide to Director William Casey told him, "We do have the proof, but we can't expose it."

MacMichael pounded enough desks to win approval of his paper for a short time. In the wake of events such as the overthrow of the Shah of Iran, in which the CIA had been caught without even an inkling of the brewing upheaval, one of his superiors told him, "I don't agree with what you're saying, but it's a good idea for us to have an alternate view in the files." A copy was even given to Anthony Quainton as he assumed his post as US ambassador to Nicaragua. The paper was at the printer in October 1981 when Nicaragua's government arrested several union and business leaders for alleged CIA connections and declared its state of emergency. The paper was pulled.

He goes on, "The next thing that really ticked me off was a document that went out in the spring of 1982, with the conclusion prepared by the guy who was at the time the head of the Central America working group, a highly placed analyst who today holds an even higher job in the agency. On the basis of two unevaluated pieces of raw intelligence with which I was quite familiar, he put together this piece of so-called finished intelligence which said that the high-level flood of arms continued. But the evidence didn't support that."

In the document, says MacMichael, were two photographs, "half-page pictures captioned 'rural landing strips in El Salvador of the type used by the Sandinistas.' Now, there are a million cow-pasture landing strips in that country, as there are all over Central America. I sat down with him over lunch and went through the document. I said, 'I'll take your word for it that these landing strips are in El Salvador and not in Pennsylvania. But what's this *of the type used by*? Is there any evidence that these landing strips were used? Markings? Wrecked aircraft? Parachutes hanging?' He said, 'Of course we don't have the kind of evidence that's going to convince the American Civil Liberties Union. But everybody knows the Sandinistas are sending that stuff up there.' I said, '*Everybody knows* is not my idea of intelligence work.' "

MacMichael believes that the major source of "garbage" in the system is the fact that intelligence is routinely gathered by the same people who are responsible for carrying out covert operations and who "have a vested interest in seeing those operations continue." Without actually fabricating evidence in the field and without any need for the analysts back home to "cook the ingredients that are supplied," the overall conclusions from an intelligence report are skewed when it finally reaches political decision makers by the pieces of information field operatives choose to report and to emphasize, which generally reflect what they believe is wanted from them all the way up the chain of command.

Only in retrospect is all this obvious. MacMichael reflects, "You begin with the belief that you are being fed the high-level information. You are debriefing the high-level people, dealing with people coming in from the field. But you soon become aware that the system is set up so that the analytic side of the CIA—the producers of the so-called finished intelligence—are consistently being duped and manipulated, while being pumped up psychologically to believe otherwise. It is real disempowerment. And it's the same thing that happens to a vast portion of the work force in the United States, people who are designated as management but who really have no decision-making power, who are psychologically manipulated to identify with those who manipulate them."

MacMichael kept speaking out when it seemed fruitful, not only on Central America but on the danger of "letting the operations tail wag the intelligence dog." Just as his two years were finishing up, meetings were held to discuss his recommendations about the creation of an office that would review intelligence analysis independently of operations. He had even "gotten to thinking there might be a future for me" in running it. But a phone call from his supervisor hesitantly informed him, "We don't have a match."

"When you're finished with, or let go from, a specific project in the agency, you get to do what's called 'walking the halls,' " he explains. "You go around with your resume to see if other projects can use you. So I did that, and was hired to do one little study on another subject on a consulting basis after my departure." But he was basically cut loose, and was disappointed. He will never know whether events unfolded as they did because he was "an independent and cantankerous thinker" or because, at the equivalent of a GS-14 civil service level, he would have been a large item in the budget. He believes a major factor was that "I was flying in the face of established wisdom at a time when operational decisions were being made" to go ahead with the contra war.[4]

MacMichael has operated most of his life on two incompatible wavelengths: he at once seeks out structured environments and drives himself to outpace and challenge whatever structures he lands in. Most of the time he manages to outrun the contradictions. Born in 1928, he was raised in a middle-class New Jersey suburb, in a proud union family which believed in "the Democratic ideal." He was taught an emphasis on "coloring within the lines" by organizations like the Catholic church and the Marine Corps. From these came the tacit assumption that "if you do each day's tasks reasonably well, there's some automatic scheme of advancement." He has an embattled quality, and a touch of cynicism, as he adds, "I believe a system should function as it should. I know that's very unrealistic of me. Consequently, I've had a tremendous number of disappointments."

His critical side, like his structure-seeking side, came from very early experiences. As a Catholic youth ("so-o-o Catholic," he sighs), he was condemned to Protestant-run public schooling by a feud between his father and "the old Nazi who was our parish priest." He learned to feel different, outnumbered, and defensive from the day he was first ordered to join the Protestant version of the Lord's Prayer. The ritual became a daily choice between human wrath and eternal damnation, a constant reminder that voices of authority can clash. "I learned very early to say 'Wait a minute. Is that so?' That whole experience left me with a tremendous sense of apartness and defensiveness," he reflects. "I wish I had the capacity to be a true believer. I often think, 'How happy I would be if I didn't have that ragged-edged critical mind running all the time.' " But instead it has run faster and defined for him a narrower road as the years have passed.

He describes his younger self as a loner except for the camaraderie of tireless ball playing—football, baseball, basketball, stickball. The Marine Corps attracted him first as "an extension of the playing field." It was also a way, after the death of his father, to finance an education on the GI Bill. Seeing older cousins go off to "the great adventure of World War II," while he was painfully too young to serve, whetted his appetite for military experience. Only in retrospect does he note that the fantasy was formed with almost no concrete images of who the enemy was or what actual combat would be like. In the Korean War era, he "assumed it would be with the Soviet Union, but that wasn't really the issue."

"Were you an idealist?" I asked him.

"Oh, yeah. A. J. Squared-Away, that was me. But the ideal was training and performance as ends in themselves."

Those ideals were sharpened by a series of what might understatedly be called character-forming experiences. MacMichael started working for a living as a teenager, after his father took sick and died. He almost died, too, of nephritis at age 16, which was generally at least crippling in the days before antibiotics. The doctors told him, "If you live, you'll lead a very restricted life." He battled back to health and joined the Marine Corps, where he "pulled a little wire" to be sent into combat in Korea. Ten days later a shell blew him apart, and he was back in the hospital for another year.

His now characteristic combativeness was born in those battles and was sharpened in college. He began his studies on the GI Bill, but at first spent half of each week playing football and the other half recovering. He was almost ready to drop out when a friend convinced him to give it one more try. He transferred to a little-known corner of the universe called Hampton-Sidney College in rural Virginia, and something fell into place in his mind—equal parts self-discipline and fear of failure, he speculates. "I decided that, if I was going to do the thing, I might as well give it a good shot, so I stayed out of the bars and knuckled down and graduated Phi Beta Kappa."

MacMichael's first critical perspectives on US foreign policy came from his post-college employer, the Marine Corps. He re-upped after graduation still holding the not-uncommon assumptions that the corps served as a protector of freedom, a builder of character, and a solver of the problems at hand. He was quickly disillusioned by training programs for platoon leaders that appeared to exist solely as a draft dodge; "Wednesday afternoon athletics," which translated into golf or fishing; and amphibious exercises whose training value was completely undermined by the installation of communication systems ahead of time to make things run smoother. In the physically demanding field of amphibious reconnaissance, MacMichael won a reputation for trying to out-marine the rest of the marines, campaigning for higher physical-conditioning standards and frequently writing blistering letters to the *Marine Corps Gazette*.

Rising to the rank of captain, he found it natural to manage people by involving them in the decision-making process, but was surprised to find that this was not a universally accepted concept. "I've never liked being the boss," he says. "It's just my personality. I've always been perhaps more willing than I should be to assume responsibility, but I'd rather not be in authority. And in the Marine Corps everybody seemed to want to be boss. I've got a middle-class education, but at the same time I've got a foot in another world which is real to me. I don't think it's right to define reality for others. I don't think that it's the function of an elite to define reality for others."

If the Marine Corps of that era sometimes seemed banal and mindless, it was also at times surreal. In 1953, MacMichael was part of a detachment of troops flown to the Nevada desert to watch a nuclear bomb detonation and test fighting conditions in its aftermath. He remembers it in every detail.

"It felt just unearthly, like no other experience I've ever had. They started by exploding one hundred tons of TNT on the site—and that's an enormous explosion—to give us something to compare it with. You feel a little jolt, you see a flash. Then comes this forty kiloton thing, four hundred times as much. But it doesn't just magnify it. It's qualitatively different. First of all, there's this jolt that's just all-encompassing. It doesn't come from any direction. You're in it, like a hammock. The ground is swaying under you. And the light doesn't come from any direction. You're bathed in it. It invades you, it surrounds you, it's liquid, it encompasses you, all while you're crouched in a goddamn hole. Everything that's not tied down starts blowing over you. Whoosh. More than hurricane force. Then it stops. But that's when you have to make yourself stay down. Because it all comes back again, you see, to fill the vacuum that's been created. Then came the cloud . . . "

It would have been a traumatic enough experience if all had worked out as planned, but it didn't. "At the climax of this whole thing, we're supposed to do a 'tactical walk' in these conditions, when all of a sudden the wind shifts and the cloud starts blowing back on us. That means Condition Black: Everybody scramble like hell to get on trucks and out of there. I was saying, 'They're telling us we're going to fight under these conditions? Give us a break.' "

During his years as a marine officer, MacMichael made his first trips to US outposts in the developing world and experienced anti-Yankee sentiment "so real you could smell it." In Vieques, two of his men on liberty were shot dead by Puerto Rican *independistas*. In the Virgin Islands, purchased by the US in this century, he found that "locals who were used to living on their little scrubby piece of beachfront, growing what they needed to survive, or trying to, couldn't quite understand how it was that some 'continental'—that's what they called the whites—could come down and take over that land and build a hotel in which they could then work as chambermaids or bellboys. And I realized I didn't understand that either."

In the Dominican Republic, he remembers a particularly difficult scene. "I was commanding the marine detachment on the USS *Galveston*, and we made a port call at what is now Santo Domingo City. We were briefed by a very nervous naval attache from our embassy who said, 'There's some political unrest in the country, but if you see anything strange, just look the other way.' It was to be a weekend of major government-organized political rallies. My job was to organize the shore patrols. Well, on my second day there, I'm sitting in my headquarters and an army truck pulls up and they drag out this poor guy all trussed up like a turkey. They dump him in the middle of the barracks yard, and I'm standing there watching them beat this guy literally to death with their rifle butts, fifteen feet from me. I said, 'Holy smokes, this is some country.' "

MacMichael spent ten years in the marines—much of it with a wife who found the unsettled life difficult. He realized it was time to get out the day he had made arrangements for his detachment to attend a training in the States while the ship was in dry dock; his commanding officer vetoed the plan because "there would be nobody on board to clean their spaces if they left." As he stood trembling with anger on the deck, MacMichael realized, "the psychology of the thing was broken. My idea of being in the marines was to accomplish any assignment, obey any order, and I could no longer do that and maintain any integrity. I just couldn't do it."

He left the Marine Corps and enrolled in a doctoral program in history at the University of Oregon. There he focused on Latin America and the Caribbean, but concluded with disappointment that the "standard works in US diplomatic history are an exercise in pure apologetics. Everything the US ever did is somehow portrayed as right."

After earning his PhD, he was hired to teach history at a small Catholic women's college. But the environment was difficult for him— "a former recon marine in the company of nuns." His pay was low, while the economic pressures he felt by this time as father of three were considerable. And the students, many of them young ladies who seemed interested only in marking time before marriage, activated an admitted misogynist streak in him.

Studying and teaching history reinforced his conviction that "policies of intervention and control are both unnecessary and dangerous." By the 1964 presidential election, MacMichael regarded the war in Vietnam as a bad idea that a smart leader ought to break with, and he voted for Lyndon Johnson as the peace candidate who had promised to do that. When he saw that promise broken, his own trust in elected officials likewise took a dive, and he began attending demonstrations with some regularity. But when the opportunity of his professional life came, it ironically led straight into involvement with the war that so outraged him.

The opportunity was a job with the Stanford Research Institute (SRI), which over the years produced both visionary studies of utopian futures and tactical support for the bloodiest war in history. SRI had just received contracts from the Defense Department for studies involving Central America. His work formed part of the basis for massive changes in the thrust of military aid programs after the Cuban revolution, changes which included the creation of the Alliance for Progress. He made his first visits to the region, to Honduras and Panama.

Then, from 1966 to 1969, the institute sent him to Thailand to work for the US embassy's Office of Special Assistance for Counterinsurgency. He is merciless in his assessment of the ethical and intellectual climate. "I was up against the lies, the bullshit, the whole number." But he is equally unforgiving of his own role. "I knew the Vietnam War was a scam from the beginning. And yet I participated in it." He is articulate about his reasons: to be sure he wasn't missing some crucial insight, to go where the action clearly was, to get back into a more masculine world. Besides all this, it seemed to him like one of the few occasions in which life was playing by the rules; he had done good work as an academic, and he was being rewarded with expanded opportunity—indeed, an opportunity for him and his family to "live like royalty over there."

His current perspectives on Central America and the sources of error in the intelligence system were influenced enormously by those years. One of his first assignments was to help Thailand's government design a security system for the country to stem the flow of arms and supplies to the insurgents. The Thai government, he says, "was insistent that all the problems it was having had to be directed by Vietnam or China; they had no indigenous roots. 'Our niggers would be okay if it weren't for these outside agitators,' that was the view." In that assignment, he learned the accepted methods for tracing the supply system of an insurgency, for identifying the arms bazaars and clandestine supply bases and sources of support both inside and outside the country.

MacMichael learned firsthand about some of the limits inherent in intelligence gathering, and about the ways the process could be subverted by "our side"—people in the field who were invested in continuing their projects and often regarded Washington as the enemy. "For instance, in violation of US policy, which was to try to limit the amount of US military personnel in Thailand, US military helicopters were being used for the transport of Thai security forces in their operations. It was strictly a no-no, but it was going on. After a while, some of these choppers started getting hit by ground fire, and word came from Washington that this had to stop.

"Well, the ambassador was very much opposed to stopping, because he had his own ideas about what ought to be done, so he demanded that all people operating out of various US agencies in the country provide reports of all Thai security or security-related activities that had failed, or had been less than successful, because of the absence of US helicopter support. As you can imagine, quite a lot of fiction got written."

At times, creating similar fictions seemed to be part of his job description. He tells of being on the team selected to brief a visiting senator, Abraham Ribicoff. At the session, the question of corruption in the Thai government arose. "Around the table, everybody echoed, 'What? Corruption? Oh, no-o-o. No corruption here.' Now, I had just returned from a trip around Thailand, talking to local officials and community leaders and asking them about the problems they saw. I had taken the time to learn the language so I could read the newspapers and have some idea what was going on in the country. And everywhere I went, people said to me, 'Corruption is a big problem. It's creating a real opening for the communists.' So I said to the senator, 'Let me tell you my observations . . . ' Immediately after he left, the word came down: 'Do not put MacMichael on any more briefing teams.' "

His experiences left him cynical but still outspoken. In the late 1960s, when antiwar students were pushing the university to divest itself of Stanford Research Institute, his manager "invited" SRI's professional staff in Southeast Asia to sign a statement expressing confidence that their work helped keep the free world free. MacMichael was one of only two who refused. "I said, 'I don't know about anybody else who signed that thing, but I'm doing this job because I'm being paid very well to do it. As far as defending the free world, I can't really see what this miserable dictatorship has to do with it. And I'll tell you something else. If this were before the Second World War, and the Third Reich were putting out contracts for studying the best design of gas ovens, you'd be in there bidding on those contracts.' "

Although MacMichael has from time to time worked for enterprises whose larger purposes he would prefer not to think about, his self-respect has depended on at least admitting that fact. "Look," he says a bit wearily, "the essence of power is being able to define reality for other people and force them to accept it. That's when someone has power over you. If you have any concept of yourself as a free person, that's what you've got to resist. I say, 'Okay, you can tell me to be in here at eight in the morning. You can tell me to do a routine, a certain quantity by a certain time. I can agree to all this without any essential violation of my integrity. But if you're going to tell me that black is white, and I have to say yes, then no. That we can't do.' "

Home from the war, MacMichael used his experience to speak out at rallies and forums on Vietnam in much the same way that he later would on Central America. But by day he continued to work for SRI. As the war wound down, he shifted into "a welcome focus on my own country." He learned futures methodology and turned out some studies he is still proud of, including one on pesticide abuse which is well-regarded in futures writing. As work fitting his background became more sparse at SRI, he supplemented it with "that genteel form of unemployment known as independent consulting." His clients, when he had them, were varied and included the CIA.

His first marriage collapsed at about the same time as his twelve-year consulting career finally dried up, and he found himself in the midst of midlife crisis in California as the New Age dawned around him. The human potential movement interested him for a time as a structure, of sorts, in which to operate, but he was soon disillusioned by what seemed to be too many people using revolutionary new ideas and technologies for the same old self-serving purposes. Asked, for instance, to review a book on "humanistic capitalism," he fumed, "I find it impossible to take seriously any treatise on personal economics that does not have the word 'risk' in it once."

By this time on the far side of midlife crisis and divorce, MacMichael had loosened the grip of his Catholic upbringing enough to see life on earth as something other than a vale of tears, and sought to get back on track with a career that would be useful to the world but fulfilling and secure as well. That meant pulling together his eclectic achievements into a coherently marketable package. He learned to enjoy the role of "free-floating big thinker," but at times floated a little too freely and began to blame himself for what seemed a lack of continuity in his career. "My generation grew up thinking it was easy to get rich. If you didn't, you just weren't paying attention. Well, I wasn't paying attention." He resolved to start doing so, but wondered at times if his fortune weren't reflected in a half-remembered movie scene.

"There's this British movie—Peter O'Toole, I think—where the guy has just had it with corruption and the banality of his work. He marches up to the top of the skyscraper to tell the boss it's over. And here, in the penthouse, is this very fat, cigar-smoking character, played by Orson Welles, getting a massage from two women. Peter O'Toole says, 'That does it! I'm going to go find myself an honest job.' The boss looks up very calmly and says, 'My dear boy, there aren't any.' "

The tension he has experienced between integrity and worldly success is not so unusual, but he is unusually tormented by it. He tried to market himself as a futurist in corporate settings, but thinks he was "too honest about what I saw as the limits of the methodology." By 1980, having concluded that his background and style were more suited for government than industry, he headed accordingly for Washington, DC. Soon after his arrival, an acquaintance who worked at the CIA told him about an internal job posting, saying, "I can't tell exactly what they're talking about, but it sounds sort of like what you do." He was sitting with a copy of the job description in the Reston, Virginia public library when, quite by chance, in walked a CIA contact with whom he had worked closely in Thailand years before. An interview soon followed. "They made me a very, very attractive offer," he recalls. "And this was not going to be just day-to-day intelligence analysis. It would be examining the big picture. We'd be a small, elite group of highly qualified people drawn from all over the intelligence community and outside, who'd be advising at very high levels of government."

In the waning months of the Carter era, working in the agency seemed to MacMichael a relatively benign opportunity to exert a positive influence from within while paying off some bills. It was also a chance to settle an old score. He confesses, "They had tried to recruit me right out of graduate school. I was teaching at the time, and had been running with a lot of personal crisis stuff since the Marine Corps from the pressure of trying to keep food on the table. They gave me an elaborate battery of tests, and they seemed startled—rushed me off to the shrinks, in fact—so I knew I was not coming off as a very controlled person. But I don't like rejection . . . "

He had gone to Washington in search of a structure in which he could function with some kind of integrity. And so, when rejection came again, it was devastating—and enlightening. He had been around this block enough times to sense that he could not keep living in a state of "moral ambivalence."[5] A sense of unfinished business and a drive for vindication led him to Nicaragua to see the situation for himself.

A new word came into use in rural Nicaragua in the early 1980s: *paracaldista*—parachute jumper—referring to a person who seemed to drop from the sky, often with a new backpack and tape recorder and Spanish-English dictionary, to check out the revolutionary scene. In the mountain town of Esteli, MacMichael appeared as a high-profile *paracaldista* during the summer of 1983. Beverly Truemann, then on the staff of the Nuevo Instituto de Centro America (NICA), a Spanish-language school there, remembers him as an unusual figure—older than most visitors to Nicaragua, traveling solo, asking a lot of questions, taking a lot of photographs. Although he did not mention his most recent employer to her, she recalls, "I for one wondered whether he was a CIA agent."

Joanne Sunshower, another staff member at NICA, shared some of those misgivings but says, "I've spent too much of my life working inside the Catholic church not to recognize a convert on the brink when I see one. David was hard to deal with in some ways. He would try to draw out a tremendous amount of information about other people without revealing much about himself. But when I challenged him on that, he revealed a lot more. It came across that this was a highly emotional time in his life. He seemed to be paying a lot of attention to the quality of his personal relationships. He talked a lot about his children and how important they were to him. He was allowing himself to be moved.

"What impressed me about the integrity of what he was doing was that he wasn't making some kind of grand tour, meeting with heads of state. He was finding out by spending time with the people, and he would spend enormous amounts of time talking to people who were of no strategic importance to either side. They were just people. There was one old man who lived on the edge of town, and David would make the half-hour walk out there many times to spend the day with him."

That trip to Nicaragua convinced MacMichael not that it was a paradise on earth but that, by any reasonable criterion for judging a postrevolutionary society, it was open and generous. He struck up a lasting friendship with Danilo Urrutia, an Esteli native who taught at the school and who honored MacMichael as godfather of his newborn baby. Of those days, MacMichael says simply, "We hung out; we wandered all over. There was an openness about the country. We were in and out of churches—Catholic, Pentecostal. They weren't afraid, they weren't intimidated.

"We wandered into two tobacco factories in Esteli, one privately run and one, which had been owned by a Cuban buddy of Somoza's, was state-run. Well, we're just poking around and talking to the workers in the state-run factory. Now, you have tobacco coming in from the curing barn in bales, very dry. A tremendous amount of dust comes out of this stuff, and then you have a misting system to keep the air moist so the leaf doesn't crumble. Clearly, it's not the healthiest environment. I was kind of surprised to see that the workers weren't wearing their face masks, and I asked why. Well, the damn face masks were no good, they said, and their health was terrible and nobody cared about them . . .

"I said, 'What about your union?'

" 'The union? Those bastards. All they care about is increasing production.'

"Well, what about your Sandinista Defense Committee? What about getting some help directly from the *Frente?*

" 'The *Frente?*' they just laughed. 'Those people don't know anything.' They were clearly ticked off and they clearly felt no inhibition about saying it. We had a very open conversation, there in that state-run establishment with the quotes from Marx and Engels on the bulletin board and the big poster of the Sacred Heart of Jesus right next to them."

Up north in Ocotal, where contra attacks on farms and cooperatives had become common and the military presence was heavy, MacMichael remembers a young army lieutenant. "He took me around and showed me the old Somoza headquarters where the National Guard had kept prisoners. We had quite an interesting talk. I've still got his picture. I said to him, 'These were Nicaraguans and they were doing it to other Nicaraguans, so what's to tell me that your bunch isn't going to do the same thing?'

" 'No,' he said, 'you don't understand. You don't understand. Those guys were trained to be against the people. We are the people. We're not going to do those things. And our revolution is not going to be over until in this whole world there is not one hungry child.'

"Early revolutionary enthusiasm doesn't mean it's going to work that way," he admits. "There have already been tremendous problems with what they call 'bureaucratism.' But the openness is still there. You can go anywhere. You can talk to anybody. You can bring in any literature. Just try carrying literature that's printed in Nicaragua into Honduras or Costa Rica and see how fast the police are on you."

Back in the States, feeling vindicated but emotionally raw, he tried halfheartedly to look for work. His "squared-away" self said, "Okay, so I'll write a few letters to the editor and get on with my life," but Nicaragua stayed on his mind. He took himself over to the office of Witness for Peace, the religious network that organizes a permanent presence of Christians in the war zone, and offered his services as a clerical volunteer while he sorted things out.

The Witness for Peace subculture is spiritual but not "churchy." Because the organization's raison d'être is exposing comfortable North Americans to realities that will lead them to question their place in the global scheme, its volunteers and staff tend to be at least open to that questioning and more concerned with integrity than material success. MacMichael felt, for the first time in recent memory, supported in an open-ended search for answers and "liberated from any need to deal with bullshit." His months there were a time of uncertainty about whether he could offer more playing ball on the inside or by adding his voice to the public debate.

Yvonne Dilling, then staff director of the Washington, DC Witness for Peace office, remembers, "It was very clear that he was searching and didn't have any answers, that he needed time and space. Just to be around and listen and talk; he was willing to do a lot of volunteer work. He stood at the xerox machine and xeroxed for me endlessly. He ran errands. He appeared to be a man who was used to having a secretary wash out his coffee cup, and here he was volunteering in an organization where people washed out their own coffee cups."

At Witness for Peace, MacMichael also ran into activists who were uncomfortable with his past. Dilling remembers, "Some people in the organization said, 'Until he's made a public break with the CIA, we can't trust him.' My response was, 'Until we trust him, he won't take a stand.' Finally, for me, it was a faith issue."

MacMichael remained ambivalent on the question of going public, but realized he wasn't finished with Nicaragua—or it wasn't finished with him. He resolved to go back, this time less as a detached researcher and more as someone who could do something helpful. He applied to participate in a coffee-picking brigade in the early spring of 1984, but was rejected when he wrote down "Central Intelligence Agency" as his last employer. Finally he made another trip on his own. He was there when explosions in the port of Corinto were traced to CIA-planted mines. As the stakes climbed higher, MacMichael realized during a discussion with a friend in Managua that he was in an absolutely singular position to challenge the escalation of the war.

His revelations in the *New York Times* brought him invitations to appear on "The Today Show," "Good Morning, America," and "All Things Considered," as well as a brief write-up in *Time*. The CIA has had very little to say in public about the episode. Phillip Taubman's report in the *New York Times* says only, "Although the CIA would not officially comment on Mr. MacMichael or his accusations, intelligence officials privately confirmed that he had worked as an agency analyst from 1981 to 1983. They said his contract was not renewed because of questions about the quality of his work. Other agency officials said Mr. MacMichael was let go because he had repeatedly challenged established policy and pressed officials to produce intelligence data to support their conclusions about Nicaragua."[6]

MacMichael was invited to testify before the International Court of Justice when Nicaragua brought charges against the United States in 1985 for mining its harbors. The case, a rallying point in the public relations war between the US government and the Sandinistas, was highly charged from the beginning, when the United States announced that it no longer acknowledged the jurisdiction of the court. Nor did the Nicaraguans come out of the proceedings untarnished. The US justification for its actions was collective self-defense against a power portrayed as expansionist and untrustworthy. One of the prime arguments for that untrustworthiness was Nicaragua's alleged support for the FMLN, the crux of MacMichael's dissent in the CIA.[7]

As MacMichael tells it, "It had been generally understood that, during the period of the failed final offensive in 1980 and up to January 1981, the Nicaraguan government had been actively in support of the FMLN. Paul Reichler and Abraham Chayes, two members of their legal team, said as much in a press conference in Managua before leaving for the Hague. So everyone assumed that would be stipulated. But the counsel for the Nicaraguan foreign ministry came over at the last minute and said, 'No, we're going to deny ever having done it.' MacMichael ended up being a partially hostile witness, then fielding a barrage of criticism in the US media, including a letter to the *New York Times* by a former US ambassador claiming that "Nicaragua's witnesses lied through their teeth."

MacMichael wrote back, "Not having been a member of the US foreign service, I am not accustomed to lying under oath, through my teeth or otherwise."[8]

While disturbed by Nicaragua's performance at the Hague, MacMichael quickly lost his inhibitions about saying publicly that he found the Sandinista government not only legitimate but made up of "exceptionally superior people." He tells with obvious emotion of accompanying the *Via Crucis,* Foreign Minister Miguel D'Escoto's forty-day march of prayer and fasting, during its final few days in 1985.[9]

"It's a dark night, with heavy clouds overhead. There were maybe eight thousand in front of the cathedral. That, in itself, tells you something. This whole 'evangelical insurrection,' it's Miguel's. It's not the *Frente*'s. If they had wanted to pack the plaza with thirty-five thousand people, they could have. But they're very thoughtful in the way they do things.

"The mass was concelebrated by fifty priests, all up on a long platform which was brightly lit. It was like a last supper. And all the people were holding their little pine splinter torches, smoking and flaring away. Very eerie.

"And then Miguel comes on to speak. Now, he's a little man. But when he hurled his challenge at Archbishop Obando y Bravo to stop being a priest of death and start being a priest of life, the prophetic voice was within him. You could watch him grow. It was like watching Martin Luther nailing the theses to the cathedral door in Wittenberg. There was that much power there."

By this time, MacMichael had fallen into a role best described as "freelance foreign policy consultant," working with anti-interventionist think tanks such as the Council on Hemispheric Affairs and the International Center for Development Policy. Speaking invitations kept coming in, but no matter how much he spoke or how much his eloquence was appreciated, he felt inadequate to oppose the momentum of the newly packaged, media-savvy "Nicaraguan resistance." He published an op-ed article in the *New York Times* urging the Democratic party to recognize and run with the political opportunity offered by the administration's "four years of hyperbole and deception."[10] But the congressional debate remained cautious and focused almost exclusively on means, not ends. MacMichael, a frequent spectator, was drawn deeper into the fray by the sense that he was watching the perversion of democracy and by a growing understanding of the way the perversion had taken place.

At times it seemed, as it had in the CIA, that the structure of the proceedings biased their outcome regardless of the intentions of individuals. At the peak of public concern over the $100-million aid package, he sat with mounting outrage through House hearings in which all the administration spokespersons had the floor first, winding up their presentations about the time the news people had to pack up their cameras to meet their evening deadlines. "And then there came some of the most knowledgeable people on this issue—Robert White, the former ambassador to El Salvador, Colonel Edward King, who has helped draft an enormous amount of legislation—speaking to an almost empty chamber."

Other times, the distortion seemed less due to chance or ineptitude and more to a conscious abdication of responsibility by lawmakers—even at those same hearings, which he calls "a most amazing spectacle." Michael Barnes, the chair of the subcommittee, started his questioning of Assistant Secretary of State Eliot Abrams by asking, "Well, Mr. Abrams, you've been before this committee many times, and we've never gotten any information out of you. Will it be the same today?" "Yes," said Mr. Abrams. "At that point," MacMichael fumes, "if I had been Mr. Barnes, I would have had the sergeant-at-arms escort him out of there."

The official position continued to be that evidence of the Sandinistas' export of revolution existed but was too sensitive to reveal. Said MacMichael with a chuckle to a magazine interviewer, "One of Damon Runyon's old stories has to do with a gambler named Rusty Charlie. Rusty Charlie is a very big, tough guy, and occasionally he drops in on the crap games. Now, he always walks away a winner, and the reason is that he throws the dice in his hat. And he is the only one who gets to look at the dice. This is an old, familiar story in dealing with the government on controversial overseas policies."[11] Whatever evidence the government may have, it still has not been made public. Even Roger Miranda Bengeochoa, who defected from the Nicaraguan defense ministry and made a series of State Department–sponsored public appearances in 1987, contested the administration's intelligence estimates on several fronts, reporting that Nicaragua had exactly twelve Soviet and three hundred Cuban military advisors, and denying that it was a significant supplier of the FMLN.[12]

With the downing of US mercenary Eugene Hasenfus over Nicaragua, the contra funding debate shifted focus from the contras' battlefield behavior and capabilities to evidence of illegal supply networks involving the CIA, other intelligence agencies, private mercenaries, and perhaps the US military. The Iran-contra scandal brought MacMichael a rare opportunity to expose more of the truth—or burn himself out trying. In 1987, he became coordinator of a major investigation by the Christic Institute, the nonprofit, interfaith law firm which is taking many of the architects of the contra war to court. Its twenty-nine defendants include John Singlaub, the retired major general and founder of the World Anti-Communist League; Richard Secord, another former major general and arms merchant; and others implicated in the contra support operations spearheaded by Oliver North from the National Security Council.

Daniel P. Sheehan, Christic Institute founder and chief counsel for the lawsuit, cut his legal teeth as a researcher defending the *New York Times* for its release of the Pentagon Papers. A tough-talking litigator with a cherubic face and degrees in both law and divinity from Harvard, Sheehan is living proof that there is a fast lane in public interest law. His clients range from Attica prisoners to sanctuary workers, and he won big with the damage suit filed against Kerr-McGee by the family of Karen Silkwood for her apartment's contamination with plutonium shortly before her death. He is the legal strategist who came up with using the Racketeer Influenced and Corrupt Organizations (RICO) Act as the basis for civil action against the alleged secret team. He is also at the center of a burgeoning personality cult among followers who have come to be known as "Christies."

The starting point of the Christic civil suit is an explosion at a 1984 press conference in La Penca, Nicaragua, held by dissident contra leader Eden Pastora. The bomb was apparently intended to wipe out Pastora but instead killed several journalists and wounded others. Tony Avirgan, an ABC camerman whose hands were seriously injured, and his wife and colleague, Martha Honey, investigated the blast with the help of the US Newspaper Guild. Their quest took them into unexpected realms, including the ranch of US expatriate John Hull, who has been accused of running a contra supply depot and who immediately responded to their charges with a libel suit in Costa Rican court. With Sheehan representing the defendants, Hull was defeated. Avirgan and Honey have concluded that the bombing's plotters included US mercenaries, Cuban exiles, at least one contra *jefe,* and numerous former high-level operatives in US intelligence and military circles.

But the bombing is only the beginning of the Christic Institute case. It alleges that the "enterprise" charged with providing arms to Iran and money and sundry other favors to the contras was not born in the 1980s, but is one of many incarnations of a floating semiprivate paramilitary infrastructure which has helped keep unpopular foreign policies afloat, from the Bay of Pigs to Southeast Asia to the present.

Sheehan has portrayed the case as a mega-Watergate. Some aspects of his public spiel depend on circumstantial evidence. But many of his claims have been corroborated by the oceans of mainstream journalism still pouring forth on the contra support network. In *Crimes of Patriots: A True Tale of Dope, Dirty Money and the CIA,* veteran *Wall Street Journal* reporter Jonathan Kwitny writes, "What we are seeing today is not an aberration; the aberration is only that we are seeing it, and what we are seeing is still not most of it."

A movement has grown up in support of the lawsuit, backed by gargantuan labors in grassroots organizing, fundraising, and consciousness raising. Thousands of house meetings, forums, and fundraisers were held around the country in the year before the trial opened. That movement, in turn, has begun a push for accounting of the Iran-contra scandal as a symptom of systemic problems, not just the work of a few renegade national security officials. And it has given voice to the heretical notion that the victims of covert operations deserve redress. While Sheehan and his wife and partner Sarah Nelson were crisscrossing the country to raise funds and build support, MacMichael and a team of over fifty lawyers and researchers were deposing hundreds of witnesses and building a case expected to find its way into court in mid-1988.[13]

The strengths of the Christic Institute's campaign have been in its tenacious search for patterns behind the seemingly incomprehensible events and its insistence that the pursuit of "national security" interests does not automatically provide immunity from either the law or public scrutiny. The frailties of the campaign have been in the virtual impossibility of documenting, in detail, a secret transnational enterprise spanning continents and decades. "There are all kinds of problems with conspiracy theories," MacMichael is the first to admit. "But as time goes on, I have more and more trouble with coincidence theories too."

Described by one journalist as "the ambassador to Danny Sheehan from the world of level-headedness," MacMichael has argued with his boss over some details of the suit.[14] But he appreciates it, overall, as a means of overcoming widespread denial about the erosion of democracy in the United States in the 1980s. "Hearing about this case and its implications is a lot like going to a counselor because your child is behaving strangely and being told, 'You have a problem of incest in your family.' People can't hear it. They go to a different counselor. They grab at any other explanation. It's too painful."

Although he is not wide-eyed about the potential of his new career for changing the world—"sometimes I think I gravitate to this issue because it's a loser," he once acknowledged—he becomes animated when discussing the lawsuit. Besides being a source of vindication (and "some measure of revenge"), he regards it as one more chance at his lifelong dream of seeing a system work the way it is supposed to. "We have agreed in this society that court is where evidence is brought and transmuted into proof. It's where we get beyond rhetoric. We're going to go into court with this and we're going to win and go on and put some of these people into jail, but, see, what's more important is that we have on the record that these claims are true. It's not just what D. C. MacMichael or anybody else thinks."

He was, and remains, torn between "going on" with his life and facing the degree to which these battles have become his life. He has struggled on many levels in an effort to help achieve justice without martyring himself. His pre-CIA style, which he characterizes as "moral ambivalence," has given way to the opposite, a deeply felt need to choose a side and be true to it, in spite of the naggings of critical consciousness and the attractions of a less driven life. He was remarried in 1985 but separated the next year because, he says, "I was finding things to do at the office until eleven at night, and that didn't make me a very easy person to live with."

The life he has chosen is one which calls forth MacMichael's characteristic combativeness and creativity but also plays on his characteristic self-doubt. "The major change in me," he says, "is that now I have a more or less constant need to justify myself, to myself and to a lesser extent publicly. Before, I could say, 'I work for SRI,' or 'I work for a government agency,' and that would be it. Now the question, 'What do you do?' is one I have to answer for myself every day. In this type of work, you have to keep asking, 'Why am I doing this?' You've got to think. That's the biggest difference."

"You must love this work," I ventured.

"Nope. I don't love it. I just do it," he responded flatly. For all his passion on these issues, MacMichael can envision a life that isn't based on struggle, and at times waxes wistful about that vision. "I remember driving out into Virginia to visit someone recently, and seeing this guy standing out in his yard with a highball glass, just checking out his crab grass and watching the sunset. I remember thinking, 'I love that guy. I'll bet he's happy. I hope he's happy.' " MacMichael has no shortage of alternative ideas for filling his time. He loves movies and fiction, runs regularly, and is a self-described "great time-waster" who can lose himself for hours in a London *Times* crossword puzzle. "People will say to me, 'Maybe you're just a system fighter,' and that's not true. In many ways I'm a very passive person for long periods of time. I put up with a lot. But I do feel that anything worth doing within any structure depends on that structure having a certain integrity, and if that integrity is violated I get extremely uncomfortable."

5   A SOLDIER OF FORTUNE
JOHN GRAHAM

The Lions Club of Whidbey Island, Washington does not like to think of itself as a breeding ground for revolution. When the club invited John Graham, a former US foreign service officer and resident of the island, to speak at its dinner meeting, he was expected to raise the audience's adrenalin levels with stories of his years in Libya and Vietnam and with adventures from his lifelong hobby, mountain climbing. That expectation was not disappointed. But Graham's biggest adventure story was qualitatively different, and from it he drew a passionate moral with the power to unsettle as well as inspire. The story began on a cruise ship.

"At 2:00 AM, we were awakened by an announcement: Fire in the engine room. It had been put out, but there was a lot of smoke, so we were supposed to go up on deck while they blew smoke out of the cabins. We went up without any extra clothes or anything. But when we got on deck any fool could see there was more smoke, not less. They were lying to us. And this was the Gulf of Alaska in October.

"A plane dropped in firefighting gear. We were standing around getting looped on brandy, trying to keep warm. The ship's orchestra was playing 'Oklahoma!' Then we were ordered to go to lifeboat stations and we made it, somehow, into the lifeboats. About ninety people in this boat made for fifty. The fire, which had been burning steadily, finally broke through the fire doors and the whole ship's infrastructure went in about five minutes as we watched from the boats."

The ship was the *Prinsendam*. Graham and 523 others lived through what *Readers Digest* later called "the greatest air-sea rescue in maritime history."[1] His willingness to tell the story over and over on the lecture circuit can hardly be separated from his own healing process, but it also fits into the radically different life this ex-diplomat has built for himself since his encounter with death. Graham's is a classic story of adventure and betrayal with a highly unorthodox climax: a spiritual turn and, with it, a brand-new sense of his own destiny. It is a metamorphosis from self-described soldier of fortune to educator, grassroots activist, and catalyst in the quest for a better game than war. The climax on the boat was a turning point long overdue.

All through that morning, helicopter rescue crews lifted one person at a time up to safety as the waiting boatloads fought off the wet cold and exhaustion. Graham's was one of the last lifeboats to be rescued. "It was a race against time because a typhoon was blowing in. By noon we were in the middle of it: thirty-foot seas, forty-mile-per-hour winds. By 3:00 PM, the helicopters had to stop; they just couldn't fly anymore. There were eight of us in that last boat. No flares, the radio didn't work. There was about half an hour of daylight left. Tomorrow, all they would find was a bunch of corpses." Graham had just left the foreign service, following an instinct to pursue some higher calling. While waiting for it to take shape, he was earning a satisfying income lecturing on world affairs to cruise passengers wanting a bit of stimulation between dessert and cognac. And here he was about to die.

"For the first time in my life, I thought, 'This is it.' Every other time when I've faced violent death, it would have been quick. This time, I had half an hour to think about it. So I prayed, or I tried. I said, 'Well, it could be that, at age thirty-eight, John Graham is about to be wiped out. I can accept that. But I don't understand why. I don't think the divine does nonsensical things.'

"I said, 'Why am I about to be wiped out, when I'm on the verge of becoming a teacher, of living a dream?' I was angry. I was challenging it.

"The answer came back clear, like a burning bush: 'What are you doing? You're lecturing on cruise ships and making money. If you can't see something larger, you might as well die.' The issue was framed very clearly. I couldn't run anywhere in the lifeboat. Even my anger was clobbered. I was utterly spent. I just gave in. I said, 'Okay, I accept. I have a responsibility. I know what I'm supposed to do.' At that moment, a Coast Guard cutter came charging through the fog. It would have hit us if the lookout hadn't been paying attention. We were saved."

In the years since then, Graham has been exploring what it means to go into the business of transformation.

His message to the Lions, and to the hundreds of other business and community groups he has addressed, was about risk taking, higher purpose, the unity underneath human beings' apparent separateness, and the connection—not simple, but strong—between peace on earth and individuals' inner peace. When John Graham talks about changing lives, his talk is infused with a vision of personal change on a scale broad enough to affect society as a whole. His organization, the Giraffe Project, honors people who stick their necks out for the common good and publicizes their examples creatively and widely. He says in a typical speech, "To stick your neck out to put a vision into action, to commit yourself to putting purpose and meaning in your life, can seem very risky. Not just because you may fail. The scariest part for most people is that they might succeed. That would mean shattering their perceptions of their own 'limitations' and accepting a power and responsibility they may never have felt before. It would mean changing their lives forever."

Graham is a confounding mix of the conventional and the outlaw, the spiritual and the pragmatic, the self-promoting and the modest. His publicity photo is a close-up face shot angled to highlight sharp cheekbones and a resolutely serious expression. But in person, John Graham is an appealing though not handsome man who carries his height a little awkwardly and whose smile is frequent, genuine, and shy. He has been an Eagle Scout, an altar boy, a mountain climber, a counterinsurgency specialist in Vietnam, a student of science, and a mystic. During his foreign service years, he was a diplomat, a congressional aide, and a NATO strategic planner. Now he can fairly be called a peace activist—of an unorthodox, nonpartisan sort.

Graham began his foreign service career as a self-described soldier of fortune, "wanting to serve America's aims, but mostly because that was how I assumed I would advance in my career." But by his late thirties, he had been transformed into a person who would let his career suffer rather than fail to articulate the visions that were taking shape in his mind. He has changed less in terms of his ideas about where the United States fits geopolitically into the grand scheme— though these have changed considerably—than in terms of the roles he and the rest of us can play in bringing about constructive change.

Growing up in the state of Washington, Graham was encouraged to achieve and adventure, but to do it with a certain class. He remembers a strong ethical component in his upbringing, both from Catholic education and his parents. His father, an advertising salesman for the *Tacoma News Tribune,* represented good honest labor, moderation, and discipline. His mother, "an indomitable woman," stood out as the stronger role model because "she taught me that anything worth doing is worth doing well. She pushed me. But she was never like the anxious Little League parent, hovering around." Both parents operated in a structured, authority-conscious universe and were models of the kind of good life that could be lived within it.

As a high school kid, Graham was brainy and socially cursed by being "over six feet tall, one hundred and fifty pounds, a hopeless athlete, and with a full set of pimples." One Jesuit interrupted his adolescent despair with the prophecy, "Look, you've got more going for you than all the rest of the kids in this school. One day you'll understand that." Graham became a youth driven by physical challenge. From the Jesuits in high school he also got more of that "fierce attachment to quality" which led him east to Harvard. The summer after his sophomore year, he hitchhiked around Europe and North Africa. After his junior year, he was part of a climbing team which ascended the dangerous north face of Mount McKinley. His adventures were still, in their own ways, structured: a trip here, a mission there, defined and then executed with a determination to excel. "I was having a hell of a good time, but I never dropped out. Never spaced out on drugs or alcohol. If there had been a book on how to be an adventurer, I would have done it by the book." But in living out that paradox, he discovered that beyond adventure there is passion.

"I was at the University of South Australia, working with a geologist in the outback, chasing kangaroos, prospecting, and I fell really passionately in love with an Australian girl. For the first time, I sensed what real passion is about, and it scared me to death. I proposed to Jean. But while she was deciding, I got a letter of acceptance from the foreign service. Now there was adventure, and the appearance of passion, within a nice, tight structure." The dilemma he faced was classic. "Mother and the Jesuits wouldn't approve of my making money as a newspaper stringer and traveling around. But as a diplomat, I could travel around with status. Wear a tie. Go to parties." He bailed out of the relationship in Australia and married the girl next door from Tacoma. They set about building a nest—in Monrovia, Liberia, his first diplomatic assignment.

He was transferred to Libya in 1968, one year before the revolution that brought Colonel Muammar el-Qaddafi to power. As a political-military officer, he served as liaison between the ambassador in Tripoli and the commander of the US-owned Wheelus Air Force Base. "Before the revolution, my job was taking care of minor fracases, airmen getting drunk and breaking up bars, that kind of stuff. When Qaddafi came to power, the first thing he did was ask the US to get out of Wheelus. So my role suddenly became very important. I was part of the negotiations on all the nitty-gritty of handing over the base. When do the barracks get handed over? Who gets the beds in the hospital? It wasn't a clean process, because there were obviously a lot of strong feelings involved. We didn't much like being kicked out, and the Libyans had a lot of problems with our policies toward Israel. The negotiations were very acrimonious, and a large part of the job was trying to keep your head amid all the screaming."

The life of the junior diplomat was one of orchestrating hide-and-seek games with Libyan surveillance cars for kicks, sleeping on couches in the embassy, looking out the windows at burning trucks and anti-Yankee demonstrations, and constant tension with his first wife, who, like many embassy dependents, felt the stress of the lifestyle with few of the benefits. But Graham thought of it as a career fast-track: the ambassador listened to him, he was a key player in the negotiations, and he was all of 25.

As his personal life and marriage fell into disarray, Graham had the first in a series of insights about the life he was leading. "I realized that the marriage was a microcosm for what was going on in Libya, or Libya was a macrocosm of what was going on in my own heart— frustration, powerlessness, anger. I was taking all the garbage that caused the marriage to go wrong, and bringing it out in the negotiations. I could see firsthand that one reason the negotiations were so acrimonious was me."

But it wasn't just him. He observed more generally that people's behavior at the negotiations had less to do with their own rational self-interest than with their inability to deal with personal problems. The United States needed Libya's low-sulfur oil; Libya needed US technology. "There was a clear trade-off on paper, but it never happened. Instead, you had all kinds of normally intelligent people arguing bitterly. I'm trained as a scientist. So it's my tendency to say, 'Hmmm. This is interesting. We're not kids. This is not a sandbox. And yet both sides are clearly making things worse for themselves and each other.' I kept analyzing, and got to the beginning of the realization that I was a piece in a puzzle."

John Graham still saw himself as living a Catholic ethic: achievement in the approved structures and rigorous personal honesty, at least on his own time. He struggled to keep life tolerable for his family. He devoted all his resources to "being the best foreign service officer I could be." Nowhere in his ethical system was it written that one ought to question the enterprise one works in. But his questioning was forced because he unavoidably saw that his work was not neutral. "It wasn't just that things were going wrong in Libya. I was helping make them go wrong because of the negative spillover from my personal life. Did I want to live with that?"

What he first saw in himself, he soon saw as a pattern. "Individual human beings, their own lives are screwed up. When Colonel So-and-so started shouting obscenities at the Libyans, I would remember that he had a teenage daughter who was pregnant and he was very worried about her. I looked around at these people who were involved in statecraft. And there were drunks. There were addicts. There were fairly depressed people. There were people with serious home problems. And they were all taking it out around the negotiating table. The negotiations merely gave us a dramatic stage on which to do this. We—all of us in Tripoli and back in Washington—were creating a bitter and senseless polarization between Libya and the US, in large part because of our respective failures as human beings. You have people dealing with their own anger and bitterness and ego, and all statecraft does is write this large. It also takes the morality out of it. It may be quite wrong to shoot your neighbor over a dispute, but in statecraft you can do that. There really are no rules."

From Libya he went to Vietnam, where he worked in the CORDS (Combined Operations Rural Development Support) program in 1971–72, during the period of "Vietnamization." His was at various times political officer, chief development advisor for Thua Thien province, and advisor to the mayor of Hue. His responsibilities ranged from building fish ponds and schools in remote districts to gathering intelligence on the Vietcong and their supporters in the villages. As he had in Libya, he regarded the din of warfare as his own personal background music, and from his first moment in training, he "absolutely loved" firing M-16s and M-45s.

"There were some real eye-openers on that assignment. We were always told we were civilians. We were expected to go around unarmed. But that civilian image turned out to be a total fiction. A huge part of the American effort was to prove to the world that it was safe for us to be pulling out. So they wanted to be able to say, 'Those areas aren't dangerous. Look, John Graham's up there in Hue in his civilian clothes building schools and doing great consulting work with the local officials.' But in point of fact we were in the middle of a bloody war."

If that point had not been driven home to him sufficiently before, it was during the 1972 Easter offensive, when Hue was surrounded on three sides and he was the State Department's man on the ground. With house-to-house fighting and a quarter-million refugees flooding the city, most of the civilian government simply fled.

As the crisis deepened, Graham's supreme pleasure was showing the world and himself how well he could keep his act together. It fell to Graham to try to create a rump government of the few local officials who remained—including one minor bureaucrat who was found in his underwear playing the flute as the mortars fell around him. Reports came to him that South Vietnamese divisions were looting the marketplaces, and he realized, "We had to restore order, and that meant stopping the looting. That, I thought, meant a firing squad.

So there I was in the mayor's office—he being the one official who hadn't fled—and slamming my fist down on the desk insisting that he set up a firing squad and start rounding up and shooting the deserters right away. But somewhere in between slams of my fist, this sudden thought came in very powerfully: here I am screaming at one Vietnamese to shoot other Vietnamese so they can get together and shoot still other Vietnamese, and I didn't give a good damn for anything in this war. My home was ten thousand miles away. That was a real life-changing experience."

It was life-changing because he realized that the bullets were real and that people were living and dying on the basis of his decisions, because he knew himself well enough that he had to face the reality of how little these people meant to him. He reflects, "I remember going over there, not believing in the American war efforts, but not disbelieving either. I mainly had a very Hobbesian view of the world: that life was nasty, brutish, and short. Vietnam was a great example of that. At the same time, I was beginning to acknowledge that I was very tough and resourceful and, if anyone was going to survive, it was going to be me."

But most of all, the moment in the mayor's office was life-changing because it forced him to face the fact that he, altar boy and Eagle Scout, was getting off on the violence. And one reason war could hold such charm is that Graham never considered the possibility that he might be a victim. Having been through so much, he had come to regard himself as indestructible. But Vietnam demonstrated that he was at least expendable. As a public administration advisor for the city of Hue, for instance, he remembers being approached by city administrators planning a big meeting. At first, he puffed up his ego with the thought that they wanted consultation on some important policy matters. What they wanted, in fact, was Coca Cola for the meeting.

And this was only a trivial example of how his concern for individual power and its limits forced him to think about the purposes to which he was putting his own power. As the US position deteriorated, he began to notice that most of his friends in the military seemed to rely on private supply lines for their necessities and luxuries, and on private arrangements such as special boats hidden for their escape in the event of the emergency that seemed imminent. His sense of himself as a civilian development worker, as one who could say "this isn't my war," had long ago evaporated. He began to "feel like a pawn" and eventually "like a hostage." He realized that, in any evacuation scenario he could imagine, he very well might have to shoot a few of the people he was trying to help, in order to get on a helicopter.

The atmosphere was rife with the kind of mistrust that encourages questioning, if only in the name of self-preservation. Hue, the northernmost city in South Vietnam, was politically and militarily an embattled environment, still in active mourning three years after the Tet offensive. It had a well-established underground support network for the National Liberation Front. One of Graham's major roles was to help gather intelligence on protest movements, which meant trying to penetrate the networks of Buddhist monks during the period of their protests by self-immolation. He tells of waiting alone in the middle of the night in Buddhist temples where he was summoned to pass messages and perhaps receive a hint of a puzzle piece for his own use. In a situation where he could have been killed by either side, he credits his survival with his usefulness to both. His life was "lonely and dangerous." Years later, watching a TV documentary about the Vietcong underground networks, he would recognize his friends and neighbors as having been among them.

Ironically, as his skepticism about the war effort peaked, so did his responsibility for getting out information about it. It was a truism that sending information via Saigon meant submitting it to any number of editorial slashings. So Graham developed channels for sending dispatches to Washington directly. Still, he felt tension between what he wanted to say and what he thought his job required. During the Easter offensive, he was the US spokesperson whose views were broadcast on Walter Cronkite's news program; in careful diplomatic language he revealed that the hour of victory was not at hand. He characterizes that statement as "not fully honest about how bad it was, but going much farther than the US government wanted me to." Anger at "feeling like a hostage" was high on his list of motives for saying more than he was expected to say. But once he had made a dissident public statement, he felt compelled to consider his own words.

Graham's time in Vietnam turned out to be an extended identity crisis. One of his most vivid memories is of sitting in his living room with a bottle of scotch, listening over and over to the one tape he owned, Gordon Lightfoot singing "Sit down, young stranger, and tell me who you are."

Who was Graham in those days? He was a survivor, physically and bureaucratically. He was a man who could function at his peak in the structures in which he operated. Because of his obedience and discipline, he regarded himself as a principled individual. He could content himself with humanitarian achievements of a certain kind, such as maneuvering to prevent a friend's girlfriend being sent to the Con Son Island tiger cages as a suspected Vietcong sympathizer. He says, "I look back at myself as having had integrity in my direct dealings. I wouldn't falsify reports. I would die rather than lie. I would tell the truth to reporters.

I would get someone out of a tough situation if I could. But I had no integrity at all as far as caring one bit about the larger aims I was serving. I would have given my eyeteeth for a job like the one Oliver North had in the National Security Council, and I was good enough to land one. I know exactly how he felt, how his blood ran when he saw his operations working."

For his service, the State Department awarded Graham a little recovery time in the form of graduate school after the war was over. He went to Stanford University and picked up a master's degree in systems analysis while carrying the investigation into his identity a few steps further. By now, something was clearly out of balance in his life. He had become a caricature of the "adventurer" style he had so carefully cultivated. He was isolated, vigilant, braced for combat, wired. He recalls, "I would walk down the shady side of the street in Palo Alto to avoid sniper fire. It was classic Vietnam-veteran stuff, but it went deeper, into the gnawing question of who I was. There were some incredibly formless thoughts beginning to surface: Am I too self-involved? Is this good? What do I do with all this violence?" He credits his first wife, Claire, with "dragging" him to support groups and workshops, which eventually helped him heal some of his accumulated fear and confusion.

At the end of a week-long retreat in the mountains of northern California, during which he had "spent most of the time trying to impress people with what a great guy I was and telling war stories," he joined thirty men in a workshop which addressed the Jungian concept of "masculine" and "feminine" in the human personality. Abruptly, the group leader said, "Okay, I want you all to pick out the man in this room who you think is the most feminine." Thirty men pointed to Graham, who ran out of the room as if he had been given a death sentence. "I screamed at these people that they were idiots and their exercises were stupid and they hadn't heard a thing I'd said all week. Then I ran out into the woods. About half an hour later, I realized that a huge weight had been lifted from my shoulders. These people were right and I knew it. They had given me permission to begin exercising another part of myself."

Intuitively, he "got" it as soon as he ran out the door. There was a side of him that was spiritual, intuitive, capable of being deeply moved. It occurred to him that his attraction to violence was somehow connected to his suppression of that part of himself. But these insights required him to look long and closely at this other dimension. "What did these guys mean about me being the most feminine? They meant a whole lot more than just that I should learn to cry at movies."

After his sabbatical year in California, he headed back to Washington, DC still puzzling over the newly emerging dimensions of his personality. Outwardly he was the same old guy: he still liked to climb mountains, he still saw himself as reliable under fire. And he could still talk about the chilling realities of war in a dispassionate, strategically sophisticated manner—as was required by his next assignment: political-military officer with NATO's Nuclear Planning Group.

He lived in Washington but shuttled back and forth to Europe, one of two State Department employees at his level dealing with nuclear strategy for the alliance. "It was a real plum. I would get to be part of these top-secret meetings in castles in Norway or England." He was responsible for dealing with political questions arising from US deployments within the alliance, which meant predicting the effects of new weapon systems on international stability—or "What are the Russians going to think we think they think we're thinking?"

As part of his training, Graham was sent to New Mexico for two weeks to learn how nuclear devices are made and how, in the generation since Hiroshima, humankind has learned to adjust its weapons of mass destruction for calculated effect. He found that his job involved thinking about those effects on a regular basis. "If you want to take out buildings, you do this. If you want to take out people, you do something else. There are all kinds of switches in the weapons to allow them to cover different areas and so forth, and it all has political overtones. How many civilians do you want to kill? How many military do you want to kill? Is it better or worse for our interests if we knock all the buildings down and don't kill the people? If both sides have exchanged"—he reverts to the planner's terminology even now—"and they're a smoking ruin and we're a smoking ruin, and we have a few rockets left, where should we aim them for maximum demoralizing effect on the remaining Russians?"

Graham remembers at one point spending a whole week discussing what to do in the third month of a nuclear exchange. And while the absurdity of that discussion did not register in his conscious mind, he remembers a detail that did cause him to think: the meeting had to be cut short so that the colonel in charge could get home to coach his son's Little League baseball team in the Virginia state championships. For all the cold, analytical attention these planners gave to the hypothetical murder of three hundred million people, for all the numbing that was required so those thoughts could coexist with images of home and family, and for all the zeal some of them applied to proving their will to annihilate those numbers were it deemed necessary, he noticed that "what was preoccupying him and the rest was being good husbands, good fathers, good people." That understanding eventually led him to conclude that the path to peace lies not in working against those planners and people like them, but in showing them new options.

His work life was heady, and in an entirely different way so was his leisure time. Claire became interested in a spiritualist group called the Inner Peace Movement and convinced him to attend a meeting. He was "entranced," figuratively and soon literally. "I found out very quickly that I have a lot of so-called psychic ability. One weekend, we were on a farm in Virginia, and a little kid burned his hand badly on the tailpipe of a tractor. I took his hand in mine and healed it." At first he experimented with his power as "a new toy" but soon learned to treat it with more respect. Nightmares crashed in on him. He once was awakened by the physical sensation of a freight train bearing down on his room, with the room filled with "smoke that wasn't there." He began to study the literature of mysticism and parapsychology with some seriousness.

John Graham makes much of his scientific training, first in geology and then in systems analysis. It finally was scientific method that led him to accept psychic phenomena as real. "I had so many experiences that I realized the simplest explanation for what I thought I was experiencing was that I was actually experiencing it." From that point, he says matter-of-factly, "I read every book on mysticism that I could get my hands on. I read Elisabeth Kübler-Ross on life after death. When I had an out-of-body experience, what I would see out there was what mystics have seen since the beginning of time. There were bright lights and all the rest. This lent credence to the fact that it was real. What it did, finally, was provide a metaphysical underpinning for my life."

His Hobbesian view was blown apart by the sense of unity he experienced, both within himself and with the external world. Instead of dark forces, he found light. "The nature of the universe was uniformly positive. The stuff in our existence that we were interpreting as coming from evil forces—wars, acid rain, potholes—those things were coming from us. We made the decisions that created those things. Seeing that was a real metaphysical change in my life." He does not claim to have found an airtight philosophical explanation for the problem of evil, but only to believe that human choices play an unexpectedly large role in the problem and any solution. "We are all one. We lose sight of that oneness because of fear and anger and other earthly ills from which we can, through our choices, break free. When we do that, and when the illusions of separateness and powerlessness are dispelled, taking risks for the common good is a natural fulfilling way to live one's life."

Only with detachment can John Graham today describe the person he was then: a spiritualist on his own time, he earned his living envisioning possible nuclear wars as if it were all "a chess game." The tension he sees now between the values he professed and those he served was not then apparent because, in his fierce efficiency, he kept his life compartmentalized and asked only the questions that were necessary to get the job done. "My supervisor kept kidding me about whether I was going to come into the office burning incense and wearing a long Indian jacket or something, but really there didn't seem to be a conflict at the time. I was capable of the most Jekyll-and-Hyde type behavior. I was a really good soldier. I never questioned those doctrines or the people working with them. I never said, 'This is ridiculous, you guys. A five-year-old knows there isn't going to be a protracted nuclear war.' I think it's because I loved the game so much."

But the longer he looked at the world through his new sense of its oneness, the more he remembered the lessons from Vietnam and saw that his own actions had effects. He came to understand that he "couldn't be a freebooter." The troubling side of that conclusion was that he had to reassess his work. But the payoff was "a new and vibrant sense of optimism about what I could achieve," even before he knew what that would be. His NATO assignment came to an end, and he was sent to Capitol Hill as part of an exchange program between the State Department and Congress. As legislative aide to Representative Don Bonker of Washington and Senator John Glenn of Ohio, he took his first steps toward bringing his emerging vision to bear in his work. One of his most satisfying memories is of writing legislation to limit US arms sales to the Third World. "Not too much of it got passed, but we had a good shot at it and I learned an awful lot about how Congress works."

He noticed that he was less inclined to see it all as a chess game for his own entertainment, but found it even more satisfying to use his capacity for playful competition when it was in the service of human well-being. He even "began to regard the nuclear thing as idiocy, although I realized that as long as I was using words like 'idiocy' I was also part of the problem." His ideas continued to evolve, and he kept looking for arenas in government where he could develop and promote them.

He continued to angle, as well, for "plum" assignments, and while still in the foreign service took a position as deputy to Andrew Young, then US ambassador to the United Nations. He was chief of the section for African and non-aligned affairs during three of the "headiest" years for peace initiatives through official structures. The Camp David accords between Israel and Egypt were being negotiated, the Carter administration's human rights campaign was at its peak, Rhodesia was becoming Zimbabwe, and the US mission's youthful staff was involved in many of these developments. Graham had enormous latitude to use the consensus-building skills he had learned in Congress and to test the insights that had been gathering in his mind. As US observer to meetings of the nonaligned movement and as a representative on UN committees involving Third World issues, he was the same lone operator he had been back in Libya, but with an entirely different purpose. Instead of implementing the goals of his employers uncritically, he used what he knew and paid attention to what he felt in the hope of serving the greater good.

From the moment he arrived in New York, the adventure did not unfold "by the book." One of his first discoveries was that his Soviet counterpart at the UN was "a real mystic," and a friendship based on that common bond soon grew strong enough to survive the hostile speeches both men were routinely expected to make. "We would read these anti-Soviet or anti-American speeches, because that was part of our jobs, but then we'd go have a beer and forget all that."

Through that same, by now natural, personal involvement, he got to know the Third World representatives, and put in the hard work and time it took to gain their respect and affection. In a rare position of being allowed to file diplomatic cables straight to Washington, he began to lay out his views on the failures of US policies toward the Third World, "the racist elements in those policies, the lack of attention to the needs of their economies. I tried to explain the venom of Third World people toward the United States in terms of their experience. Here's this Third World diplomat screaming obscenities at the United States. I'm not excusing the behavior, but I am saying we have to look at what's going on in his country. We've refused to give him a dam he desperately needs because he won't vote our way on this anti-Russian issue. Well, he can't. He has his integrity."

As he had been in Libya, Graham was embroiled in a rancorous international arena which was also a tangled interpersonal one. People came into meetings laden down with the baggage of their national histories, cultural interpretations, and personal troubles. While there were no bullets whizzing, Graham's skills at keeping his sense of balance while under fire paid off enormously, as did his enlightened cowboy style. At a meeting of the nonaligned movement in Havana, where he was an observer without voting power, Graham tells of being banned from the official sessions and doing all his diplomacy in bars after the meetings. He took pride in being "the only western diplomat the Third World UN diplomats felt they could trust"—and in narrowly escaping several threatened bar fights with those whose trust was less than complete.

Graham's efforts bore fruit, especially when he maneuvered a resolution through the Security Council's Committee on South Africa, which briefly removed loopholes in the then-existing arms embargo against South Africa. He achieved this by collaborating with his friends in the nonaligned bloc and drafting an arms embargo they all could endorse, then presenting it to his US bosses as though it had come entirely from them. After the victory his African colleagues publicly cheered him, and his superiors in the US mission quietly offered him a new post—as number three on the embassy staff in the Congo—but Graham decided it was time to move on. Soon after his departure, the resolution was dismantled by combined US, French and British efforts.

Graham drew two morals about international politics from that experience, one from his short-term success and another from its reversal: Change is always incremental, and large-scale change is made up of incremental personal changes. The arms embargo had passed because he had made the effort to listen to and build trust between himself and Third World delegates in support of a goal they all shared. It had been reversed by his own country and its closest allies because "that level of trust just hadn't been built. I tricked them instead of trying to win them over."

In the light of his growing spiritual perspective and his insights about the personal underpinnings of political behavior, he was able to understand the tensions and egos and blind spots in the UN with a clarity that had eluded him in earlier assignments. He was able to see in these diplomats' behavior the image of his earlier self, and to respond to their anguished thrashings with a certain generosity as a result. He saw them not as evil or foolish, but as lacking in a certain body of illuminating experience he had been lucky enough to step into and live through. He concluded that people were digging themselves into divisive relationships because they hadn't had a sufficiently compelling experience of unity. People were hooked on violence, conflict, and functioning in crisis mode to convince themselves that they were alive, because they hadn't yet learned about less violent forms of risk taking. People were bringing their personal baggage to bear in their efforts at statecraft because they hadn't taken the time or learned the skills to do an inside cleanup job.

During his final months with the State Department, Graham played a dual role which was as confusing to him as the public. He had always done considerable public speaking in his official capacity, but he also began to accept invitations to address peace rallies and church groups as an individual, and what came out of his mouth on those occasions was what he thought. Some audiences were fascinated, others visibly hostile to him as a State Department employee, regardless of his views. "If you can't accept converts," Graham asked, "how is your movement going to grow?" Those "angry peace people"—their ineffectiveness in influencing him and the paradox they represented—reinforced the lesson that one can't preach global transformation and at the same time hang onto old habits. His speeches also made final his rift with the State Department. He remembers a particular rally at New York's Riverside Church in front of two thousand people, in which he expressed his honest view that it was time to normalize relations with Cuba. "But I realized I couldn't do that as a serving diplomat. It wasn't fair to anybody."

He resigned and tried to set himself up in New York as a consultant on Third World issues for business and governments. He had the experience, the savvy, the contacts. But not a single client even nibbled. By this time, his marriage was no longer functional, and divorce further drove home the need for some real housecleaning. His years of jetting around the globe—and too often regarding home as a base of operations—had exacted their price. His two children, Mallory and Jason, went to live with his ex-wife in the state of Washington. His father was dying. The failure of his consulting business was totally baffling. It was a point in the life cycle when many executives would take a long vacation. Or a cruise.

"You know," said a friend, "you can make good money lecturing on cruise ships. People want a little stimulation and fresh perspective from someone who's knowledgeable and knows how to entertain." Here was a chance to express his views in a noncombative arena, to earn plenty, and to take it easy for a season. He embarked on his first cruise, to Tokyo, with his daughter Mallory, but the night before his debut the fire alarms sounded and his harrowing turning point occurred.

Graham's journey began with his awareness of the relationship between personal wholeness and political behavior, his own and others'. In uneven steps, mostly when he was pushed against some kind of imposing wall, he changed the direction of his life for the combined purposes of personal healing and service to humanity. At first, his understanding of the connection was intuitive. It became conscious—and his changes speeded up sharply—when he discovered spiritual realms. From that point, his story thumbs its nose at interpretation. Looking back, he sees many of his earlier successes, failures, and decisions as pure destiny. "Why did the consulting business fail? It had everything going for it. It failed because consulting is an ostrich thing to do, keeping your head in the sand instead of sticking your neck out."

He began searching more purposefully for ways to implement his newly conscious philosophy. John Graham Seminars, his first vehicle, taught skills—public speaking, community organizing, lobbying—to those who sought them. It was satisfying, but not quite enough.

Graham soon met Ann Medlock, a journalist who had just been through a divorce and was also looking to put her considerable energy into a project worth doing. She and Graham had been thinking along complementary lines about how to contribute to social change and, it turned out, about what they wanted in a life partner. They were married in 1982.

Medlock, a writer and editor who broke out of a "no juice, no verve" publishing job into self-employment in 1966, boasts a resume that ranges from speechwriting for the Aga Khan to running a public relations firm in Princeton. When they met, she had just left the latter situation—and a marriage, with one child finishing high school and the other starting. With a sense of calling similar to Graham's she had moved to New York, hoping to "play jacks with the big kids in the world of communications" but at the same time to create a job that would contribute powerfully to global healing in ways she could not yet imagine. A vibrant woman with the unusual ability to speak at once precisely and passionately, she says about her motives, "It is terribly important for me not to be among the living dead. Life is too short not to be doing work that matters. I used to think I was unemployable; then I realized I'm an entrepreneur. A lot of people are coming to the same realization these days, and inventing their own jobs, because the things that most need doing don't yet have job descriptions attached to them." The Giraffe idea, when it came, was the first of her many experiments that intuitively felt just right.

From that point of commitment onward, Graham's life unfolded in a way that is common for religious converts. Success came to him when he stuck to the "right" path and eluded him when he did not. A heartwarming sort of success has been his with the Giraffe project, Medlock's idea which soon became their collaboration. It is a "nonpartisan, nonprofit, nonsecular program that inspires people to stick their necks out for the common good." As executive director, Graham covers the speaking circuit of Rotary and Lions Clubs, churches, and campuses, giving what he bills as "apathy-busting" talks. Medlock publishes the *Giraffe Gazette* and runs the Giraffe Broadcasting Service, cranking out radio scripts and taped spots which celebrate imaginative risk takers all over the political spectrum and all over the globe: an itinerant theater troupe which performs in prisons with material helping inmates take charge of their lives, a homemaker who spearheaded her town's campaign against a radioactive waste disposal site, a Polish dissident poet, a Los Angeles project to help warring street gangs make peace, and a first-grade teacher who educated herself about the nuclear arms race and founded Citizens Network.

Graham, Medlock, and their growing staff—now four—catalogue and celebrate stories like these, whether they involve international campaigns or one-time, local acts of courage. The motivating concept for the Giraffe Project is the moral John Graham drew from his near-death experience in the lifeboat: if you can't see something larger, you might as well die. Or, in more positive terms: if you can see something larger—and can be helped to identify with it—you will find a new, invigorating perspective on being alive. Giraffes are creators of new mechanisms to help people deal peacably with each other—to create, in a very concrete sense, a better game than war.

These themes are hyped—and the organization's $160,000 budget raised—with the aid of Giraffenalia, from coffee mugs to sweat shirts. Isn't all this a little lightweight? Medlock addressed this concern in a recent newsletter.

> Laughter is literally disarming. We get in under people's radar in a way we couldn't with a name like the International Society for the Fostering of Courage and Service. Besides, I've learned to be suspicious of people who are solemn. The people who seem to me the most effective and powerful in getting good things done in the world fairly radiate good humor. It's been a great lesson to meet activists I've heard are living, breathing saints and find that they laugh more than most of us.

The vision of the Giraffe Project is nonviolent, gradualist, cheery. But Graham and Medlock hope and believe it is a harbinger of revolution which the Whidbey Island Lions Club and similar groups can welcome, and might even lead. "One of the most fertile breeding grounds for Giraffes is the business community. I think that's where we'll see a lot of leadership for positive change," speculates Graham. "There's a tremendous reservoir of good will out there in the business and professional communities. It's just that a lot of people get caught up in power ladders and working themselves to death." But how, he was asked, does Giraffe positivism deal with people who are not just disempowered but have an agenda that goes against the interests of the majority? Can someone sit down with General Pinochet of Chile and say, "Come on, General, stick your neck out for the greater good and start respecting human rights"?

"I can't and you can't," admits Graham. "But maybe some other general could, after developing a relationship of trust with him."

The Giraffe philosophy of changing the world is a grassroots approach: national institutions will change when people change them, and that will happen when people learn to overcome fears, acquire skills, think strategically, and enjoy working together. As an experiment in empowerment, not ideology, the project teaches skills, encourages networking, and suggests strategies for problem solving. The premise is that if barriers are removed, people will act in their own best interest. At the local level these solutions tend to defy the labels "liberal" or "conservative," because they not only involve but require dialogue across those boundaries.

But this doesn't mean that everybody in the world who takes initiative qualifies as a Giraffe. Graham himself preempted any attempt to nominate Oliver North for that honor by writing, in early 1987, his observations of similar personalities.

> In the years that I worked in Washington, the Oliver Norths didn't work for Ronald Reagan, they worked for Jimmy Carter. They pursued liberal goals with the same high-handedness that today's Oliver Norths used to funnel arms money to the contras . . . The Oliver Norths I knew weren't operating for the common good. And they weren't patriots, not in the true sense of the word. They didn't love their country so much as they loved their plans for their country, their roles in those plans and, most of all, the personal power those roles gave them.

Since the birth of the Giraffe Project, Graham and Medlock have lived through the occasional week of uncertainty about where the grocery money would come from. But for the long run they have set themselves up in relative security by selling off a town house in New York, the last remnant of Graham's fast-lane life, to build a home on the rural island north of Seattle. Their temporary dwelling above the Giraffe Project's office is small but linked via picture windows with the vast forest lands of the Pacific Northwest. Bookshelves with a goodly portion of fiction and a basket of knitting in the living room indicate that these people do sometimes relax. But their work is much more than a nine-to-five enterprise.

The John Graham who now lugs around a six-foot inflatable giraffe on the lecture circuit is a recognizable descendant, not too far removed, of the John Graham who justly prided himself on his dynamism and persuasion in Libya, Vietnam, Europe, and the United Nations. He uses his own story and those documented by the project to inspire and empower. He is convinced that wars will end when people no longer "think they need violence to get their jollies," and he is working to market an alternative that will be self-perpetuating. The kind of role model Graham provides isn't a neat, prepackaged one, but the image of a man letting himself outgrow old expectations. The phrase "stick your neck out" pops up in Graham's language regularly, as though he may be reminding himself as well as his audience.

At times, he still looks the part of the soldier: disciplined, contained, taking care of business. He admits that his transformation—from soldier of fortune to soldier for the greater good—is still very much in progress. Tough times still shut him down emotionally and send him into combat mode. He tells the story of a financial downturn early in the project's history. "Not long after we had moved here and put everything we had into building this home, we had a period of time when the money just wasn't coming in. We had made a choice to rely on donations; we really didn't want to owe our souls to some corporate Medici. But it was rough at first. There were a couple of weeks when we had to borrow from Annie's parents to buy groceries.

"At one point during that period, we heard a storyteller on the radio talking about the Spartan boy whose father told him not to go into the woods. Well, he did, and found some cute little fox cubs, and brought them home inside his jacket. While he was talking to his father, the fox cubs began to gnaw at his ribs. And he—living the Spartan ideal—fell dead rather than uttering a sound. Through this whole period of money worries, I was being a lot like the Spartan boy—outwardly positive, but inwardly very frightened. And then this particular morning Annie reaches over and touches my stomach, and it's like a drum, and she looks at me and says, 'Fox cubs?' And all I can say is, 'Yeah, that's it.' "

John Graham believes not only that individual transformation is a possibility to be taken seriously, but that it is the only real avenue for social change. He has become both an advocate and role model for such change because he has seen it succeed and its alternatives fail. What he and his cohorts are hoping to promote is "a healing . . . not just in high government circles, where the courageous compassion of enlightened leaders might 'trickle down' through society, but also in the grassroots, where we can start a great bubbling up of boldness, caring and service in the ordinary actions that shape our lives and the society we share."

6   SOLVING PUZZLES
IN THE DARK
THOMAS GRISSOM

Tom Grissom is a gentle intellectual. His thinning hair is the color of sawdust. His face is deeply wrinkled but not unappealing. His smile is completely unpretentious. He dresses in corduroys and nondescript pullovers, presenting himself to a stranger with a slightly shy formality but turning on almost instantly to the substance of the conversation. He seems most animated when he is talking on a level that is both philosophical and personal, that weaves together experience, literary references, and tales from his youth in an endless waterfall of ideas and feelings.

Both his gentleness and his spark showed when Grissom gathered together his staff of sixty at Sandia National Laboratories in New Mexico and told them why he was leaving his $75,000-a-year job. He was manager of a major department at the lab, the group responsible for developing state-of-the-art nuclear weapon triggers. Grissom tried to avoid making grand pronouncements about the morality of the work he knew his staff would continue without him. He acknowledged that the decision was a complex and individual one. He had made it, fundamentally, to preserve the quality of his own life. Even some who knew him well were shocked when he shared and spoke about a just-written letter headed, "To a Few Friends."

> The present course has become odious and alarming to me, as well as intellectually unsatisfying. I cannot accept the premise that we are any longer engaged in a labor of deterrence, with some measure of moral justification, but rather, it seems to me, merely in the self-serving perpetuation of a military-industrial establishment which by

its very nature and staggering enormity must ultimately result in our own destruction. In this I can find no historical solace for my fears.

That conclusion represented the sum of a series of large and painful steps for Grissom, a scientist who has always loved science and for most of his life had considered its fruits to be beyond ethical controversy. Some of his most fulfilling moments had been while working on a research problem in comforting solitude, marveling at the seemingly superhuman feats that could be brought into the human repertoire— what J. Robert Oppenheimer called "the sweet ideas of technology."[1] And in this respect, while his fascination and commitment might be extreme, he points out that he and his former colleagues at Sandia are not too far out of line with the culture in which they exist. "Look," he says, "if you show people a film of a nuclear explosion, whether they're scientists or construction workers or whatever, their first response isn't horror or outrage. Their first response is excitement at what a big boom it makes." It is this fascination that drove Tom Grissom to a career as an experimental physicist—and to compile an impressive collection of patents and research papers, produce two published books of poetry, and win major professional honors.

Grissom found in science an avenue for the achievement to which he felt driven as a child and then as a serious young man. His father, a middle-class farm-goods salesman in Cleveland, Mississippi, taught that one owes one's community hard work and that in exchange one's community owes one liberal amounts of money and prestige. Grissom, who was always shy, brainy, and sensitive, realized early that he had a better shot at that success in physics than in football, and drove himself accordingly.

Although focused on science, Grissom also found great delight and comfort in culture, history, and philosophy. With his two brothers and sister, he shared a natural skepticism, a critical consciousness. "I remember wanting to believe everything I read, to believe everything I was told on authority, but I couldn't, because too much was unsupportable and I could think of too many exceptions," he reflects. That was even true of organized religion. After a few months of being "enamored" with the teachings of a local fundamentalist minister, he came to the conclusion that whatever the essence of the universe, it is a lot more complicated than any orthodoxy likes to admit.

Grissom grew up flexing his imagination, first by entering the worlds of literature and later through meeting people who encouraged him to stretch his mind by thinking about real-world issues. Two early influences in that direction were college professors at the University of Mississippi during the height of the civil rights battle. Alexander Duff Gordon, his philosophy teacher, was the first person Grissom remembers who spoke out in uninhibited moral terms against the racial bigotry of the South in the early 1960s. When Grissom began to think about bigotry, he realized that one of the primary examples of it in his experience had been the attitudes of his own father, in whose footsteps he was following. Gordon left his imprint by encouraging the white, middle-class youth to think about his own "particular participation in the social order" and by his willingness to express unpopular opinions out loud. So did history professor James Silver, who stood up in Mississippi and identified the state as a closed society run by a political machine and uncritical press, and was vindicated in that view by being driven from the state by physical threats.

As a young man, Tom Grissom became a bit of a local star for his scientific prowess, and the Selective Service thought him promising enough to allow him to fulfill his military service requirement as an air force reservist while earning first a bachelor's and then a master's degree in physics. His attitude toward the military was that the government defines national defense and the citizen serves dutifully when necessary. He describes himself as always "uncomfortable" with the idea of nuclear weapons, but that discomfort was kept in check by the assumption that the people in charge of defense approached the problem in the same careful, systematic way that he approached a physics problem and so had it under control.

Grissom is an experimentalist, a physicist whose business it is to obtain, repeat, and interpret results rather than to refine theories in the abstract. But concern about results—say, the precision with which the path of an electron can be measured—is not the same as concern about the uses to which experimental results are put. For years, ethical considerations about his work were a non-issue. Grissom shared with most of the scientific community the assumption that its work of amassing knowledge benefits humanity, regardless of the uses to which the knowledge might be put. Most of his physics interests, such as a lifelong fascination with neutron generators, could be turned as easily to civilian applications like medicine as to the making of bombs. He says, "I think the sad fact is that the degree to which I thought about it was determined by the parameters that everybody obeys: I thought, 'How can I make a living doing this?' and 'How much money can I make?' " When he emerged from the University of Tennessee with a doctorate and looked around for suitable work, he sought a place "where I could do good physics, where I could have the resources to support my need for physics."

From the start his resume reflects a generalist's wide range rather than a specialization in nuclear problems. Taking off a few years to earn some income between getting his master's degree and beginning his dissertation, Grissom did nuclear physics measurements for the army's missile command. But in the same period he held civilian jobs developing instruments for mapping the cornea of the eye, a new time-keeping concept which he sold to Bulova Watch Company, and other devices. While at Sandia, he continued to develop—and enjoy developing—such civilian applications as medical instruments and a random-number generator for computers. He considered it a great advantage of working at a national laboratory that it could afford to subsidize civilian research. Nevertheless, most of his work was either "pure" research or directly applicable to weaponry.

It was for the most prosaic reasons that he ended up at the nation's largest weapons-design lab: it conspicuously had the resources to keep him working happily, he had a friend there, they were hiring. The problems he was brought on board to address were open-ended and grew naturally from his research in graduate school. He believed at the time that "no one was going to require any particular or immediate applications" of them. And so he could say, "I actually went to Sandia with little if any conscious thought of what the lab does as its end product. All I was really looking at was what I was going to do there. And that's a characteristic of the national laboratories: they're sufficiently big and multidisciplinary and diverse" that this nearsightedness is the rule. But in retrospect, Grissom sees it as curious that intellectuals who clearly think in broad terms about many things seem to think so little about the results of their labors. "You don't really go to one of these laboratories without being aware that they build weapons. You might or might not know whether you personally are going to be contributing to the building of weapons. But the real issue is why the question doesn't occur to people more often, why it doesn't seem to matter."

Grissom himself spent five or six fulfilling years there before the first signs of discomfort showed, and in that period he established a career of considerable prestige. Starting out as a solitary researcher, he became supervisor of a fifteen-person division working on hybrid microcircuits, and finally managed a department called Neutron Devices and Technology, with a technical staff of sixty and a budget of $15 to $20 million a year. He oversaw major aspects of the research and development of a new generation of nuclear weapons. He worked with other Department of Energy (DOE) facilities that produced the plutonium and components to make the bombs. He traveled frequently to other national labs such as Lawrence Livermore and Los Alamos, and to Washington to coordinate the scientific efforts. His peers were prestigious scientists, technical managers, government liaisons. He had a Q-clearance, the highest possible among DOE staff.

In that microcosm, his power was considerable. "There was practically nothing I ever wanted to do, nothing my colleagues ever wanted to do, that we couldn't do because of money constraints," he says. It was a heady life and materially rewarding. Besides the budget and autonomy, by 1985 he was bringing home $75,000 a year. His first wife and three children enjoyed shopping, valued expensive Christmas presents, and affirmed his chosen role as provider. He rejoiced in his alchemist's ability to turn plutonium into money. "It wasn't the money per se, but the fact that it was a societally accepted form of acknowledgment," he explains. "Your peers are saying you're doing a good job." He became increasingly caught up in building monuments to that recognition, in the form of fancier and fancier houses. "The cement would barely be dry on one before I'd be itching to move to a 'better' part of town, every two or three years at least."

At the same time, another part of Grissom's personality began to rebel. He owned four cars, but his favorite was a beat-up old Pinto. He continued to buy goodies for his family, but noticed more and more discomfort with the gulf between his children's consumption and the frugality of his own upbringing. Symbolic of his understated rebellion was the fact that, in a neighborhood where everyone else had swimming pools, Grissom could not bring himself to put one in.

And at the lab, a variety of managerial issues irritated Grissom throughout his career. Sandia is run by Western Electric along a model based on "a very rigid management structure, very bureaucratic. Top management gives permission for just about everything."[2] The first clashes he remembers were over the lab's seemingly arbitrary and constricting approach to classifying research papers, which ran counter both to his ideals and to his need to talk physics in detail with as many peers as possible. During his first year, he and his boss, Gordon McClure, did a research report—measuring the energies of ions generated by a particular process—and, as part of standard procedure, were asked to specify a distribution list. Since the paper was unclassified and a major researcher in that subspecialty was in Leningrad, Grissom naturally put him on the list, whereupon "a few months later, Gordon McClure got a phone call from his boss, who said he was having trouble sleeping because he couldn't figure out why we were sending it to Leningrad." Another time, Grissom, who knew the classification guidelines inside out because he had helped write them, sent a paper to Poland before sending it to the lab's classification people. Another brouhaha followed.

As he moved into management, Grissom became more and more troubled by the criteria he was expected to follow for reviewing and promoting employees. "If an individual came to the laboratory and made a good first impression, he or she would get rated well and it wouldn't matter later whether that first impression was right. So you had a lot of frustrated people running around"—late bloomers who never received adequate recognition for their growth and others who had been placed on a fast track whether or not their current performance merited it. He saw it quite simply as "an abomination," but despite his prestige as a researcher and his management level, he was powerless to influence policy.

While those practical complaints were widely echoed, he heard very few openly discordant notes about the underlying purposes of the work. But when scientists went on recruitment trips to campuses, they frequently came back disgruntled because some talented graduate student had turned down weapons work on principle. "Sometimes," Grissom recalls, "the recruiter would refuse to be drawn into that conversation, and therefore would miss out on talking to a talented student. Other times, if the recruiter was a typical Sandian, there would be a certain ego involvement in the idea, 'What I'm doing is okay and I can convince this person.' " Discussions of those discussions would cycle endlessly around the lab when the recruiters returned.

In these, Grissom generally played the militant cold warrior, even when the part began to seem like devil's advocacy to him. "I would use all the stock arguments: If I don't do it, somebody else will. We've got to do it, it's a dirty job. If we don't recruit some good talent here pretty soon, we'll have a mediocre laboratory and then the other side will get ahead of us in this game." Hearing himself wage those arguments made him uncomfortable, and eventually he concluded it was because he didn't believe most of them. "I realized that, forced into a corner by someone who was really critical, I would say all kinds of stuff that was really crazy."

Ironically, it was not the moral underpinnings of the work but the lifestyle that first began to unravel. Pushing forty, Grissom noticed that he wasn't very happy, wasn't getting excited about his life or work any more. The work environment struck him some days as rigid, fiercely competitive, and divorced from any purpose—or at least any purpose that anyone wanted to talk about. There was, in fact, an uncomfortable silence surrounding a question that had begun to nag at his conscience: What were they all there for, anyway? "In all my fifteen years at the lab, there never once was a meeting in which anyone questioned the appropriateness of a given weapons system," he reports. "No one would say, 'Why the hell would anyone want more nuclear weapons?' " And once he began to let those questions in, he found them difficult to contain or neutralize. "I sat myself down and started thinking, 'Why am I doing this? Is this acceptable to me any longer? What is it that I find unacceptable about this? Is it the moral and ethical implications of my work, or is it simply coping with all the needs and problems of these other people?' "

Why all this broke loose when it did remains a bit of a mystery. He knows it began after he had achieved all the goals of his youth, from a doctorate and published work to a nice lawn and talented children. "Some people describe this reassessment as midlife crisis," he says, "but to me it was a natural evolution, going back to ferret out the source of this dissatisfaction, because I could see that it was rooted in the fact that I didn't really know how I behaved and why. I had become very selfish and consumed by self-centeredness." Although he did not have words to describe it at that point, he began to understand his malaise in terms like those used by Joanna Macy in *Despair and Personal Power in the Nuclear Age*: "The conspiracy of silence concerning our deepest feelings about the future of our species, the degree of numbing, isolation, burnout, and cognitive confusion that result from it—all converge to produce a sense of futility."[3]

Grissom sought to get a handle on his questions about identity and values in the way that came most naturally: he gave himself a series of homework assignments. First, he set out to write down the goals he actually pursued in the course of his life and work. He ended up with a "fairly conventional" list: achieve scientifically, publish papers, get raises, be respected at work, bring home good money—in short, "the values of the society in which I participated." Then he gave himself the harder assignment of listing all the things he really *liked* to do before he got caught up in all that stuff. He realized, "I liked thinking more than doing. I liked daydreaming more than planning a career. I liked plays and drama. I liked music. So I asked, 'What happened to all these things?' "

He began reading about human development and hit upon R. D. Laing's *The Divided Self*. It spoke to him. "On the one hand, I was this person who could play a game and succeed at it. On the other hand, there was another part of me who had principles, but who didn't generally acknowledge them. Once I came to realize that split, I realized that I really disliked that actor part of me that was succeeding, and I liked this other part of me that had values. Take the nuclear weapons issue: the principle I was acting on was the one society bought, that we needed these weapons in order to prevent someone else from attacking us. The principle I found I really believed when I examined it more critically was that that was absolute absurdity and nonsense. The possession of more and more of these weapons was going to guarantee their use, not prevent it. But I was acting as if I believed that the whole enterprise was okay."

The work itself kept him going with a certain businesslike cheer. Besides being intellectually challenging and therefore emotionally sustaining for him, there was a lot of it to do. Grissom was busy enough thinking about physics, supervising larger and larger groups of scientists, deciding how to get his papers published, and planning his travels that he could easily hold off thoughts about what all this effort served. And this, too, had been the pattern of his life. "In high school I worked very hard to be sure I could go to college. In college I worked very hard to see if I could get into graduate school. When I got into graduate school, I worked very hard so I'd get a PhD. And so I spent the first thirty years of my life always scrambling, always working, always competing. And when I got into Sandia the whole thing started again: I've got to be a physicist, a division supervisor, a department manager, a director. The whole thing is a consuming process. You never sit down and think, 'Why the hell am I doing this? I'm behaving like a rat in a maze.' "

Grissom's first answers to that question, to his surprise, took him straight back to Cleveland, Mississippi and the stratified society in which he had grown up. "You see all these other members of society who don't have anything, and the generally socially accepted explanation is that they don't have anything because they don't work for it. They don't try hard enough. It's not that we've prevented them from having all those things. So, when you're a member of the fortunate part of society, the fact that the other part exists tends to fuel the idea that you've got to be competing."

When he started thinking about why his life wasn't working, Grissom found himself looking back to his first visions of justice and his early Mississippi role models, who never seemed to hesitate to look below the surface of their lives or to be intimidated by the consequences of saying what they saw. He became "less pragmatic." He pulled back from his breakneck schedule of overtime and lab-related socializing. He became a bit of a recluse and read hungrily.

At first, he read without clear direction; in fact, the point was to cast about for something that struck home, for some ideas or stories of experience that would cast light on his own. Allowing himself to wander the library and take from the shelves whatever his hands were drawn to, he gravitated mostly to modern authors. What he tended to pick up were attempts, through literature, to deal with the violence of the twentieth century, the powerlessness felt by individuals, and the meaning of human bravery. He read American literature by the carload: Faulkner, Poe, Hawthorne, Twain, Robert Frost, Stephen Crane, Robinson Jeffers. He read Toynbee's histories. He read Bertrand Russell and Camus and R. D. Laing, devouring each in turn.

Among his greatest sources of consolation as well as insight were the existentialists, because he saw in them the courage to confront the absence of easy answers. Though he knew it had become cliché, the word "absurdity" really did sum up for him the fact of two technologically and culturally advanced nations threatening each other with annihilation in the name of human values. There was no other term for the stockpiling of nuclear weapons beyond overkill, and he concluded, "You may think —you may know—that, in somebody's lifetime, these weapons are, by their very existence, likely to be used. But you don't make that the reason for sitting down and calling it quits. You continue to work as if that doesn't have to happen." Reading "The Myth of Sisyphus," he saw in Camus' metaphor of pushing the rock uphill his own search for a coherent life and the effort it would take to wean the scientific world away from its fascination with weaponry. "We're all born to die. But as long as you're alive you have to confront the absurdity of it all and do your best. To do less is uncourageous . . ."

Much post–World War II existentialist literature examines the question of responsibility for the atrocities of that war and the moral status of the "good Germans" whose position seemed ambiguous at the time but in hindsight looks so clear. It occurred to Grissom, "If there's a nuclear exchange, and if there are survivors, they will have every right to think of me—of all of us who worked on these weapons— as war criminals. They will have every right to try us. They will have every right to hate us."

Around this time, Grissom also began writing poetry as a loner's way of getting at the confusion, guilt, and anger that were surfacing. No matter what he wrote about, his poetry flirted with the abyss—but with a certain exuberance. In "A Mystery to Cling To," he writes:

> The danger fills me
> With a delicious joy
> Of what it means to be alive
> Now, at this moment, as I
> Make my way down the beach
> Dodging thunderclaps in the rain.[4]

In "Themes," he confronts the chaotic nature of his changes, the lack of simple, linear, reasonable explanations that he as a scientist was attached to, and the uselessness, much of the time, of analytical discussion.

> Solving puzzles in the dark
> from pieces upside down
> dreaming poems
> that go unwritten
> out of words
> that never come
> to escape from being alone[5]

Thus he began to confront the thoughts, fantasies, and fears he couldn't raise in the lab cafeteria. His search was for a new philosophy to live by. His particular concerns—why he felt so uneasy, whether his job was defensible, how one human being could influence the global situation—would be answered as a byproduct, he felt. He entertained the idea that there might not be answers to all his questions, that there probably was not a divine scheme and maybe not an objectively right way to live. He thought about what an honest human being ought to do in that case. He thought about who runs things, both politically and cosmically. He thought about whether there was a connection between the broad imponderables and the fact that, close to home, his life wasn't working. "All of it made connections with what I had thought I was about at one time. I decided, 'Hey, I'm this way still. I'm somebody who's interested in the human condition. It's just that I deny that part of myself in order to go out and make a living.' "

Grissom did not intentionally embark on an inquiry into the ethics of working in a weapons lab. He embarked on a search for an anchoring set of values, a vision that could give sense to his life and restore the integrity and purpose he had once known. But particular stories hit a nerve and pointed uncompromisingly toward his work as the source of his discontent. When he reread the dialogue between Thoreau, in jail for refusing to pay taxes to support the Mexican War, and Emerson, visiting him ("What are you doing in there, Henry?" "What are you doing out there, Ralph?"), it was impossible not to hear Thoreau's voice as the more empowered and independent, while knowing that Emerson's spoke for the life he was leading.

Grissom perceived this process of questioning as emotionally necessary but professionally dangerous. He saw the climate at Sandia as one with very little tolerance for hand wringing about the meaning of it all. The story of Bill Riggan, a former colleague and close friend of Grissom who works on testing devices for nuclear weapons, illustrates several points about the sociology of the lab, even though Riggan can not for a moment be described as a typical Sandian. Bill Riggan is "an Idaho farm boy who never got a college degree" but who, through his talents, rose to staff level. As many researchers are, he is grateful from the heart for the opportunity to do high-powered science at Sandia. Riggan, who considers himself a testimony to the lab's openness to dissent, is an atheist, a socialist, and a voracious reader whose cubicle is wallpapered with clippings, cartoons, and bumper stickers criticizing the arms race. Riggan once marched into the library at Sandia, deadpan, and convinced the librarian to order a scientific journal called the *Bulletin of Atomic Scientists,* whose monthly arrival a few Sandians awaited like a samizdat newsletter in Leningrad but whose circulation list hovered stubbornly at around four people. "When it comes to dissent here, there's no problem," he insists. "People put up with me as an eccentric, but they put up with me because I do my work well."

Riggan characterizes most of the lab personnel as "good Republicans" for whom concern about nuclear weaponry is "a non-issue." But in reconciling his own position as a scientist who opposes the arms race yet contributes to it on a daily basis, he maintains that the tide can only be turned in Washington. Of Grissom's stand, he only says, "I guess what troubles me about it is that it doesn't trouble me more."

Grissom reflects, "I think that if I had told people in the laboratory about it when I first started to think this way, they would have recommended that I go see a psychiatrist and take it easy, that maybe I was coming apart under the stress." And so for more than half of his fifteen years at Sandia, Thomas Grissom led a divided life, and to do so he shut down more and more of his playful, experimental side, the side that let him enjoy science in the first place. Instead of growing, his concern became coping. And he understood that the deterioration in the quality of his creative life was directly tied to the need not to think about what he was creating. Grissom's state while working at the lab was the subject of many verses, including "Real Death":

> Physicians of the world
> debate
> when death occurs
> with electrical impulses
> from the heart
> and brain; but
> this is only
> biological death—
> real death
> is of the mind and soul
> and often
> comes much sooner.[6]

He wrote poetry in bursts, then tucked it away self-consciously with the suspicion that it wasn't very good. But it kept flowing from him and felt more and more legitimate as time went on. He had a breakthrough in his attitude toward the whole expressive process when he stopped "just writing" and started writing to someone: his teen-aged daughter. Another breakthrough came after a long period of hiding the poems away, when he decided to collect and put them into an order that reflected their evolution. Reading the poems that way, he saw something there: perhaps neither literary value nor elegant metaphor, but honesty. He found a publisher in New England who felt the same way, and then the realization crystallized: If I've put all this effort into making these statements of my values, and if I read them and, yes, they do ring true, then these are the guiding sentiments and principles by which I ought to live. At first, Grissom did not know exactly how he ought to change his life, but he did know that he was unlikely to have a harmonious future in the job that had made him feel such conflict.

As he turned away from his professional path, Grissom's relationship to his family changed too. His confusion came out as inarticulate anger toward his wife, which exacerbated long standing differences, leading to their separation in 1978 and divorce four years later. "I was still struggling to put it all in a framework. I wasn't able to say what was going on in a very coherent way at the beginning, and so a lot of animosity and frustration developed between Joanne and me. Whatever I tried to say came out as finger pointing, and my changes were such a shock to her that she thought I was blaming it all on her," he remembers with sadness.

It was a messy divorce, and in the late 1970s, his life fell into considerable disarray. He retreated more and more deeply into books but found significant sources of support in friendships at the lab as well. Bill Riggan was one because he could be such a strong devil's advocate in argument and at the same time such a good-natured friend. And a couple of years before his resignation, Grissom found validation for his doubts from an unexpected source: his close friend and mentor, Gordon McClure. As he neared retirement after twenty-seven years at the lab, McClure's first doubts about his work surfaced. Like Grissom, his love affair with physics had been lifelong and unconditional. He wondered, thanks to a question by his son in the mid-seventies, why so many thousands of nuclear weapons were necessary. But when he gave any thought to the applications of his own work, he assumed he was contributing to global security through deterrence.

By his retirement in 1982, however, McClure admitted to friends at the lab that he was troubled by the "technical approach" to international security represented by "nuclear weapons that were smaller, lighter, more resistant to hostile environments, more accurate, more reliable, safer, and longer-lived." He retired not to a life of relaxation but to a full-time, self-imposed second career of researching, writing, and speaking against further weapons development, and addressing specifically the responsibility of scientists. In an "open letter" sent to sixty of his former colleagues, McClure wrote, "We have all—citizen and scientist alike—participated in attaining our present world status. There is no justification for finger pointing in any direction. I think it's high time for a change and I think the weapons labs people can have a major input into constructive change. Perhaps the job of ameliorating the U.S.-U.S.S.R. confrontation cannot be done without the intensive involvement of weapons labs personnel. But

I'm confident that labs people will have to move to other institutions—possibly create them—to induce change."[7]

Another powerful influence on Grissom's final decision was Chuck Hosking, a Quaker who with typical Quaker tenacity stood vigil daily outside the lab through every kind of weather, short of an all-out blizzard, for years. "At first, the signs he held put me off, things like 'You can't hug your children with nuclear arms.' They were a little simplistic," Grissom recalls. Still, he watched the man in growing fascination as the years passed and he remained a constant presence. But actually talking to the lone figure, getting close enough to his vigil site on the edge of the base, required a conscious decision. For years Grissom watched him with curiosity and growing respect, but did not make a move.

"When I did talk to him, I had made my decision intellectually but hadn't verbalized it. He became a symbol, his persistence. The first thing that caught my attention was that, when I told him what he was doing was very courageous, he took strong exception to that. He said, 'It's not courageous at all. It's a duty, an obligation, to exercise your rights in a country where you're able to.' "

Hosking is a pacifist in the purest sense. Grissom even today does not describe himself that way. In discussion after discussion, probing that pacifist conscience with all manner of questions—"What if the Russians invaded? What if someone were to take a shot at you?"—he found Hosking's positions hard to accept, but saw the man himself as "very rational, very articulate, not the least bit mystical or foolish." And for Grissom, meeting a human being who represented a coherent set of ideas meant feeling responsible for coming to terms with those ideas.

Grissom was naturally inclined to give it time, to look for reasons why he was wrong, and to seek what wisdom the eight thousand people who went to work with him daily without apparent conflict could impart about how they did it. But his discomfort increased. And in his search for an intellectually satisfying solution to the problem, he discovered the clumsiness of human emotion. As he puts it, "I got interested in this idea that there are more approaches to questions than just pure reason." Or, in free verse,

> I don't know—
> I honestly don't;
> But I think
> and feel
> and believe;
> knowing isn't
> important
> to me anymore—
> caring is.[8]

He began sending out resumes, and his combined expertise in physics and poetry led Evergreen State College to offer him a job. Slowly he understood that he was preparing to say goodbye to Sandia.

One morning while he walked to work, the text of a statement began to form in his mind. By the time he got to his desk, he was furiously writing what would be his letter of resignation. In it, he said:

> After fifteen years I am leaving Sandia. The reason is very simple—conscience and honesty demand it. No longer can I suppress my true feelings and my apprehensions and continue to participate in the blind realization of more and more weapons, nuclear or otherwise. I have examined my beliefs and found them sincere. If I would be regarded seriously, I must be willing to act accordingly.

He pointed out similarities between the dutiful weapons engineers and the dutiful German citizens who built the ovens and camps. He did not let his audience slip off the hook with the claim that they were caught in a terrible dilemma, that it worried them too. He wrote, "I do not observe individuals straining against their consciences . . . Instead, I observe people who derive enormous stimulation and personal satisfaction from technically challenging and interesting tasks, and from the exercise of power, content not to examine too closely their own motives and constantly reinforced by other like-minded individuals. How many would evidence the same degree of conviction if the pay were only half as much? And how many would exhibit the same courage as the pacifist outside the gate at the risk of any personal loss or inconvenience or embarrassment?"

He left with the knowledge that he was in no position to be judgmental. He could not find it in his heart to condemn the people he had been so attached to, whose work he had admired and motivated. "My decision," he wrote, "is not meant to pass judgment on others . . . I regard my behavior as moral in the existential sense; as a universal prescription, humanity would surely benefit. Yet I recognize the existence of evil in the world and harbor no illusions that my actions can ever constitute a universal moral imperative . . . "

But he ached to see other people take notice, reflect on what he had done, and figure out what they could do. He ached for something that would disrupt the serenely suicidal obedience that had come to characterize the lab in his eyes. He saw the players in the arms race—the weapons labs and their lobbyists and the members of congress who depended on them for campaign funds and the Pentagon and the friendly journalists and the rest—as threads in a tapestry that had entangled the economy, the culture, and the media. He saw them as sleepwalkers who said yes to participation in it because they hadn't figured out yet that it was possible to say no. He closed his letter to those few friends with these words: "There are certainly alternatives to our present policies regarding nuclear weapons, and some are straightforward, but all require a degree of collective self-confidence and belief in ourselves of which we seem incapable, and all of them threaten the self-interests of powerful economic factions woven tightly into the fabric of our entire society. Dealing with them may require unraveling the whole cloth and beginning anew. I am reminded of an admonition by Edward Abbey in the introduction to *Desert Solitaire*: 'This is not a travel guide but an elegy. A memorial. You're holding a tombstone in your hands. A bloody rock. Don't drop it on your foot—throw it at something big and glassy. What do you have to lose?' "[9]

As he emphasized in his farewell address, Tom Grissom left the lab and began a teaching career, but he did not quit the lab for teaching. He quit the lab to straighten himself out morally, to bring his actions into line with his emerging beliefs. It was the first time in his life that he had initiated a major change of direction that way, a change not required by the conventional path of his career.

His new job is teaching undergraduate physics at Evergreen State College in Olympia, Washington. It is an experimental school in many respects. Faculty are hired on three-year contracts without tenure or rank. The place reflects a set of values Grissom has come to take very seriously. Instead of specialists, Evergreen cultivates generalists. A student can't graduate without studying the history and philosophy of science as well as its methods, without looking across the boundaries of disciplines, without doing some research that is original, without making some value judgments about it all. By teaching science holistically and very well, Grissom hopes to contribute, however modestly, to a future in which scientists are more aware of the human significance of their work, less compartmentalized in specialties, and therefore less able to "participate in an organized evil without even being aware of the fact that we are doing so, without any personal, individual culpability."

A major source of support and vitality in Grissom's new life is his second wife, Donna, who worked on the publications staff at Sandia. She became a natural ally for him because of her "strong streak of rebellion" and ability "to cut through nonsense." Like him, she was uncomfortable with both weapons work and materialism.

Grissom was respected and missed at Sandia. According to Riggan, many people who were profoundly uncomfortable with his politics found identification and comfort in his poems. But the dimension of his courage that is most appreciated by his colleagues at the lab is the upward mobility he sacrificed. Riggan concludes, "If Tom had tried, if he had played the game, he would be up at the director level by now."

Grissom believes that the compartmentalization of an institution like Sandia quite effectively keeps people inside from having to look at the meaning of their work. So does the competitive pace, the hierarchical structure of a lab and an industry in which somebody else is always in charge, and the consensual belief in an unlimited Soviet threat as a rationale when one is needed. Taken together, these structural characteristics and human decisions add up to a self-reinforcing system. "And it's fundamentally grounded in our social values," he adds. "Look at the military complexion of American society, at the number of TV commercials that use military metaphors and symbols. I guess it's an understandable outgrowth of two world wars and a cold war, but it's really kind of frightening to consider the portion of our society that thinks in military concepts."

Grissom looks back less astounded at the fact that it all goes on than at the fact that he broke out of it. "You're in there with eight thousand other people, all of whom are there because they've chosen to be, all of whom reinforce each other. 'We're all good people. We love our families. So how can this be wrong if we're all doing it together?' Furthermore, the country reinforces you, the president tells you you're doing a great job, the Congress sends you billions of dollars. Your fellow citizens don't ostracize you. It's everybody's acquiescence in this enterprise that gives it legitimacy, that takes the edge off."

When confronted with the questions of what his action will mean and what he anticipates doing further to improve the world's chances for survival, Grissom is subdued. When he first settled in Olympia and began his new career, he saw no way of affecting the course of history except perhaps by teaching. "I'm not sure that much can be done. I have given a few speeches at rallies and so on, but I frankly think that the climate inside the weapons labs and the companies that produce new generations of warheads is so blinded to the nature of what's going on that I don't know what it will take to awaken them." On an equally skeptical note, Bill Riggan adds, "When Tom left, I lost a manager and an eloquent spokesman, and he left an opening for someone more hawkish to take his place . . . Management's attitude toward Tom's leaving was concern, but it was more an embarrassment than a moral concern."

Yet Grissom has not been able to let go of the question, even though he is emphatically not an activist by temperament—"I went to hear Helen Caldicott speak once and kept asking myself, 'How does she do it, night after night?' " Like the existentialists who had inspired him, he could not let his skepticism serve as an excuse to give up. The impact of Chuck Hosking on his own life deprived him of the rationalization that one person can't make a difference. "It's not my makeup to try to reform society," he begins, "but then I think, 'Well, you ought to become like that. Somebody ought to be doing that, going around telling these blokes that they're out of control.' "

He is trying on the role by speaking to journalists and addressing forums from ethics classes to rallies, drawing on his own experience as a dissenter and his expertise as a physicist. Because the state of Washington houses the world's largest atomic complex, the Department of Energy's Hanford reservation, nuclear power and weapons are a charged issue economically and environmentally as well as ethically. Grissom has already played an important role in one battle, over the reopening of a Chernobyl-style graphite reactor on the Hanford site. The only purpose of the old reactor—built without a safety containment vessel in the 1950s—is production of weapons-grade plutonium. It was Grissom, in speaking to a Seattle-area reporter, who shifted the terms of the debate by reminding the public that the current generation of nuclear weapons had been sold to policy makers largely on the grounds that it required less plutonium than its predecessors. [10]

Tom Grissom still takes his life one careful step at a time, still believes that whatever fulfillment he has gained stems from thinking out his actions very clearly. On the question of nuclear weapons and his own modest contribution toward turning the tide, he has moments of optimism and clarity, alternating with others when all he can muster toward the weapons industry and his former colleagues is a quiet, baffled sorrow. In "All My Friends," a poem about a former student visiting the professor who left the bomb factory, he writes:

> He felt anew the empty longings of homesickness
> The way he had those first few times he'd severed
> Ties and struck out on his own. He didn't
> Miss the work. He'd done it for the money
> Much longer than he meant to, and for the
> Others, and the loyalty and friendships,
> Until he could not do it anymore. No,
> It was only the people he missed, the ones
> Like Josh who understood—him best of all—and
> Nothing changed between them. They sat in awkward
> Silence. "Sir," the youth at length broke in,
> "Is something wrong?" "No," he said, "I'm sorry,
> It's just that I was thinking—how ironic and
> Strange it is—that all my friends build bombs." [11]

7 A DYED-IN-THE-WOOL DEMOCRAT
BILL PERRY

When William Perry became director of public relations for Lawrence Livermore Laboratory in California, both he and the lab's management thought it was an ideal match. Livermore is one of two enormous national laboratories run by the Department of Energy to research and develop state-of-the-art weapons and delivery systems, and to investigate the basic physics underlying them. The lab's chosen middle name is excellence, and so is Perry's. A black writer who set out in the early days of the civil rights movement to become "the best damn communicator around," Perry is a shaman of words and images. "The place dealt in magic. I was magic. I was pretty sure an hour after walking in the door that they would hire me."

But barely a year later, in the spring of 1982, a demoralized and angry Bill Perry dictated a letter of resignation, through his lawyer, and said goodbye to the ruins of a dream job. He left, the letter said, "to seek other opportunities," and these came—in management consulting, writing, and an executive job in a growing computer graphics firm. But his resignation was not for the sake of career mobility; in conventional terms, Livermore was a pinnacle. Perry left the lab because he could no longer bear to work there. His was a precise 180-degree turnaround. It left him positioned, if not compelled, to become a primary public challenger of the hall of magic where, a year earlier, he had gone to work with such excitement. He emerged as a sought-after public speaker on the dangers of the nuclear arms race and the fallacies of defense through deterrence, and then as chair of the Marin County Nuclear Weapons Freeze campaign. What had happened?

Four years after his resignation from the lab, I went to see Perry at his job as marketing manager of a Berkeley company called General Parametrics, which makes flashy computer graphics packages. Almost immediately, I understood the charm that had made him such an asset at Livermore. Perry sat me down, turned on his terminal, and under the guise of showing me his work, playfully keyed in my name in giant script. "Okay," he said, "pick a color." I went for purple. At the touch of a few buttons, the letters were transformed into gothic type and highlighted in purple on a field of bright blue. I had my name in lights.

Bill Perry is an average-looking middle-aged man with beefy build and a hook nose, but he manages to be good-looking by the sheer power of his joie de vivre. It shows in his clothing—peach silk shirt, blue-gray tie, jewelry just this side of ostentatious—and in his way of making eye contact that says there's a person behind the face and you're going to have fun together. Intense without being intimidating, he is a stellar communicator who is equally at home with intellectual complexity and plain English and is skilled at combining the two. His voice has the resonance of the veteran speaker he is, and a typical Perry monologue manages to roller-coaster you from euphoria to outrage without ever losing balance.

"What makes Sammy run? What makes Bill Perry tick?" He turns my question over for a second and answers, "Fun has a lot to do with it. My mother always accuses me of thinking life is a party, and I have to admit she's right. I seek a certain comfort level, a convenience level—I don't need a lot, but I want the basics to be there—and that comes a lot from the years I spent as a starving writer."

Perry roundly denies having any grand life plan, but his road to Livermore was shaped, as was his life, by the pragmatism he had to develop as an unusually talented black person wanting the good life for his people but seeking it through a path of achievement rather than sacrifice. He gravitates to situations where he can exercise his talents and where he can feel that his efforts are directed toward solving significant human problems. He believes there is room in this society for many people, including him, to live rich and exciting lives while using their creativity and the resources of society as a whole to help others become more self-reliant. In short, he says, "I am a dyed-in-the-wool Democrat—embarrassingly so."

Perry was raised in New Rochelle, New York in a small subculture of black families who were acutely aware of racial divisions—many worked as servants—but who raised their own children in an atmosphere that creatively combined the genteel with the outrageous.

"Ours was sociologically a very interesting group. If you meet any one of us, you'll say, 'Wow, this is not your typical black person!' " The Perry home was full of books and insulated from the worst wrath of the depression. During his childhood, the most common recreation was acting out Shakespearean plays in the living room. He grew up seeing the world as a place where injustice happened and people got hurt, but also as a place with enough maneuvering room that you could do an end run around the worst of the misery. His upbringing gave him a sense of life's wondrous possibilities, an appreciation for the richness of language, and an unusually sophisticated awareness of the fact that social norms are not carved in stone. As he describes that lesson, "I've always had confidence, always. My education helped. Sports helped. But one of the major contributing factors, I think, was the fact that in high school, when everybody else was playing the dating game, I was having a full-blown affair with a friend of my mother's, with my mother's tacit approval. It was wonderful."

Along with that sense of outrageous possibility came the understanding that it takes work to weave the possibilities together into a coherent life, especially if you are black. Much of this wisdom came from his grandfather, John Edward Perry, an entrepreneur who lost a fortune in the depression and ended his career as head custodian for the New Rochelle public schools, wryly describing himself as "an old black janitor."

John Edward said, "When you walk into a room, all the people who had assumed you were white are going to have to deal with the fact that you're black. That gives you an automatic thirty-second advantage. Use it."

John Edward also said, "If you fail, nobody will give you a hard time. There are always excuses available for black people who fail. It's your choice."

Bill Perry chose success—in a big way. He cultivates peak experiences as daily fare. He admits having done so as a survival mechanism, and he does it very well. He floats on good timing and luck—the luck of a man who has taught himself how to get lucky.

"I never had a real job until I was thirty-two," he says. "Nobody hired black people in real jobs anyway." Instead, he holed up in a Greenwich Village apartment all through the 1950s and early 1960s, soaking up poetry and fiction and cultivating his own writing craft. He remembers the young James Baldwin, Lorraine Hansberry, and Siobhan McKenna. They all lived the same way: holding down survival jobs by day and "writin' our thing," or acting, or painting by night.

Perry's youth was free enough of overt discrimination that he remembers his first experience of it, while in the navy in 1947, as "a stunner." He says, "I was in Washington, DC in uniform. I went into a drugstore and ordered a milkshake at the counter, and the waitress said, 'You'll have to get it to go.' There I am, in the service of my country, literally in the shadow of the Capitol, and I can't get a fuckin' milkshake in a drugstore."

His introduction to the civil rights movement was through white friends, led by his Irish second wife, Peggy Perry, who spent all her free time at the Greenwich Village NAACP. He was "dragged kicking and screaming into being black" by her invitations to picket Woolworth's, by the pervasive spirit of Martin Luther King, and by the words of a fellow struggling writer.

"What do you want to write about?" James Baldwin asked over drinks one night.

"I want to write about people, real people, but not just black people," said Perry.

"What's the matter," Baldwin shot back, "aren't blacks people?"

Perry's whole life seems to be about responding to that challenge, balancing his personal drive with the civil rights era vision that blacks ought to be able to hang onto a larger dream if anyone can. William Perry's major literary work, a novel in progress called *The Eighth Sea,* is a story of racial identity which he has been working on for ten years. Its thesis is that American culture tries to make you choose a color, a loyalty. The central figure of his book, Nelson Chambers, is a black man who figures out that he doesn't have to choose.

Perry's career has been built on that premise.

He emerged from his Greenwich Village years committed to being the best possible communicator, but unlike those who were discovering and celebrating their blackness, he wanted to excel in the most mainstream, pragmatic, and—he is the first to admit—whitest possible way. He wanted to be the best public relations guy in the country. That aim started to coalesce when, bored as a teletype operator, he visited business trade shows and fantasized. Eventually, he bluffed his way into a job as editor of a magazine about business systems by using a fake resume of defunct periodicals. From there, he was lured away by IBM and introduced to the public relations business.

From IBM, he found his way into the nonprofit world via a remarkable opportunity in private industry. "I happened to go to work for the Bell System at the right time, in 1965, in the middle of the civil rights movement, and I just fell into wonderful things. The Bell System was at that time in history becoming very, very involved in urban development. And what are they creating when I walk in the door as a public relations person? They are creating the largest urban affairs department in corporate America." For five years, his job was to dole out checks for thousands of dollars to ghetto social programs and to jet all over the country to check on their progress. He moved into public relations at the Urban League and then to the Mental Health Association in Washington.

Perry came of age as a liberal, and remains one. His involvement and investment in civil rights grew in tandem with his own self-image as a successful black professional. The sit-ins, the pickets, the meetings were dedicated to winning a fairer share of wealth and opportunity for blacks, including himself. He is resolutely casual in insisting that his early civil rights work was self-serving—"It got my wife off my back, satisfied some curiosities"—but before long, his imagination was captured by a larger vision.

"I think it started to mean something to me when the sit-ins started in Alabama, and we did a companion one at a Woolworth's in New York. I was one of the founders of a CORE chapter in Westchester County somewhere in the sixties. And through my job with the Bell System, I was very active in traveling through the South to many of the riot cities, writing a lot of reports. I was on Vice-President Humphrey's task force on youth motivation, traveling to a lot of black colleges, meeting a lot of youth. I wrote a magazine piece, 'Black After Five,' addressing the duality of black life as we experienced it. Here we were, doing our corporate bit during the day and then, after five, going to CORE and all kinds of other meetings and plotting to overthrow the system we worked for all day."

Martin Luther King's murder stunned Perry and called his liberal vision into question. As city after city caught fire in the sumer of 1968, he remembers thinking, "White America has lost its best friend." His response, on the surface, was a moderate one: he united with half a dozen friends to form the Council of Concerned Black Executives, explicitly as "a middle-class response." It wasn't black power and it wasn't demonstrating in the streets, but it was for Perry a precursor of the Livermore conflict because it was the first time he had felt forced to choose a side. "The ethic of my generation was to work like hell to become as white as you could. The civil rights era changed all that."

Perry finally resettled in the San Francisco area in pursuit of not career mobility but romance. "I had met the woman who was to become my third wife. Sharon lived on the west coast. We decided to move closer together the month our combined phone bills topped the eight hundred dollar mark."

Through a search firm, he heard about a super job that for some unknown reason had gone unfilled for a year at a place called Lawrence Livermore Laboratory. He was led to Livermore by a naive desire for marvelous toys and a nice sandbox. It ended up by far the most controversial and troubling job on a resume not noted for its blandness. Perry was hired, at the peak of public agitation against the arms race, to improve the image of the primary design contractor for the neutron bomb, Strategic Defense Initiative (Star Wars), and other toys too marvelous for even the imaginative mind of a Bill Perry to fathom.

In *Star Warriors,* written during the period Perry worked at Livermore, *New York Times* reporter William Broad unequivocally describes the lab as a weapons-design facility. Founded in 1952 because H-bomb inventor Edward Teller fought for it, the lab has been "a child of the Cold War" ever since.[1] As Broad sketches the sociology of the remote, top-secret compound, it is a world of old-guard atomic scientists—powerful, entrenched, and convinced of the wisdom of deterrence—and of youthful whiz kids about whom Broad writes:

> Many professed concern about the future of their country. At times they seemed almost too wholesome; none of them smoked. Their worst addiction seemed to be the consumption of soft drinks by the case and the ingestion of large amounts of ice cream. Most striking, they were charged with enthusiasm for their common goal of using their technical advances to protect the nation from the horrors of nuclear war.
> But their excitement also had a dark side. They could be arrogant. At times they seemed to believe that their labors gave them the power to save or destroy the world. They enjoyed black humor. Mimicking a greeting-card slogan, they liked to say the bombs of Livermore were the way to 'send the very best.'

Though the lab's nuclear emphasis would become obvious, Perry went to work at what he believed to be a multifaceted hall of science, aloof from real-world politics and technology. "I wasn't naive. I knew big science was tangled up in weapons. But I figured everybody's doing a little something with weapons, and Livermore was no different."

No one disabused him of that assumption. When he called the search firm before the first interview and asked if there was anything to be on guard about, his contact said only, "Well, if you have any negative feelings about nuclear energy, I probably wouldn't bring them up in this context." And in two solid days of interviews at the lab, more than half of which were with the five top directors, he remembers exactly one mention of nuclear weapons, a low-key question by director-at-large Michael May, "How do you feel about working in a place that has something to do with nuclear weapons?" Says Perry, "The question was so soft, and everybody seemed so concerned with other things, that I almost gave him a flip answer. But I didn't. I said, 'Mike, I would really prefer that there not be nuclear weapons anywhere in the world. But, since there are, I would prefer to be at the place that's best at making them, and I assume that's Livermore.' "

That answer turned out to be nearly perfect. And it kept further questions from arising while he settled into an office so spacious that he joked about needing a telephone to communicate across it, got to know his nine secretaries and staff of thirty-five, and began to figure out how to spend a virtually unlimited budget.

What Perry first came to know about Livermore was the aspect he was hired to promote: "the magic show," the glamor that is naturally attached to any establishment employing over two thousand PhDs with an $800-million-a-year budget. The aura shines even brighter at a place like Livermore, working at the far reaches of the subatomic and supersonic. "It was a very heady place to work, probably for anybody, but certainly for a black dude who had come of age in the civil rights movement and devoted his life to being the best," he says. Little manifestations of that headiness preoccupied him for months—like the time he said casually to his secretary, "Boy, would I like to have that computer system," only to find it ordered, delivered, and installed within days.

Perry soon found out that much of the lab's bread and butter came from designing bombs. Shop talk about surgical strikes and collateral damage was routine, but it was conducted in such morally neutral language that Perry, emulating those around him, didn't blink. The first time he remembers nuclear weapons development addressed as anything controversial, it affected him quite a bit. The incident occurred during a press seminar he had set up, where reporters sharply challenged the lab's executive director on the percentage of Livermore's budget that actually went to nuclear work. According to Perry, the director started out maintaining it was less than 40 percent and ended up estimating 65 percent. Perry came out of the meeting thinking, "If he admits to 65 percent, and there's that much confrontation about it, I bet it's at least 90 percent."[2]

Bill Perry's belief in the lab and his role didn't come undone all at once. He says, "I've told reporter after reporter that I wish I could point to a particular morning when I woke up transformed. But it didn't happen that way." What did happen was a series of unravelings, all intertwined—unravelings of his beliefs about what in fact went on at the lab, about the motivation and worldview of the scientists and directors, about their role in pushing for new generations of weapons rather than just carrying out the will of the people, and about his own personal responsibilities and options.

The first of these unravelings had to do with a handsome, well-dressed woman in her late forties with shoulder-length dark hair and a tasteful string of pearls. Perry had traveled to Washington, DC with an assistant to network with scientists who could help him enhance the lab's image. On the podium at a press conference on nuclear arms control sat this most impressive woman, staring him down with an obviously charged gaze. He looked back. She stared harder. He drew the obvious but laughably wrong conclusion: "I thought we had an eye game going."

The woman was Dr. Helen Caldicott, author of *Nuclear Madness* and *Missile Envy,* at the height of her fame. Perry heard a capsule biography of Caldicott from his staffer. She had been a cystic fibrosis researcher, become concerned about the medical effects of radiation, led the movement to stop nuclear testing in the Pacific, helped revive Physicians for Social Responsibility. His assistant had just whispered, "We're not interested in anything she has to say," when Caldicott stepped up to the podium. Helen Caldicott makes people uncomfortable in two ways: by talking in excruciating detail about nuclear war as a real possibility in our lifetimes and by insisting that "each of us must take total responsibility" for preventing it.

"When she laid out her spiel, you talk about cognitive dissonance! It was so different from anything I had ever heard at the lab. It was the first time my confidence, or at least my belief, in my world was shaken even a little bit.

"I got furious at Helen, which was how I met her. Somebody in the audience asked her a question, 'How do you know what you say you know?' and she gave an answer I thought was very arrogant. She said, 'Well, I'm a physician and a scientist.' I thought, 'Goddamned answer. I'm going to meet this lady and tell her what I think of her answer.' "

Perry marched up to Caldicott in full dragon-slaying armor and received his second surprise. "Despite the militancy of her speech, she was soft, she was warm." She admitted the arrogance of her answer, then took charge again. "Mr. Perry, do you have any children?"

He has three.

"Have your children asked you about where you work?"

They hadn't.

"They will, you know."

He headed back to the Bay Area determined to check out Caldicott's scientific credentials and to deal with the substance of her charges one way or another. But returning to the lab, he found a fortress preparing for siege. Major demonstrations were being planned, spearheaded by an outfit calling itself the Livermore Action Group. His job would be to "handle" the demonstrations in the press, to minimize their impact.

The Livermore Action Group, a grassroots coalition which still functions in the Bay Area, had targeted the lab for an ongoing campaign in active nonviolence. Its tradition was that of Gandhi, Dorothy Day, and Martin Luther King, who toward the end of his life took increasingly strong stands against the Vietnam War and suggested that there might be connections between a society's warmaking and its racism.[3]

Perry set out to know this adversary. He expected to find Berkeley students, hippies, and misfits, but the demonstrators who met his gaze through the fence seemed middle class and, above all, serious. He filed that impression away in his mind and set out to reclaim the moral high ground on behalf of the lab. The demonstrators challenged the weapons designed at Livermore as a provocation to war and the philosophy behind the weapons—deterrence—as morally reprehensible and unreliable. In countering their arguments, Perry was forced to defend the lab not only as a detached hall of science, which nobody seemed to believe anymore, but also as a designer of state-of-the-art nuclear weapons intended to preserve the peace.

"Did you believe in deterrence?" I asked him.

"Of course I believed in deterrence, starting the first time I had to deal with it at the lab. Before that, I hadn't thought much about it. But that's how I do my job—by believing in whatever it is, so strongly that I could convince even you."

Besides relying on the deterrence argument, the lab defended itself by means of its image of excellence and by out-liberaling the opposition. To the demonstrators' outrage, the lab responded with calm. To the demonstrators' black-and-white morality, the lab responded with a tolerance for all points of view. To the demonstrators' urgency, the lab responded as an entity that had the status quo on its side—which it did.

Perry still chuckles at some of the "genius things" his staff pulled off, like creating a special press room inside the lab where journalists would be welcomed and briefed and could see the entire event literally from the lab's point of view. "There wasn't anything you could want for in that press room: donuts, coffee, typewriters, beautiful women. I said to the photographers, 'Man, you come in here and, instead of photographing the backs of heads, I'll give you face shots.' I said, 'You want a scientist's opinion of the demonstration? I'll give you Roy Woodruff, the top weapons designer in the country.' Roy would say all the right things. He would say, 'One of the reasons Livermore was built is to protect the right of Americans to demonstrate freely.' "

No amount of genius could cancel out the emotional intensity of those demonstrations, not only for the participants and press, but also for the community of people who made their living at Livermore. In normal times, conversations in the cafeteria might be about Beethoven and Debussy or about quarks and neutrinos; it was rarely about the morality of the lab's work. During the demonstrations, those normally unspoken concerns rapidly surfaced. A common argument was that the demonstrations should be in Washington, not Livermore, because that's where the decisions about weapons policy were being made. Perry remembers answering huffily at one point, "If you guys weren't coming up with these new generations of weapons concepts, the politicians wouldn't have 'em to play with!"

While everybody in the lab stepped into debates like this from time to time, Perry's job forced him to deal with the issues eight if not twelve hours a day, and he found himself more and more confused. In the emotionally charged state of mind that was becoming his hallmark, Perry visited Dr. Edward Teller. "Edward," he said, "I am very concerned about nuclear war. Should I be concerned? Tell me how you deal with these questions."

He says Teller answered, "Young man, you are concerned about the wrong things. You should be concerned about the Soviet threat. Even in the event of an all-out nuclear war, only ten percent of our population would be killed."

Perry thanked him and walked away numbly. But on the way back to his office, the response sank in. "Only ten percent" of the population! In the United States, that would be over twenty million people.

With each monthly demonstration, and with each onslaught of increasingly knowledgeable reporters, the lab's staff became more polarized about how to handle the whole mess. Perry's job began forcing him to take actions he couldn't justify, not even in terms of the goals he thought he still shared with his colleagues. In March 1982, for example, a demonstrator with chutzpah and a point to prove about nuclear security scaled the fence surrounding the Livermore compound, marched into the lab's main building, entered the office of the chief weapons designer, and managed to throw some lab documents into a courtyard before he was caught. It fell on Perry to try to contain—and thus to acknowledge the importance of—a story he personally considered trivial.

In the ensuing months, the fence was given a new topping of barbed wire, security personnel speaking in arcane codes through walkie-talkies were placed around the perimeter, a virtual SWAT team was created for special incidents, and a holding cell was set up for arrested demonstrators on their way to jail. Before long, philosophical differences between Perry and the lab's chief of security blew into the open over a press request to photograph demonstrators in the pen, and Perry found himself ordered to deny the cell's existence to a veteran reporter who had seen it a few days earlier.

Livermore "absolutely won in the press," at least by Perry's scorecard. But in his own mind, the victory was not so clear. Under the surface of the public relations man who had everything under control, uncontrolled and largely unconscious changes were taking place.

He recalls, "I met a woman at a speaking engagement a few months after I left the lab. She said, 'Remember me?' I said, 'Refresh my memory.' She said, 'We talked across the fence at one of the demonstrations, and you told me, "Some day I might be where you are." ' I have no memory of that conversation, but I'm sure it happened."

Walking back to his office after one demonstration, his assistant said, "If Martin Luther King were around today, what do you think he'd make of this?"

Perry, who had met King, said, "I think he'd be out there demonstrating."

"Where would that put you?" his aide asked.

"I don't know, Judy. I don't know."

Between demonstrations, the public relations work of the laboratory revolved more and more around antinuclear initiatives. Proposition 12, a referendum expressing support for a nuclear weapons freeze, found its way onto the California state ballot, and the phone rang off the wall with invitations for nuclear scientists to debate the question. The basic public relations approach was to create a speakers' bureau of famous scientists, coach them on dealing with lay people, and turn them loose. But the basic approach resulted in disaster. "My guys were coming back and saying, 'We're losing our ass out there. The freeze people are using their half-hour slots to show a film, and you can't compete with that.' "

What the opposition was showing was the cream of the nuclear-war consciousness raisers from the early 1980s, *The Last Epidemic,* a simple black-and-white film narrated by Dr. Jack Geiger of Physicians for Social Responsibility.[4] *The Last Epidemic* starts with a question: What would happen if a one-megaton nuclear bomb were dropped on the city of San Francisco? The answers are given in meticulous detail: people and animals blinded from the blast, third-degree burns in epidemic proportions, hospitals demolished, water supplies contaminated, doctors in the same shape as everybody else.

"Get me a copy of that thing," Perry directed. Not wanting to "contaminate" his staff—and mindful of the fact that lab management, in response to a peace group's request to show the film on site, had banned it—Perry set up a screen in his office one day after hours, alone, and ran the film.

"I was absolutely blown apart. I was gone. When it was over, I couldn't move. I sat looking at a blank screen for an hour. Just kind of sat there. Then I wandered around the building for a while. I was stunned."

Never before had Perry thought in such concrete terms about what, specifically, he was promoting. Even now, his articulateness fades on the subject. "I'd never really, really made the connection between what was being done at the place where I worked and . . . I mean, I'd never made a nuclear weapon myself, but I was contributing to the process of making a weapon that could, that could . . . I felt . . . "

Tangled up in all the unearthly horror, the scenes too painful to comprehend, were images of more mundane losses which made the whole appalling thing real. "I found myself thinking about my record collection. I have about two thousand albums, real collector's items. It's taken me years to build it, and it stands for the way I see life, as a total symphony. I thought about never being able to play my record collection again, of seeing it all melted down. It was not just that things were being destroyed. It was humiliating that anybody would design anything that would be so quickly destructive, after all the centuries it's taken us to get where we are.

"I could absolutely feel the heat. I felt outraged, I felt like I'd been violated, I felt out of control. I felt that somebody else was controlling the world I lived in, and control is a very important issue for me."

Next morning, he quietly told three or four key staff members of the experience and admitted grave doubts about staying in his job. They convinced him to show it to the whole public relations staff, which he did, carefully keeping his mouth shut until they had seen and discussed it. Reactions to the film were mixed, as they were to Perry's revelation about his own feelings, but at least his concerns were out of the closet. Soon after that, Perry went to the office of one of the directors and laid out his conflicts. "He didn't say much. That was the first time it occurred to me that the lab might be bugged. He just said, 'Let's not talk about it here. Let's make a tennis date.' "

The tennis date never happened. Perry quit his job within a month of showing the film. Ironically, his resignation had no surface connection whatsoever to nuclear weapons. It had to do with a spat over personnel policy with another of the lab's directors, Jack Kahn. Perry says, "We were having a meeting about how to handle a personnel problem. It was strictly about business. Somehow, we blew into a heated argument, like one of those arguments that happens in a marriage. Nobody knows why it explodes. But we were obviously feeling more tension than we realized." The discussion became an argument and then a blowout, long after the original issue stopped mattering.

"We got down to the 'fuck you' level. At some point, Jack said to me, 'If that's your goddamn attitude, I'd find my way out of this lab.'

"I said, 'Jack, are you firing me?'

"He said, 'You know what I'm saying.'

"I said, 'No, I don't know what you're saying.' "

The spat solidified into a power play between two stubborn men who were both accustomed to winning. Perry called up his lawyer and friend of twenty-five years, Kurt Melchior, and laid out the situation. Melchior, knowing that a good lawyer is also a good counselor, hit him with the one question that mattered: "Bill, if you really want to go to war, we can fight it as a labor issue, we can fight it as a race issue, we can win hands down. But the question is, do you really want to work at the lab?"

Perry had said yes to working at Livermore because a search firm offered him the opportunity and billed it as golden, because he wanted to live on the west coast, because the power and the salary were enormously attractive, because no danger signals had gotten in the way of that yes. But the lessons of a year had not been wasted. "The question was so refreshing, so thunderous, that it kind of shocked me. I said, 'Well, no, I don't.' "

The mental equilibrium he had been maintaining shifted at that moment, so stunningly that Perry could only sit there and beg his lawyer to buy time while his emotions caught up with events. In a matter of forty-eight hours, his situation had deteriorated from a job that he had qualms about—qualms which could be reconciled in their own good time—to a job and career that were disintegrating under his feet. He stewed all weekend.

On Monday, his lawyer called and said the lab was demanding an answer that day. "What we have at that point is a film being played at very high speed, and it's my life. Even my lawyer is pressuring me. I said, 'Kurt, what should I do?'

"He said, 'As your lawyer, I can only advise you of your options.'

"I said, 'Kurt, we've been friends for twenty-five years. I don't want options. I want somebody to tell me what I'm supposed to do.' Realistically, nobody could tell me what to do. At one moment, all the options looked dark. Five minutes later, all the options looked bright. The situation seemed to be deteriorating very fast. All I could see was money going away, and erosion of power, and embarrassment. I had long since lost sight of what the issues were."

Finally, sitting in his living room and looking out over the placid houses of Mill Valley and the green hills of northern California, Perry realized that no right answer would drop from the sky. It was his choice. Did he want to work at the lab? In the context of that question, all the ferment he had been able to neutralize for months surfaced. *The Last Epidemic*, Helen Caldicott, the demonstrators, feelings I'd had for months, Kurt's question—in a quiet moment, it all came together, and I called Kurt, and I said, 'Write a letter to the lab. Deliver it by messenger. Tell them that, as of today, I have resigned. Negotiate whatever severance you can get. I'm out of there and feeling good.' "

Every ending is the beginning of something. Perry had no idea that his resignation would matter to more than his family and former colleagues—until he went out on an errand and came home to find his living room filled with TV cameras. It was inevitable that the reporters who covered the lab would notice his absence, but he was not prepared for the degree and suddenness of his notoriety. "These cats descended like hordes—print, radio, TV. I still have clippings, mountains of them, and I haven't saved half the stuff. Look: 'Inside the Bomb Factory: Revelations from One Who Got Away,' 'Lab Aide Quits as Matter of Conscience,' 'Balancing Bombs and Beliefs'—that's one of my favorites."

Cut loose, Perry felt the euphoria of one who has just had an aching tooth pulled. At first, he had no plans whatsoever about taking a public stand on anything. He expected to kick back, collect a not insignificant sum in severance pay, lie on the porch for a few weeks, and get his head straight on possible futures. But neutrality eluded him.

Opportunities to take a public stand not only knocked; when he hesitated, they came into his life through the windows. First he was invited to join the studio audience of a local debate show, "Say What You Think," featuring a Livermore scientist and an antinuclear activist. But, chatting before the show, he found himself at the center of attention. When it came time for audience questions, he thought of such a probing one for the Livermore spokesman, Dr. Robert Barker, that no amount of discretion could keep him from opening his mouth. "Dr. Barker, I hear that Livermore is planning a conference of scientists called 'Upgrading Lethality.' Could you explain what that conference is about?"

As Perry remembers it, "Bob Barker is a heavyweight scientist, and he handles himself very well in public. But he broke into a visible sweat at that question. He said, 'That doesn't really have anything to do with nuclear weapons. That conference is about conventional warfare.' I said, 'Even if it's about water pistols, *upgrading lethality* means finding more efficient ways to kill people.' "

After the show, he was invited out for drinks by some economist-scientist-activist types who work together as the Mid-Peninsula Conversion Project, studying and publicizing questions about how to convert Silicon Valley's heavily weapons-dependent economy to a civilian base. He was invited to speak at the group's next lunch time meeting in the little town of Mountain View. "What do I know that people want to hear?" he asked, and was reminded, "Most people have never been inside a nuclear weapons facility, even most people who argue about the issue. You understand the philosophy and the psychology of the lab, what the people in there think about."

"Understand it? I helped create it," said Perry, accepting the invitation but thinking it would be a minor episode in his life. He arrived at the meeting and found a message, through his attorney, from the lab: "If Perry gives that speech as planned, we will play hardball." The ultimatum gave him visions of his severance pay—a generous sum—taking wing. But at the same time there was the question of whether he would let himself be silenced. The ante was raised when he walked into the meeting room to find hundreds of people, TV cameras, the wire services. Bill Perry found himself giving the most carefully balanced talk of his life—and taped it, for extra protection. Even with that care and balance, the words that came out were dramatic.

He talked about the good things at the lab, its genuine commitment to excellence, its sense of unlimited creativity. He talked about the demonstrations and his own conversion. He compared his relationship with Livermore to a courtship and marriage, and only after the marriage does the mother-in-law show up. He maintains that he tried to portray his former employers not as bad people, but as people who for all kinds of reasons didn't take full responsibility for—and maybe didn't comprehend—the magnitude of the destructive potential they were unleashing. That's what he tried to say, but it didn't come out quite right. "I said, 'The whole answer that we are scientists and as scientists we don't decide what's to be done by the nation, that doesn't seem to work. Another time in recent history, in another country, just following orders got scientists in particular into a lot of trouble.' It seemed to me quite honestly that there was a lot of Nazi-like thinking going on at Livermore, and I said so. Of course, the headline writers turned that into 'Bill Perry Calls Lab Nazis' . . . "

As the 1982 elections heated up, Bill Perry threw himself into nuclear freeze speechmaking, but he is the first to admit that his motivations were only partly altruistic. One major factor was his emerging "hardball" relationship with the lab (whose meaning he never found out). Another was the fact that his peace work, the weaving of words and the strategizing of campaigns, was exactly what he had loved in his job and had suddenly lost. But, in addition, there was a feeling of integrity, of coming home, of making amends, of having earned the confidence of his convictions once again. A few months after leaving Livermore, he was invited to attend a fund-raiser and introduce the main speaker, Dr. Helen Caldicott, whom he hadn't seen since that Washington encounter. Humbly, he handed her a red rose and said, "I wish my friend Judy Collins were here to sing one of my favorite songs, 'Both Sides Now,' because I have seen this issue from both sides now, and I believe in our side with all my heart."

Press interviews begat speaking invitations—sometimes three in one day. "I plunged into it," says Perry, "the way I do into most things, not even taking time to wonder when it would end, or how." At some point, he telephoned Daniel Ellsberg and arranged for a briefing from the former defense analyst on the state of the nuclear stalemate. "My life became terribly disorganized. I had had nine secretaries. Now I didn't have any. There were occasions when I scheduled myself to show up in two places, fifty miles apart, at the same time. Occasionally, when I would get a moment, I would wonder what it all meant, wonder if I was making any contribution. At some level, I probably believed that if I worked harder and made more speeches, I could stop the arms race all by myself. It didn't matter if that was true. That's what was driving me."

He worked with a frenzy that recalled his early days in public relations, biting off challenge after challenge for its own sake. The rewards of activism—the speechmaking, the flow of creative juice, the strategic challenge—were not so different from the rewards of his job at Livermore. The freeze resolution passed in Marin County. The freeze campaign went on to organize—and win—a referendum "with some teeth in it" to turn the county into a nuclear-free zone. From time to time, he and Ellsberg would escape to a favorite restaurant in Berkeley where they would "get lots of parking tickets and just talk for hours about how intense it all was."

By 1985, Perry's cash reserves were dwindling and he began to wonder if there was life after the peace movement. "I'm going to have to either sell a big piece of writing or get a pretty groovy job pretty soon," he remembers thinking. His family was not, by that point, unscathed by the pace he had been keeping. "I think it's hard in any marriage for anybody to live with somebody who is operating off pure passion. The reason Sharon and I have hung together is that we know we really want to be married to each other. We've independently raised a lot of kids and done a lot of stuff . . . "

He found himself a job and entered another of his periodic retrenchment phases—tinkering with his novel, revising the manuscript on Livermore, reading, spending time with his family. Peace activists are still among his closest friends, but the friendships no longer revolve so rigorously around saving the world this minute. "There's a group of us who go to Yosemite every year at Halloween and have a costume party. That grew out of the peace movement. You need a cadre of close personal friends, people who can understand what you're trying to do but who can also laugh with you. Your public persona needs to able to say, 'I'm doing serious work on serious issues.' But you also need to be able to laugh."

How and why did Bill Perry change? First of all, his basic factual understanding of the world began to unravel. He started out believing that he worked for some neutral scientific enterprise, dimly connected to weapons research but fundamentally above that and any other real-world application. The new information he received began making an impact when it was addressed specifically in an ethical context, when reporters confronted the lab's management about weapons work, and not when it came up in the morally neutral context of shop talk.

The problem was that, as part of his daily responsibility, Perry had to come to terms with those facts, to formulate positions about the lab's work, to refine them as the debate evolved, and to defend them with an air of confidence. To do his job at the level he demanded of himself, Perry had to believe in what he was selling. For a while, he maintained enough belief in something: first, that the lab's research was "pure" science; then, that the scientists at Livermore just executed what Washington, as the voice of the public, mandated; later, that even if the lab was not only designing but lobbying for nuclear weapons, no one would be sufficiently callous or detached from human sensibility to use them; and finally, that somebody was in charge of the situation and could make sense of it, even when he began to realize he couldn't. As each of these beliefs in turn unraveled, Perry fought harder and harder to keep functioning, largely on adrenalin. In the end, the conflict he hadn't yet consciously faced erupted in his sudden loss of finesse, and he was squabbling over not bombs but a seemingly peripheral issue.

Of course, Perry's relationship to the lab existed on many levels, and so did its unraveling. Tangled up in his shift in attitude about the morality of building and lobbying for nuclear weapons—feeding that shift and fed by it—was a change in his own professional relationship to the laboratory. In the pressurized atmosphere of the demonstrations, differences in style and management philosophy surfaced and so did plain old irritability. As his attitudes and feelings toward the lab began to sour, so, inevitably, did his working relationships.

Perry was uniquely isolated, not only by his anguish over nuclear weapons, but also as spokesman for an enterprise whose ideals he was coming to doubt. With his isolation came a growing sense of vulnerability. His dispute with Kahn only made clear that corporate power struggles tend to favor top executives over public relations directors. If Perry had seen a chance of winning that battle, his decision to leave would have been tougher.

Bill Perry has never claimed to be a candidate for sainthood. For all his articulateness about the details of his experience, he is wise enough to know that he will never understand it completely or live up to his own example. He wants to have enough of the good things in life. He wants to have fun. He wants to feel in control. Yet he doesn't want to feel that these things are being purchased at the expense of other people's well-being, and prefers to think he is sharing the wealth instead of merely amassing it. He came to Livermore convinced that personal success was consistent with helping humanity. He left because neither personal success nor service to humanity seemed possible there. After months of trying to hold his finger in the dam, his lawyer's question—"Do you want to work at the lab?"—forced him to reexamine his position and choose a side.

In the years since his resignation, Perry has worked on a manuscript, still in progress, about how establishments like Livermore create their mystique. The cornerstone is a chapter called "The Fence." He writes:

> The fence was the great divide . . . it created mental, spiritual, and emotional gaps which may never be closed . . . One of the many illusions created by the fence is that it is transparent. Outsiders believe they can look in and see something they might understand; insiders believe they can look out and see something they feel they already understand too well. People on either side may be able to look, but what reality either sees is questionable because the fence, at least metaphysically, is a mirror. Some people look into the mirror and see themselves locked out by their government from stopping the work of people who are plotting the extinction of all life. Others look into the mirror and see themselves protected from suspected lawbreakers who question not only the usefulness of the lab's work, but also, they feel, the seriousness of the Soviet threat. Viewers on either side claim theirs is the only way to peace . . . The fences of Livermore harden the hearts on both sides, and polarize patriots inside and out.

By now, Perry has found some peace in his relationships with those who still drive out daily to that fenced-in compound in the desert. He has reflected at length on the professionals at Livermore, and says, "I think the guys who run the lab are extremely political men, part scientists but mostly businessmen. They spend an awful lot of time lobbying to get more money into the lab. They're the old guard nuclear establishment. They are brilliant. Many people in the peace movement seem to think, [baritone voice] 'The gods of fire are at Livermore. They're evil, evil men . . . ' I do not think they're evil, inherently. I think they're misguided. They're stuck back in 1945."

He sees the working scientists in a much different light, as much less versed in the details of the disarmament debate, more oriented toward buying the freedom to do science and feel good about it. "Do you realize," Perry asks, "that many of the people at Livermore are only twelve years old emotionally? Twelve is the age when they got their first Gilbert chemistry set for Christmas and turned their rooms into laboratories, and ever since—from kindergarten through PhD— they haven't had to be in contact with the outside world. I have seen thunderous examples of people like that who grew up with no responsibility. First Mom and Dad took care of them, then the school and the scholarships, and then they get invited to a place like Livermore, and they're challenged to make more speed, more heat, more light than anybody's ever seen. It's heady."

Bill Perry is still a dyed-in-the-wool Democrat and an incurably cheerful man. He has donated countless hours to antinuclear organizing, but he still reserves the right to live comfortably. He drives a burgundy Datsun 280Z, maintains his record collection, writes fiction to relax. He has pulled back from public visibility, saying he prefers to collect clippings about his kids' accomplishments instead of his own. Whenever he's asked to, he makes a speech on the threat of nuclear war. He hopes it's doing some good. Even so, Perry believes there will be a nuclear exchange of some kind in his lifetime. He has thought a lot about how it could happen. "I think it will be on the small end of the scale—maybe a hundred thousand people killed. It will probably take place in a desert country, maybe in the Middle East, because the white people who own most of the establishment do not like to blow up property too much. And it will probably take place somewhere where the deaths are of indigenous people, say Arabs."

Then what?

"Then," he says, "the world will come to its senses. I have too much faith in humanity not to think so."

8 *TO TAKE A CHANCE*
LOU RAYMOND

The coastline of southern Rhode Island and eastern Connecticut is one of the most military-dependent economies in the United States. General Dynamics' Electric Boat shipyard in Groton, Connecticut employs eighteen thousand people building Trident submarines and other nuclear systems. Over the border, the Electric Boat plant in Quonset Point keeps eight thousand Rhode Islanders working, making General Dynamics the largest industrial employer in each state.[1]

Until 1982, Louis Raymond was one of those workers, a supervisor in the salvage yard at Quonset Point. Raymond drew tremendous satisfaction from the tasks, the friendships, the pay and benefits. But he and his family were also Catholics whose faith had been deepening and playing a more practical role in their lives for some years. Ultimately, his faith led him to quit his job.

Raymond, 45, is a small and stocky man with a generous grin. Several miles down a country lane, he lives with his wife, Mary, and four children in a shingled ranch house he built himself. An oil painting of Jesus adorns one wall of the living room, haloed by a ring of smaller photos of their now teen-age offspring—Katie, Tim, Greg, and Steve— through the years. Shelves and sideboards full of figurines, framed landscape prints, and a flocked gingham wall covering are evidence of the care and attention that have been put into this home.

Lou and Mary Raymond met at Warwick Veterans High School in a suburb of Providence in 1961, introduced by friends who had matchmaking in mind. They spent their first date riding the merry-go-round at a local park, and Lou jokes, "We've been on a merry-go-round ever since." Both working-class Catholics with the same simple vision of making a home and raising a family, they fit another visiting

145

journalist's observation about Rhode Islanders: "They're not crowd pleasers. They're not rebels. They're just real, centered people."[2] They were open and thoughtful in talking about their joint decision that Lou's working on a nuclear sub was inconsistent with their Catholic faith, a decision which Lou characterizes as one of the major turning points of his life. But he cautioned right away, "I'm not sure how much light I'm going to be able to shed on this. It's been a while, and a lot of the real nitty-gritty changes were unconscious."

Neither of Lou Raymond's parents finished high school. His father, a carpenter, and his mother, a homemaker, instilled in him the kind of work ethic which emphasizes "doing whatever you need to do to provide for your family." The idea that one's choice of profession might have ethical dimensions never intruded in his upbringing.

All his life, Raymond has had a vague but persistent attraction to the helping professions. He started community college after high school with plans to be a social science major, but after a year, the Vietnam-era draft interrupted his education. He spent two years in the army at Fort Knox, Kentucky, supporting the war in spirit but feeling no particular desire to be involved firsthand. He came back to Rhode Island and, with his brother, went into business building houses, loving the independence and doing well enough financially until the housing industry collapsed in the late 1970s. By then, Raymond was a father of four and not in a position to be selective about a new career. When a friend offered him help in finding a job at Electric Boat as a rigger, he was delighted.

Working for other people was an adjustment after having been his own boss, but Raymond enjoyed the companionship and the sense of mission as well as the paycheck. After a while, he moved up into a clerical job and then became head of the salvage yard, selling off salvageable materials and supplies left over from the massive sub-building operations. "It was excellent," he says of the job. "The pay was good, at least after I'd been there a little while. They had outstanding benefits, a good retirement program."

The Quonset Point plant builds sections of Trident submarines, which are then shipped to Groton for assembly and launching.[3] The overall mission of the shipyard played little role in Raymond's choice to work there, but it harmonized with his values and worldview at the time. "I had been kind of hawkish as a young man. I remember during the Vietnam War thinking that we really should have gone in there and done far more than we did. I figured that the United States was strong, so why didn't we go in there and destroy the whole place? I felt we were in the right. The peace people, or whatever you call them, I could never really understand"—he loses words temporarily—"The way they dressed, everything about them. They were just different." The word "different" is often used in the Raymond family to describe the otherwise indescribable. It is not exactly a condemnation, but neither is it an expression of praise.

The details of the debate over Trident, or even nuclear weapons, were never a conscious concern for Raymond. But Trident is a cornerstone of the Reagan-era nuclear buildup. At 560 feet from end to end, the sub equals nearly two football fields in length. Two generations, Trident I and II, differ in their firepower, but both are a quantum escalation from previous nuclear subs. Trident II contains 24 missiles with 14 independently targetable warheads on each. A single Trident II can incinerate 336 Soviet cities, dropping the equivalent of five Hiroshimas on each one. It can do so in under fifteen minutes. The cost of two Trident submarines is equal to the cost of running the entire public school system for a year. Congress had authorized funds for a dozen Tridents by the end of 1986, and the Navy's "wish lists" for the program range between twenty and thirty subs.[4]

The massive system represents the state of the art in submarine-launched ballistic missile (SLBM) technology, and is the same one which moved Lockheed engineer Bob Aldridge to quit his job designing the system out of concern over its aggressive potential. In *First Strike!* Aldridge writes,

> The characteristics that make SLBM's likely to be the first weapons used in limited nuclear war are the same that make them the most probable choice for use to initiate a strategic first strike. First, the location of the submarine that launches them is much less certain to the Soviets than the US silo-based missiles. Soviet radar would have to provide surveillance in all directions from which a SLBM might possibly come. It is possible that they would not even detect a SLBM until it was too late. That would mean that Soviet land-based missiles would be destroyed before they could be launched. Likewise, communications centers would be annihilated before they could send the launch command to Soviet missile-carrying submarines.
>
> The second very important advantage of SLBM's over land-based ICBM's in destroying land targets is their shorter flight time. That is made possible by the shorter range from which they can be fired. Whereas ICBM's take about thirty minutes to get from one continent to another, SLBM's travel from the submarine to their target in ten to fifteen minutes. This pares down warning time . . . to as little as five minutes.[5]

Paradoxically, Trident has mobilized many extremely knowledgeable people such as Aldridge to join the peace movement, while remaining nearly invisible on the national debating agenda.[6] The very qualities that make Trident so upsetting to many peace activists also make it a symbol of patriotic nuclear deterrence and a sacred cow for legislators willing to oppose many other nuclear weapons. According to Joanne Sheehan of the National Coalition to Stop Trident, the system is widely considered "the Pentagon's answer in its search for the perfect weapon. For those who believe we need nuclear weapons, Trident has no serious flaws. It is technologically superior and invulnerable to anything the Soviets can produce. Opposing Trident involves not only pointing out its flaws. The problem is that Trident may work exactly as advertised, and challenging it involves exposing the strategic policies of the US and USSR, a task some activists find too complicated and difficult."[7]

Among workers at both Electric Boat plants, the big sub is proudly viewed as the state of the art technologically and strategically. Raymond remembers vividly the first time he saw and then boarded an assembled Trident submarine. "In supervisor training down at Groton, they took us through the submarines so we could see firsthand how they were put together. It was kind of awesome. When you have your first visions of a submarine, you think of the ones in World War II. They're pretty small. The ones we worked on were just huge. You feel like a little pimple on the side of this huge thing. It boggles the mind, the size and complexity of them. Seeing the missile tubes and the huge doors the missiles would come out of, I realized how many cities it could attack at once, and I understood for the first time what 'mass destruction' meant."

Sobered but not fundamentally thrown off balance, Raymond continued his job. But in other parts of his life, things were changing. Through their parish, Lou and Mary Raymond were drawn into community work and spiritual retreats. They volunteered many hours counseling other Catholic couples getting ready for marriage or dealing with hard times. Their house was frequently a way station for foster children and unwed mothers. These activities were rewarding, and in turn expanded the church's role in both their lives.

"My father was an old-time Catholic, a religious man in his way. He went to novenas every Tuesday night and church on Sunday, but I don't think his spirituality was the same kind I see for myself," Lou Raymond reflects. "I think the single thing that's added most to my spiritual life is my wife. She's very open to the Spirit. We talk about it a lot, and she's been an impetus to get me into places where I'd be led in some way." The Raymonds try to do—actively and with some degree of discipline—what many churchgoing people talk about: live a life of prayer, not only for comfort and strength, but also to seek and receive guidance on specific decisions. "As time goes on in my life, I believe more and more that God leads you to or shows you what he would like to have fulfilled in your life. You can either accept or reject it. If you leave yourself open, you are led, and I haven't always accepted the places I've been led, but when I do it seems to work out well."

In 1981, the Raymonds signed up for a two-year course called "The Spirituality of Christian Leadership" at a local spiritual life center. "It was a place to think about your personal relationship with God, where it was leading you, how you would take God's message into the world," he explains. Besides weekly classes, the program involved intensive retreats every quarter and occasional seminars as well. One of these provided Lou Raymond with his next source of discomfort about his job. "I've mostly tuned this out," he admits. "But there was some kind of a presentation about the nuclear arms race there one night. It struck me as very propagandistic, very manipulative. But the one thing that did stick with me was the fact that the military budget was taking so much money that could have been used for people who were starving or homeless. And I was making a living from that industry."

Raymond first noticed that his attitude toward his work was changing when people in the retreats asked the most natural question, "What do you do for a living?" To his astonishment, he felt embarrassed. "It just didn't seem right. It didn't jibe. I'm not a very aggressive person. And here I am making this instrument that is all destructive, or sure seemed to me to be when I thought about it."

It is not surprising that Raymond felt himself on unsteady ground working for an arms manufacturer and worshipping in the Catholic church of the early 1980s. Nor is it surprising that he has a hard time pinning down specifically the source of his discomfort. The National Conference of Catholic Bishops' famous pastoral letter, "The Challenge of Peace," whose groundwork was being laid at the time, is a painstaking struggle between theological tradition of "just war" and the realities of any warfare in the nuclear age. The church has been far from united on the ethical question of weapons work, but its climate reflects the leadership of a pope who has written prolifically on the spiritual dimensions of labor, including a poem called "The Armaments Factory Worker":

> I cannot influence the fate of the globe.
> Do I start wars? How can I know
> whether I'm for or against?
> No, I don't sin. It worries me not to have influence,
> that it is not I who sin.
> I only turn screws, weld together
> parts of destruction,
> never grasping the whole,
> or the human lot.

> I could do otherwise (would parts be left out?)
> contributing then to sacrificial toil
> which no one would blot out in action or belie in speech.
> Though what I create is all wrong,
> the world's evil is none of my doing.

> But is that enough?[8]

His discomfort was as vague as the images in his mind of what that submarine, or any other nuclear weapons, could actually do. Raymond exudes optimism and, consciously, he has not been one to preoccupy himself with something as grim as nuclear war. Once, in the army at Fort Knox, he remembers waking up in a violent thunderstorm and, for a moment, imagining it to be the final holocaust. But except for the odd unpredictable moment which he calls "silly," he never had to imagine the possibility—until 1981. To celebrate the launching of each new Trident submarine, Electric Boat traditionally holds a celebration by the water's edge as each massive vessel is lowered. A band plays. Hot dogs and hamburgers, beer for the adults and prizes for the kids, all are generously provided. The Raymonds, adults and kids, climbed into the car one Sunday to celebrate the commissioning of the USS *Ohio.*

Rounding the bend in the access road, they were taken aback to see several thousand black-robed figures—demonstrators with faces painted ashy white, gazing at the procession of party goers. They carried signs expressing the scale of destruction represented by Trident, their belief that it would destabilize superpower relations and make nuclear war more likely, their pleas with the crowd to rethink what they were building. But what the Raymonds remember most is their complete silence, composure, control. "It was a very unusual feeling. There was no sound at all. In fact, even the people going in to the launching were silent. It was very scary. There was an awesome mood to it," says Lou.

Mary remembers, "I noticed all of a sudden that we were whispering. And I think the deadliness of the image impressed everyone around us. I didn't hear anyone putting it down." The party never got very lively. On the way home, the family compared experiences, and everyone was moved. Greg reflects, "It was sad, eerie. It made you think. The silence, especially. You see demonstrators on TV yelling, and you say, 'What a bunch of goofs. They're just making it worse for themselves.' But these people were totally different."

Mary Raymond is a pale blond woman whose manner is resolutely upbeat. She speaks simply and concretely of the first time she had to think about the source of her family's income. "When he first took the job, I was just very grateful and looked at it as a paycheck every Friday. I never thought about what was going on over there," she says. Nor did she ask about the use of the components she was making in her own part-time job at an electronics plant. "I don't understand electronics, and I wasn't enchanted enough by the job to care a whole lot what we were making," she says. But a few weeks after the launching, she remembers the boss coming in and "announcing that they had just gotten a government contract, that it had something to

do with arms, but he wasn't free to tell us any more than that."
Suddenly, the everyday business of getting up and going to work
seemed, for both the Raymonds, to require new and uncomfortable
reflection. She notes, "I don't think I ever thought about nuclear war
as something that might affect us directly. I just thought about the
morality of the work. Peace and justice have to start with each of us.
I just remember thinking, 'It's wrong to be collecting a paycheck that
comes from war or from the potential for war. If we don't have peace
in our hearts, how can we expect it in the world?' " At that point,
she had already given notice to leave her job in order to spend more
time at home with a foster child. She left with relief.

Lou Raymond kept relatively quiet about his concerns, as is his
style, although there was no shortage of people with strong opinions
on either side of the issue. Specifically staying away from people who
seemed "propagandized" or "emotional," he pondered in silence instead.
The one person he confided in besides Mary was his priest, Father Fred
Sneesby. Though he never formally sought counseling, the subject just
seemed to come up whenever the two worked together on church
suppers or marriage counseling programs. "Lou is a prayer," the priest
recalls. "He really does it. I doubt that he's ever had a crisis of faith.
I think the change in his attitude about working at Electric Boat
happened so naturally, and he was able to trust his feelings, because
he doesn't rely on intellectual answers."

Raymond's feelings were distressingly consistent. The silence of the
demonstrators haunted him. "If we ever did have a nuclear attack, this
is how it would be, this dead silence. The demonstrators didn't look
human, in a sense, wrapped up in their sheets and robes. They were
something not human." That, too, sharpened his images about what
the real survivors of a nuclear war would be like.

He kept chewing on the dilemma: Thou shalt not kill, but thou
shalt support thy family and be a productive member of thy community.
Raymond recognized that his co-workers thought of themselves as
preventing nuclear war, not making it more likely. The arguments
about deterrence were not something he chose to engage on an abstract
level. But intuitively, once he understood what he was helping to
build, his gut told him that making huge state-of-the-art nuclear
hardware was not the way to avoid nuclear war. "I don't personally
think we have to have no defense, either. I don't see going that far.
But I just think we've gone beyond reason in what we're building. If
the Russians did come in, I know I'd be scared silly. Still, maybe
that's kind of what we're called to leave ourselves open to," he reflects.

Economic issues hung heavy, as did his difficulty in believing that
he could be right when thousands of co-workers seemed to go to work
unperturbed. His limbo lasted more than two years. "I don't know if

other people could tell, but I was pretty scared," he admits. What pushed him into a commitment was a meeting with his boss, who said, "We've got a new job opening up, and you're just the perfect person for it. It's quite a step forward for you." Raymond steeled himself and said, "I'm afraid you'd better think of someone else for that job. I don't expect to be here much longer." He remembers his sheer astonishment hearing himself spit out the words. "I felt as if I were two people: one saying those things, and the other standing off to the side screaming 'What are you doing???' "

He gave no departure date, and his supervisor, while expressing authentic respect for the decision, encouraged him to think it over. He felt consciously resolved—in theory. But he kept going to work.

Finally, when it was time for the next round of raises and promotions, his supervisor beckoned him in for a talk. "Look, Lou, take your time in figuring out what you need to do. But let me know. If you think you're going to be around for a while longer, I'll put in for a raise for you. If not, let me give it to somebody who is staying."

"Give it to somebody else," said Raymond. At that moment he understood that "when it comes down to decision time and you're scared stiff and you feel totally out of control, something kicks in and you feel like God is taking you where you have to go."

Raymond's loss of enthusiasm for his job had not been something he could, or would try to, conceal from the children. But the subject was not discussed until his second meeting with his supervisor. Before he got home from work that day, several friends had called Mary to ask if the rumors about his resignation were true; Lou and Mary had the choice of telling the kids that evening or letting them hear about it at school the next day. He gathered them together after dinner and tried to put his feelings into words for the first time. "I told them basically how I felt about the arms race, and how I felt it affected me. I said I felt it was wrong for me to be involved, that it was a personal thing and I didn't want to make a judgment about anybody else. I just couldn't in good conscience be a part of something that could mean risking total destruction." He remembers struggling to keep from inflating the issue, while admitting that he had never faced a decision so difficult and compelling. "I remember telling the kids that Mary and I had prayed about it and talked about it. I think the term I used was 'uncomfortable.' It had gotten too uncomfortable for me to stay there." He warned them that their classmates might give them a hard time. But the real weightiness of the discussion came from the fact that the Raymonds had no idea where the money would come from. If a new job did not materialize, health insurance would be the first loss, and then, in the worst case, the house. Tim, the youngest, remembers asking, "Will we still be able to have Doritos every now and then?"

After the family meeting, when the kids got together in their pajamas to confer, the general sentiment was relief. Katie, then 13, reflects, "I had always wondered why he worked there. It didn't seem like something my dad would do, because of the moral issues and all. When he told us, I thought, 'That's the dad I know.' "

But the period between that decision and his final day was one of escalating stress. Raymond worked harder than ever to train a replacement and to leave his work station in good shape. He kept himself too busy—or was in too much shock—to make any headway in seeking another job. Looking at himself in the mirror on the morning of August 20, 1982—his last day at the shipyard—he saw a sleepless, vulnerable face. He remembered the frustration and powerlessness of his last years building houses, when work was harder and harder to find. He had still not faced the reality of his decision to begin looking for another job. Punching in for the last time, he recalls, "was really difficult, just knowing that when I came out of there this time I wouldn't be going back in. I would be turning in my badge. I had a lot of friends there and a lot of security there and right in the pit of my stomach it was getting to me."

Final paper work took most of the day. The rest was filled up with a farewell lunch at which his foreman and co-workers wished Lou Raymond the best and talked about his decision. Many disagreed with his position, but the strongest emotion they expressed was concern for his future. One colleague, almost ready to retire, said, "Yeah, Louis, I've thought about it too, and I have my moments of feeling guilty for staying here. But where would I go? And what about all the years I have invested in this place?"

"There's no reason for you to feel guilty," Raymond assured him. "This is just what I'm being called to do. You have to make your own decisions based on your own life. Besides, I have a skill to fall back on."

Mary Raymond was waiting in the parking lot when her husband came out the gate for the last time. "That's it. We did it," was all he needed to say as he got into the car. Dinner was the same as always. The kids continued to be supportive. The news went on as usual, and Raymond relaxed as he typically did with a novel for a few hours before going to bed. As his feelings slowly surfaced, they had less to do with the grand ethical questions of nuclear arms than with the goodbyes he had just said to the work and friendships of five years. "It was a lonely feeling. You're used to losing a friend here and there, when people move away or whatever. But two or three hundred people in one shot gone from your life, knowing I would never be involved with those people again . . . "

"It was frightening," Mary recalls. "We used to joke that maybe we would end up eating at the soup kitchen where we had volunteered as a family, or sleeping in the shelter where Lou had volunteered. We lost our Blue Cross coverage. We didn't have five cents in savings. We had no security except the Lord."

"Dear God," Lou prayed that night, "I understand that we may lose a lot of what we have. Grant us the strength to handle that, if it is your will. But we ask you to look after us and let us find work to support this family . . . "

The next day, a friend of Mary's called for Lou. "Do you have some spare time?" she asked. "I've been wanting to hire somebody to build a deck behind my house." From that short-term job, others followed. Raymond bought himself a secondhand pickup truck and incorporated as Louis A. Raymond, Builder. The work orders never stopped coming in, and business has been steady enough since 1986 to let him employ his son Gregory as assistant. He sums up, "After the initial shock of leaving, I never regretted it again. I enjoy what I'm doing. It's a good lifestyle. I think I'm doing something good for people." He stops short of condemning the work he did at Quonset Point. "I can't say I was contributing to something good or something bad. It was uncertain. Maybe nuclear arms have saved us from massive land wars. But then again, what are they leading us to? Now I know I supply people with something they find joy in."

During his final years in the armaments industry and right afterward, Lou Raymond's resignation was the major crisis of his life. But with time and the discovery that he could keep the bills paid through carpentry, his life settled into a familiar, simple enough rhythm. He gives major credit to his spiritual life and his marriage. "Mary and I have tremendous faith, and somehow we call it out of each other. When things don't look so well, one or the other of us says, 'You know, God's always taken care of us in the past.' So we've kept each other straight and strong."

In recent years, activists concerned with moderating the economic and psychological influence of the Pentagon on industrial priorities have begun to pay greater attention to the lives of workers in weapons industries. These workers' political power often keeps legislators angling for submarine or bomber contracts even while supporting arms control legislation. And on a more personal level, while many workers in these industries understand and endorse the politics they are serving, large numbers struggle with guilt or the numbing sense that what they make is an unspeakable secret. In one 1986 survey of New England weapons industry workers, fully 63 percent expressed ambivalence or moral discomfort with their work.[9]

Support groups have begun to form—most of them limited by their members' status as outsiders and the difficulty faced by any missionaries making initial contact with the infidels. One such group began in

Providence at about the time Lou Raymond made his decision. Formed by religious activists—mostly but not all Catholic—drawn from many communities, the group members had been working together as a "parish without walls." They called themselves Genesis. They volunteered at local soup kitchens and homeless shelters, led Bible study groups, and traveled around Rhode Island to answer calls for help.

When the members of Genesis sat down to name their newborn support group for people thinking about leaving weapons industries, the natural name was Exodus. But that was one of the few easy decisions for the group. Organizers talked long and seriously about how to step outside their own, often passionate, convictions about the ethics of weapons work and to minister genuinely to the workers. They asked Lou Raymond to join the group, and he became the only Exodus member with firsthand knowledge of the inside world of Electric Boat. "The most important thing is not to come on too strong," he advised. After many meetings and even more rewrites, Exodus came up with a simple statement to hand workers at the gate:

> Dear Worker,
>   I am sure you have thought about your job in many ways.
>   Does your job provide you with sufficient earning power to support your family in a satisfactory manner? The answer is probably yes.
>   Does your job provide you with job advancement opportunities? The answer is probably yes.

After cataloging the pluses of income, security, and benefits, the pamphlet asks, "Does your job present you, at times, with the moral dilemma of working in a nuclear arms industry when our world is facing the possibility of a nuclear disaster?" In simple language, it introduces Exodus as a group that can help with practical support and discussion, and ends by urging, "If you say 'No, it is not morally objectionable to work in a nuclear armament industry,' please do not throw this pamphlet away. The same question just might come to mind again tomorrow."

It was still dark on the morning in 1983 when the Exodus members met at McDonald's for breakfast prior to a long-anticipated initiative: the distribution of the first batch of pamphlets. They drove up to the gate of the shipyard just as the morning shift was beginning. Once a commuter on that very access road, Lou Raymond stood by the gate with a full heart and very curious mind. "It was a group decision to do it," he remembers. "I voted for it because I thought it was a good thing in the abstract, but I knew I didn't want to do it. No way. On my own, I probably wouldn't have. I had left as a low-key, personal thing, without pointing fingers. Now here I was back with a point of view in my hand. You never know if it's going to be accepted. And you always want to be liked."

Mary adds, "The thing that was hardest for me was that there wasn't time for dialogue. People were rushing in to work."

Outwardly polite and inwardly "real nervous," Lou remembers handing out the folded sheets to those who indicated interest. At first, friends he hadn't seen since his resignation went out of their way to greet him. Many accepted the pamphlet. But soon there was a pale blue carpet of rejected paper all around him. "Hi, Lou," said a vaguely familiar voice, and he looked toward the gate to see the building security officer with a camera, snapping his picture for the record.

Subsequent leafletting sessions—once a year or so—remained frustrating yet, for the Raymonds, still compelling. The company took to increasing its security forces at the gates and even including guard dogs, leading Mary to comment, "It made me very uncomfortable that anyone would think they needed a guard dog to defend against me. If part of their purpose was to intimidate us—and I don't know, but maybe I suspect that—it certainly worked with me."

At first, Exodus also applied for grants from area churches and put together an emergency assistance fund of a few thousand dollars, to be offered as revolving loans to workers wanting to change fields but held back by financial worries. Such a fund could never completely cushion the economic shock of a job change—lost time, loss of seniority—for even a single worker. But it could provide for emergencies, keep health insurance going, cover other survival expenses, and say "You're not alone."

That fund still sits in a bank account. Exodus continues its annual leafletting but, between those reunions, organizers admit the group is at a standstill. Laments Brian Donahue-Lynch of Providence, a founder, "The military-industrial complex seems so big and so diffuse. Every mom-and-pop electronics place is trying to get into military contracting. In the short run at least, we are definitely going against the tide."

The difficulties of blue-collar workers breaking ranks with weapons industries are some of the most serious and stubborn, especially in a region like the Rhode Island coast. While Raymond's pay at Electric Boat was satisfying to him and enough to keep his family comfortable, it did not stretch to make much saving possible. Raymond was able to support his family and satisfy his conscience because he had a trade, carpentry, which was in sufficient demand again. For others at the shipyard—some without particular skills, others who had worked there all their lives—asking the ethical questions about nuclear weaponry meant asking even more difficult practical ones. Civilian jobs might be available for some, but the work force along that coastline, from unskilled laborers to middle managers, understands that Pentagon dollars are the driving force of the economy. Converting the military-industrial work force on more than a symbolic scale means converting an entire regional economy.

Louis Raymond is not particularly daunted by that reality because, unlike many who resign in protest and many more who hang onto secure jobs, he did not base his decision on its economic consequences or on its potential to influence policy. He based it on a highly personal code of ethics. But there has been one unexpected, satisfying consequence of his stance: His children have all given the issue more thought than they otherwise would have. Says Timothy Raymond now about his father's move, "I'm happy with his change. He's home a lot more. And it's not as scary as it used to be. The risk of nuclear war is still really scary, and it's still there in my mind, but somehow his decision helped a little bit."

Raymond does not have grand hopes about the potential of people like him in communities like his to end the nuclear threat—at least not by politics as usual or intellectual debate. "What it's going to take," he believes, "is for each side to take a chance on the other side. I don't know how we can do away with nuclear arms without doing that. Then I suppose I'd be worrying about how honorable each side would be. But I've always had this picture in my mind of Christ, and he gave the world that same thing. He took a chance on the world, and he was betrayed for taking that chance, but somehow the cross was what saved the rest of us. It just seems like we have to take that same chance."

9 THE BIGGER FLEECE
DAVID PARNAS

For years, David Parnas had a recurring nightmare: a letter, or perhaps a courier, would arrive in his office announcing that he had won a dubious honor, Senator William Proxmire's Golden Fleece Award for the most extravagant and blatant misuse of public funds. Parnas, a pioneer in software engineering and longtime consultant to the Naval Research Laboratory, worried about gaining that notoriety for the largest and most recent of his navy-funded projects: the redesign of a major software system that already worked well, in an airplane which was soon to be retired, in order to study design principles. Parnas, whose sense of professional ethics is acknowledged even by his critics, saw no other way to answer key questions about the reliability of large software systems. "Who has the money to build a thing twice when it works the first time?" he asks. "Only the Department of Defense." Still, he wondered whether the political science majors on the senator's staff would realize that software design is not just an aesthetic concern, but affects the economics and safety of computers and all they control.

Parnas finally did shake hands with Proxmire, but for a very different reason. He had become well known not for participating in a "fleece" but for protesting one, by quitting, with moderate fanfare, another consulting job—his $1000-a-day seat on the Reagan administration's advisory panel on computing in support of battle management. The panel, later known as the Eastport group and the subject of a major congressional investigation for conflict of interest, was a key element of the Strategic Defense Initiative (SDI).[1] He had joined the panel skeptical of, but wanting to believe in, the idea that a ballistic missile defense shield could make nuclear weapons "impotent and obsolete." But Parnas, known for his independence of mind and a style bordering on abrasive, had concluded after a few weeks on the panel that the idea was not only off base but "a fraud." And he met with Proxmire, one of the few in Washington he respects, to be congratulated for "having the guts to quit a $1000-a-day job just because what it's supposed to do can't be done."

There is a kind of Woody Allen quality to David Parnas—not the gaunt nervousness, but the same blend of irony and straight-shooting commentary, the same soft New York accent and cultivated schlemiel image, the same tendency toward self-perpetuating intricacy of thought. It is not unusual for him to show up wearing decrepit corduroys and two clashing flannel shirts for his job as a professor of computing and information science at Queen's University in Ontario. Bicycling eight miles to and from work on a fat-tired, mud-encrusted mountain bike, he enjoys his reputation for quirks like lecturing with his pant legs tucked into his socks. But he is also known for turning out students who know how to think fundamentally about computers and what they can and cannot do. The author of over one hundred technical papers and holder of a distinguished teaching and consulting resume, Parnas speaks with self-awareness and concentration, taking the time to say exactly what he means and the pains to correct any misinterpretations.

In his famous March 1983 speech, Ronald Reagan uttered the challenge, "I call upon the scientific community, who gave us nuclear weapons, to turn their great talents to the cause of mankind and world peace, to give us the means of rendering these nuclear weapons impotent and obsolete."[2] From this wishful statement came a Pentagon fiefdom, the Strategic Defense Initiative Organization (SDIO), headed by Lieutenant General James Abrahamson. It was given a budget in the billions of dollars and a general technical goal: to create a ballistic missile defense system, using satellite-based sensors and high-energy beams to neutralize incoming weapons, tied together by computer systems as monstrously complex as the concept itself.

By the time Parnas was invited aboard, SDI was already a highly charged issue. Over eight thousand scientists—eventually it would be fifteen thousand—had signed a pledge not to accept research funds from the project. The American Association for the Advancement of Science had polled experts in the fields most heavily involved in SDI-related research, such as physics and computer science, and got the response "it won't work" from fully 98 percent.[3]

The chorus of skeptical responses even included no less mainstream a diplomatic foursome than McGeorge Bundy, Robert McNamara, George Kennan, and Gerard Smith, who wrote in *Foreign Affairs* in 1984,

> What is centrally and fundamentally wrong with the President's objective is that it cannot be achieved. The overwhelming consensus

of the nation's technical community is that in fact there is no prospect whatever that science and technology can, at any time in the next several decades, make nuclear weapons 'impotent and obsolete.' [SDI], ambitious as it is, offers no prospect for a leak-proof defense against strategic ballistic missiles alone, and it entirely excludes from its range any effort to limit the effectiveness of other systems—bomber aircraft, cruise missiles, and smuggled warheads.[4]

So inappropriate was the SDI concept to its purported task that rampant speculation arose about other, shadier purposes. Robert M. Bowman, a retired air force lieutenant colonel who under the Ford and Carter administrations managed the research efforts which later became SDI, wrote that "the only believable so-called 'defensive' use of a Star Wars system is to protect an aggressor from the few missiles he missed in a first strike."[5] Others duly noted the words of Heritage Foundation consultant Greg Fossedal, who wrote in *Conservative Digest* in 1984 that Star Wars was an effective political stratagem regardless of its military value, a way to "fast-thaw the nuclear freeze movement," then at its peak.[6]

Whatever the motives of its architects, SDI triggered concern for its ability to destabilize the arms race by giving the Soviet Union every reason to worry about its offensive potential. And even if it were never to be deployed, it loomed as such a massive expenditure that Kennan et al. wrote, "The larger likelihood is that, on their way to oblivion, these schemes will simply cost us tens and even hundreds of billions of wasted dollars."

Much of this debate raged outside the hearing range of David Parnas, who has lived in Canada since he married his second wife, Lillian, an educator who had emigrated there from Hong Kong and whom he met at a conference in Victoria in 1977 after his painful first marriage and divorce. Lillian Chik-Parnas is a plain-dressing, even-tempered woman, neither noticeably shy nor dynamically outgoing but candid and thoughtful. Parnas says of their meeting. "We found common interests right away. She got me interested in some Chinese philosophers—Chuang Tzu, Lao Tzu—so much that I promised to buy some books she recommended. But she showed up the next day with copies, saying 'I know you'll never get around to buying them yourself, so here they are. You owe me twelve ninety-five.' "

Lillian is taking off a few years from her work as an educator to be the full-time parent of a precocious, bilingual pixie named Henrietta. She agrees with her husband on SDI and supports his outspokenness, but is clear that the stress on their home life is something she could do without. "When you're one of a billion, you learn to fit in with the crowd. I might disagree with an official policy, but my style is to do it more quietly," she reflects, adding with understated humor, "For a while, when Dave first got all this attention, I used to worry that he would be harassed or threatened or even killed for stepping out of line. But then I realized that anyone who wanted to could destroy him without firing a shot. All they'd have to do is get all the reporters who have taken an interest in him, and have them call up one after another until he drops dead of exhaustion."

It is not surprising that she chooses to put up with the uncertainty and stress. Among the factors that made him the kind of person who could think critically about the SDI panel's mission were the shared values which cemented their relationship: discomfort with conspicuous consumption, resolute independence from the mind-numbing influences of TV and alcohol, and a regard for work as not just a means to financial ends but a source of satisfaction and a way to contribute to human well-being.

For David Parnas, this path was clear fairly early. As an undergraduate at Carnegie Tech in the late 1950s, he studied physics and engineering, indifferent to grades but drawn to the cutting edge of theory. Physics disillusioned him after a while because his professors seemed to be "devoting their lives to adding an extra decimal place to the weight of an electron." Parnas was acknowledging a need for something different and more stimulating just as the university bought its first computer in 1959. "I was attracted to computers because you can study anything with them. You can study early childhood education. You can study natural science. You can get into a lot of fundamental concepts, think about a lot of things I like to think about." He graduated with honors in electrical engineering as the field of computer science was defining itself, and got his doctorate at Carnegie in 1965. Alan Perlis, the department chair there as well as his role model and long-time friend, remembers that he "chose his own thesis topic and developed it without the standard reliance on an advisor, and it was a very good piece of work."

Parnas was at the forefront of computer scientists concerned with fundamental issues of software design and reliability. He was an activist, of sorts, for the methodical and structured development of programs in an era when the norm was trial and error. Fred Brooks, an architect of the IBM 360 computer at the University of North Carolina, calls Parnas "one of four seminal thinkers in the field of software engineering," even though the two have debated each other on the feasibility of SDI. Parnas wrote an important early paper on handling errors in large systems—exactly the concern he would raise on the SDI panel—and pioneered the now standard concept of "information hiding," or minimizing the communication between different parts of a program to limit the impact of errors.[7] He remarks, "I'm still astonished that lay people expect computer programs to be perfect.

They may have seen a program error once; they think it's the exception. But it's the error-free program that's really the exception."

Parnas's constant questioning is that of a man whose intellect is his primary bridge to the world. But he is more dynamic than the stereotypical intellectual. "There are people who wouldn't say I'm a nice guy," he admits. "But when I think back over the people I've gotten along with and the people I haven't, intellect isn't the major factor. The people I've liked have had a certain openness, that's all. They haven't pretended to be anything they're not."

Some of his confidence and zest for argument came from his education at the exclusive Bronx High School of Science. Some came from his discovery in high school and college that "often professors would say things that weren't correct, and when I would challenge them they would generally acknowledge that I had a point." His parents, both refugees from the holocaust and physicians, left him with a lifelong appreciation of German language and culture and a strong sense of professional ethics. "I remember that my parents, who intentionally practiced in working-class neighborhoods, posted a copy of the American Medical Association's minimum fees in their waiting room— and then charged half those amounts. They were critical of American doctors as being too materialistic and not really dedicated to their profession. I think that's where I came to the conclusion that there was more to a profession than making money," Parnas reflects. His code of ethics, combined with his outspoken personality, ensured an embattled career. He wrote after leaving the SDI panel,

> As a professional:
> —I am responsible for my own actions and cannot rely on any external authority to make my decisions for me.
> —I cannot ignore ethical and moral issues. I must devote some of my energy to deciding whether the task that I have been given is of benefit to society.
> —I must make sure that I am solving the real problem, not simply providing short term satisfaction to my supervisor.[8]

Principles are not the only things that drive Parnas. He clearly enjoys being right. On his office wall, among diplomas and honors and a few understated watercolors, is a letter: "Dear Dave, Enclosed is a check in the amount of $.05 to acknowledge your victory in our bet that 'in five years there would not be a fully operational DOD weapon system with its software in ADA.' " The ADA controversy concerns a much-hyped new computer language, labeled a turkey by Parnas and now under investigation by the General Accounting Office for questionable cost-effectiveness. But in spite of his satisfaction at calling certain shots correctly, he is not so invested in being right that he is afraid to take intellectual risks. "How can anyone know everything?" he says matter-of-factly. The appeal of the intellectual life for him is precisely the chance to test theories, learn from others, engage in the delicious cross-fertilization of ideas through correspondence, lecturing, publishing, and bull sessions. It never occurred to him to take another path, and he has not regretted this one. But until he faced the dilemma of the SDI panel, Parnas never had to choose between income and independence. "I've been an idealist, in a sense, but I can afford to be," he admits.

Parnas has jumped around a good deal in his career of twenty-odd years: two years consulting for Philips-Electrologica in Holland, a three-year teaching post in West Germany, six years at the University of North Carolina, several stints teaching at Carnegie-Mellon, three years as a visiting scientist at IBM, and a part-time consulting role with the Naval Research Laboratory starting in 1972. Underlying this seemingly twisted career has been a continuity of emphasis on several themes, including the reliability of large software systems.

In his travels are a number of turning points. Philips, he says, introduced him to a whole new class of software problems and forced his work to take a right-angle turn. It also gave him the first of several cross-cultural influences. "Living in more than one country, you naturally wonder about the way social systems are set up. Why do some countries have privately operated post offices and public telephone systems, while in other countries both are public?"

Working for the navy was another cross-cultural experience of sorts, and a source of several lessons which later influenced his judgment and behavior on SDI. Naval software problems were harder than any he had encountered in civilian work. "They use militarized computers, they have real-time deadlines, and although the smartest people working there are quite good, in general they have lower-quality technical staffs. That's because the government doesn't allow itself to pay its engineers as much as it allows its contractors to pay their engineers. The navy wanted one of my colleagues to do some work, but he was too busy, so he asked me to come along to the meeting and then he disappeared. I looked at what they were doing, and they were designing an extremely stupid computer. That's my opinion, but I think time has proven me right: computers don't look like that." The project—now defunct—was the Advanced Avionics Digital Computer, a system intended to go into airplanes but highly inappropriate for the task. "The people who were working on this were being told by the contractor that they were going to be famous for revolutionizing computer science. Their egos were being fed, and they were going down this extremely stupid road. When I started criticizing their design structure, they said, 'Okay, we'd like you on board to help us.' I realize now that they were trying to co-opt criticism. But I didn't play by the rules. I kept criticizing them."

The project was finally killed by a report written by Parnas and the attempts of the contractors to counter it. He pointed out, among the design problems, a "fundamentally silly thing" in the documentation. "Some of it had been written as if there were seven index registers; some as if there were eight. I pointed it out because it showed that they didn't have a good intellectual grasp of what they were doing." The engineers heading the project wrote two separate reports attempting to refute Parnas, who notes with a chuckle, "They put out these two reports calling me incompetent. One of them said that obviously there were seven index registers. The other one said that obviously there were eight. At that point, even an admiral could understand that something was rotten."

That confrontation did not involve difficult ethical issues. He was a part-time consultant, backed up by full-time navy staff who were grateful for his outspokenness (as others later would be). And "it wasn't a public issue. It was something to be decided within the technocracy of the navy, a purely technical beef."

For most of his career, Parnas embodied a common attitude toward military contracting. In his early years, he was uncomfortable enough with the Vietnam War to be engaged in a running battle with a neighbor who regularly tore off his Eugene McCarthy bumper stickers. He has been troubled by nuclear weapons as far back as he can remember, but had always "assumed that everybody would be glad to un-invent the bomb if it were possible." Yet those issues, in his mind, were totally separate from the military work he did for a living. He remembers using the word "strange" to describe a graduate student at Carnegie who left computer science to become a full-time antiwar activist. Political activism was what one did on one's own time, even though "everybody knew the Department of Defense was the primary funder of computer science—seventy percent of the discipline, I think."

This dissonance was possible because, in nearly thirteen years of consulting for the Pentagon, Parnas never once visualized the uses of the weapons systems he worked on. This, too, was typical. Hardly anyone asked about them, and when anyone did, he duly and conscientiously responded. In 1972, a reporter inquired, "Do you want to participate in weapons development?" He answered no, interpreting the question in the most literal and limited way. "I had a purpose for doing my work. Building things that would kill people was not my purpose. I wasn't taking a stand against those things. I wasn't asking myself whether they were necessary. The direct answer was no, that was not what I wanted to devote my life to."

But the process of hearing and answering the question changed his understanding of the answer. He realized anew the fact that his work, like every basic researcher's, had applications in weaponry. He asked himself why. The answer was that the military was the primary funder of the research he wanted to do. "I had never asked myself the questions I think a lot about today, whether that's how science should be supported, whether we're taking a proper approach to making decisions about what science is done and what science is not done. That interview stands out in my mind as one of the few times anybody ever asked me to think about those things," he says.

His first encounters with those questions were muddled by the knowledge that his beloved research project in software design principles, funded by the navy, would be hard to find sponsorship for in private industry or academia. "For a while," he admits, "I didn't want to see. It was convenient to keep doing my research with the people I was doing it with, in the ways I was doing it." Juggling his research with teaching at the University of Victoria, he kept himself busy enough that his answer sufficed. But the existence of the arms race troubled him when he thought about it, and in nearby Vancouver an organization called Stop the Arms Race got him to think about it by mobilizing a demonstration of over one hundred thousand people.

His first response to the demonstration was irritation. "If all those people who are out in the streets talking to each other would go talk to their neighbors, who are unconvinced, we'd get somewhere," he fumed. Filling in for the minister of his Unitarian church one Sunday, Parnas made that argument in a talk entitled, "For Disarmament But Against the Peace Movement." Afterward, a woman in the audience rose. "Dr. Parnas, thank you for your constructive criticism. I work with Stop the Arms Race. And I'd like to invite you to come help us, advise us, work with us on strategy."

He hedged. "I really don't see anything useful for me to do. And I'm committed to finishing my research right now." But her challenge stuck with him.

That question of his responsibility as a scientist next intruded into his life at a computer conference in Germany in 1984. The topic was far from politics: marrying theory and practice to make better software. But its organizers were activists as well as academics. As one of the few German-speaking foreigners present, Parnas was invited to take part in a press conference where a reporter asked an unusual question: "Could you write a computer program ten million lines long, and make it error-free on the first try?"

"Of course not," replied Parnas without hesitation. "Why do you ask?"

"That's what your president is proposing to do with his Star Wars plan."

Parnas thought the reporter had to be oversimplifying the plan, but was concerned enough to join a discussion of conference participants about what, if anything, scientists could do to challenge weapons development they saw as irresponsible. The main debate at the meeting was, "Do we limit ourselves to technical analysis—'Will it work? Will it be reliable?'—or do we also address the political questions—'Is it a good thing?' " Nothing was settled, and nothing came of it. Parnas, while registering the issue as significant, figured there was more to the SDI story than these people knew and went back home to his naval research.

The social responsibility of the computer professional is not, for Parnas, an issue which can be addressed very usefully in the abstract. "Even now," he says, "I don't spend a lot of time asking, 'Will this piece of software be used to bomb Nicaragua or repress people in South Africa?' When you're working closer to end users, you can ask those questions; if some general in Latin America asked me to build him a database to keep track of his political enemies, I'd have no trouble saying no. But when you're analyzing error-handling procedures or writing compilers, you know your work is going to be used by the military—and by everybody else."

Against the backdrop of these low-level questions—and ironically, as he was in the middle of Joseph Wiezenbaum's *Computer Power and Human Reason,* a sobering assessment of the computer's inherent limits in solving human problems—his phone rang one day in the spring of 1985. As he remembers it, Dr. David Mizell, an employee at the Office of Naval Research working with technical officials in the SDI hierarchy, asked a memorable question: "Dave, how would you like to save the world from nuclear conflagration?"

Parnas's reactions covered every extreme, from grandiose and altruistic to self-serving and mundane. "It must be more complicated than they're saying in the press. Here's my chance to find out." "Lillian will kill me for being gone eighteen days in the summer." "The money will be nice." "People only call me in when they want me to tell them the truth. So I'll go tell them the truth, whatever it turns out to be."

Before accepting, he pointed out that, in his research for the navy, he was working on all sorts of things which could benefit from SDI funding. "Isn't that a conflict of interest?" he later asked panel convener Dr. Richard Lau of the Office of Naval Research, who he says replied, "If you didn't have that kind of conflict of interest, we wouldn't want you on the panel."[9]

He hunted down every piece of information he could find in the press about SDI. "It sounded sort of silly," he recalls, but he decided "it must be the way the media is handling it."

Hearing a roster of the other panelists deepened his discomfort. In his view, it included no well-known thinkers on software problems. The chair, Danny Cohen, had a respectable resume that included teaching at Harvard and the California Institute of Technology and several years of experience in real-time graphics and networking, but no ground-breaking work. Parnas was the closest thing to a specialist in military software. One panelist was a former student of his. "If I had been asked to put together a panel with the charge this one had, there were some people I had in mind, people in military industry who had actually worked on weapons software and on large systems. None of them were on the panel, and the people who were didn't sound right. Not being a shy guy, I asked, 'How did you pick those people?' The chairman said, 'They're all people I've worked with and I know I can trust them.' "

"Wait," said Parnas, "I don't fit that category."

"You were the only one everybody else would agree we had to have."

He reported for the first of the eighteen scheduled daylong meetings in Washington with a wait-and-see attitude. But within an hour, he had begun to see. "I was appalled by the lack of organization. You've got seven or eight people sitting around, each being paid a thousand dollars a day. You've got a big important problem. You should come prepared. You should have people to present the problem to them, bring them up to date on the state of the art, name the issues you're worried about. But instead we sat around the table, sort of bullshitting, until somebody said, 'Well, what are we going to do?' "

Parnas suggested what seemed to be an obvious answer to that question: "Let's get some briefing on the problem."

"I wonder how we can do that," mused the chairman. "The designs are all confidential. But we do have a guy who is looking at them all and making up a composite design. We could invite him in."

While waiting for that arrival, members of the panel took turns responding to the question, "What kinds of research do you think SDI ought to be supporting?" To Parnas, the presentations sounded more like summaries of the panelists' own research. "That bothered me," he says. "I had been on a lot of Canadian funding panels, and one of the clear ground rules is that you don't talk about anything related to your own projects." His concerns have been borne out by recent Senate hearings into the potential for conflict of interest in so-called blue-ribbon panels. But at that particular table, Parnas felt quite alone.

His version of what happened behind that closed door is as follows. "They came to me and said, 'What do you think we should work on?' I just said, 'I don't know what you should work on. I don't know enough about the problem yet.' And someone—not the chairman, one of the support staff, I think—said, 'Well, why don't you just tell us what kind of work you've been doing?' So I gave them a brief presentation on my A-7 work for the navy and explained the issues and why I thought this would be relevant to SDI but that I wasn't proposing anything for SDI.

"Then the chairman, one of the people I like the least in this whole game, got up and started talking about investigating something about man-machine interfaces, something extremely general. I said, 'Wait a minute. Why should SDI fund that? It seems so general.' And he gave me an answer that really bugged me. He said, 'Dave, you're probably right. There isn't anything special about SDI in this regard, but there's lots of money, and it's something I want to do. Don't worry. There will be plenty of money left over for your stuff, too.'

"That was the attitude. Nobody was ever asking, 'Is this something we should do? If we solve all these little research problems, does that mean we should build SDI?' They were just thinking about what they could spend this money on." Though he felt "betrayed by the crassness," Parnas was not at this point judging the project on political grounds or seeing trends behind the day-to-day incidents during his days in Washington. "They just didn't seem to have the right attitude," he sums up. "Here they are with a particular stated purpose, but not taking it seriously, and here I am trying to think about how we could ever do something like SDI."

Cohen's version is quite different, and the two have debated extensively and rancorously. In a policy paper on professional responsibility, Cohen writes, "In his description of the first meeting, 'Everyone seemed to have a pet project of their own that they thought should be funded.' This is true only about Prof. Parnas himself! In this first meeting, he already knew the 'solution,' the right direction for SDIO to pursue. When he presented that pet of his to the rest of the panel, his general-purpose approach was immediately criticized as being equally applicable to an intensive-care unit in a hospital, for example, and not addressing the special properties and problems of the SDI system . . . " But Cohen does not specify Parnas's pet project or discuss its merits in the paper.[10]

Parnas says he asked Richard Lau over lunch, "If we decide this thing can't be done, what then? Do we have to give the money back?"

"It's our job to spend the money," he quotes Lau.[11]

There was in the first round of meetings one presentation to the panel about the technical aspects of SDI. But here too Parnas was unimpressed. "The guy who came to make the presentation was a strange little old man who had done simulation models. He started presenting his little models, 'We'll shoot up these weapons,' all very vague. He had brought a pile of computer listings with him, so I sat there leafing through the listings and then asking him questions and pointing out factors that he wasn't taking into account in his models. Instead of being embarrassed or saying, 'Yeah, I should do that,' he gave me this smile and said, 'Yeah, that's what's great about this problem. There's always something else you can do.' "

After a few days, the panelists gathered their accumulated documentation and packed their bags, taking with them a homework assignment. They were asked to write up their ideas about the fundamental question: What research programs would move the Strategic Defense Initiative forward? For the next three weeks, Parnas put the rest of his work on hold and devoted himself day and night to that task. Armed with the SDI panel's 1985 report to Congress and an unclassified computer study, he willed himself yet again to imagine the goal: a ballistic missile defense network reliable and precise enough not to let in a single nuclear weapon, neither this year nor twenty years in the future, not prey to technical failure, able to function as an all-seeing eye in space yet invulnerable to antisatellite weaponry—a byzantine network of antimissile rays, surveillance satellites, ground stations, and linking them all together, a computer system whose software was expected to run tens of millions of lines in length.

The project seemed to go off the scale of rational human endeavor, not only in its cost and complexity but in its reliance on a technological system to solve essentially political problems. The thought of creating such a system that would be even minimally trustworthy—and when one error can mean the annihilation of cities, the margin for acceptability is very narrow—seemed a fantasy. Parnas's doubts were especially hard to ignore because he had been sensitized—at the Berlin conference, in the criticism of his "Against the Peace Movement" speech—to his responsibility as a scientist to take a critical perspective.

At the same time, his naval research was periodically stalling in ways which raised anew his lifelong questions about "what it is—no pun intended—that makes software hard." It is the same "something" which has led him to irritate many colleagues by proclaiming artificial intelligence to be a pipe dream. Even before the trip to Washington, he was on the brink of reaffirming that those limitations of digital, logical "thinking" reflected intrinsic limits to a computer's reliable processing of information and handling of routines more complex than sending out monthly bills. Though other software thinkers, including Brooks, disagree, Parnas spoke for many when he concluded, "The problems were fundamental. They weren't going to be overcome."

Parnas struggled. He tried a number of approaches which had been discussed in the earlier meetings. "What about software engineering techniques like the ones I'd been developing? What about artificial intelligence? What about program proving—programs are mathematical objects, so can you prove them correct?" The more he willed himself to write research proposals that contributed to the stated goal of SDI, the more logical contradictions and technical improbabilities he hit upon. Each time he looked at the language embodied in SDI's statement of mission, the thought forced its way forward in his mind: We can't do that. "For each of those categories, I was able to convince myself that it just wouldn't do any good. It was not too long before I realized that I didn't believe it could be done by any method. We could never trust such a system. And you can't end the fear of nuclear weapons with something you can't trust.

"Shortly before the end of the three-week period—as the date of the next meeting approached—I realized something else. I wasn't going to that meeting. I started writing up the papers I'd been working on, turning each one from 'here's what we should do' to 'here's why we shouldn't do it.'" He raced to finish in time for the meeting, feeling it was essential not to quit without an explanation. Before mailing the papers and his letter of resignation, he tested them via electronic mail with a few colleagues. The standard comment—"You're probably right about SDI, but that's no reason why people shouldn't take the money"—clinched his decision.

Parnas's position papers, subsequently published in *American Scientist,* were widely circulated among researchers on both sides of the debate.[12] One faculty member at Cornell University said she got copies from six different people in the mail the same day. They are lean, logical, and compelling in their argument that the software requirements for an SDI system make it many times more complex than the systems that human beings now routinely screw up, and they point out aspects of such a system that may be intrinsically insoluble. For instance:

—The system will be required to identify, track, and direct weapons toward targets whose ballistic characteristics cannot be known with certainty before the moment of battle. It must distinguish these targets from decoys whose characteristics are also unknown.

—The computing will be done by a network of computers connected to sensors, weapons, and each other, by channels whose behavior, at the time the system is invoked, cannot be predicted because of possible countermeasures by an attacker. The actual subset of system components that will be available at the time that the system is put into service, and throughout the period of service, cannot be predicted for the same reason.

—It will be impossible to test the system under realistic conditions prior to its actual use.

—The service period of the system will be so short that there will be little possibility of human intervention and no possibility of debugging and modification of the program during that period.

—Like many other military programs, there are absolute real-time deadlines for the computation. The computation will consist primarily of periodic processes, but the number of these processes that will be required, and the computational requirements of each process, cannot be predicted in advance because they depend on target characteristics . . . We cannot even predict the "worst case" with any confidence.

—The overall battle management system will have to integrate a software system significantly larger than has ever been attempted before.

In short, though advocates may compare the SDI mobilization to a moon launch in technical difficulty and patriotic significance, SDI is different because the effort to go to the moon was not complicated by the presence of an enemy trying, with both force and cunning, to beat the astronauts back.

When Parnas mailed off the papers, he thought that act would close a troubling chapter in his life. But he was still agitated. He sent a copy to his congressional representative in the US, where he still voted, and to the member of Parliament who served his district in Ontario. As it happened, a commission of the Canadian Parliament was conducting a fact-finding and opinion-gathering tour to decide whether or not Canada should join the United States in SDI. Patrick Crofton, the MP from Parnas's district and a staunch member of the Conservative Party, contacted Parnas for input, which was so effective that Crofton became the only Conservative to break party lines—a major breach in Canadian politics—to vote against participation.

The story was leaked twice—once to Canadian papers, and then to the *New York Times,* which "discovered" Parnas with enthusiasm. So began a period of constant invitations—to speak, to be interviewed, to testify—which had barely subsided when I met him in early 1988. "Everybody's supposed to get fifteen minutes of fame, but isn't mine up yet?" he had begun to wonder. But Parnas could not escape the fact that he had something to say.

Parnas's real radicalization, and his greatest anger, came not with his resignation but as he continued to speak out. Many public statements of SDI supporters impressed Parnas as grossly distorted in ways that were hard to see as innocent. His favorite example is the claim by an SDIO administrator to an audience questioner that a computer program can contain ten thousand errors and still work acceptably—a statement which is perfectly true as long as the errors are placed just right, known in advance, or trivial.

Only a small percentage of his challengers tried to support SDI as an effective defense. Most pointed to secondary benefits, from introducing uncertainty into an opponent's nuclear war-fighting scenario, to creating a bargaining chip, to finding technological spinoffs. But Parnas saw SDI as an obstacle to arms agreements, not a useful bargaining chip, and a source of greater uncertainty for the United States than for any attacker. As to the spinoff argument, he concluded, "You cannot spend billions of dollars without having some spinoff, but they are rarely worth the price. The Apollo program may have led to improved heart monitoring and better ways to make jello, but fifty-two billion dollars would have bought a lot more research on medical technology and food preparation."

Parnas came to believe that he was in a majority in his scepticism. He noticed the words of one debate opponent, an SDIO panel member, who dismissed the project's stated goal as "ridiculous." He remembered a conversation with a senior official at Los Alamos, who defended the lab's participation by saying he "liked challenges." He even wondered anew about his initial briefing before the panel, which portrayed not a future made bright by a curtailed arms race, but an ongoing competition in the new area of space-based defense.

These revelations, Parnas says, were the most emotional aspect of the whole thing. "I don't get angry unless I feel threatened. Nuclear weapons still seem like a more abstract threat. But one thing I feel deeply threatened by is lies, because you can't defend yourself against lies."

Each side has accused the other of defining the problem to suit vested interests. Panel chair Cohen sees two kinds of people in the world. "There are those who find [SDI] desirable, and therefore worth the effort of finding out how to pursue it, and there are those who find it undesirable and therefore 'know' that it is impossible, and that no research has the potential to further our knowledge on the subject."

Parnas portrays himself as part of a third category, one who initially found the idea desirable, then ran up against its low probability of success and from that point backed up to question the source of the other panelists' fevered commitment to it. But he is still meticulous about separating technical criticisms from political ones. "I think, when I was first writing up my views, I missed a lot of things,' Parnas says looking back. "The way I see it now, not only can we not do SDI, but trying to do it will make everything a lot worse. I didn't see that then. In the first papers I wrote, I only said we would never trust it. That was my technical conclusion. If you put up something like that without trusting it, that's destabilizing, and it makes the arms race worse."

As he continued to defend his views and watched them develop, Parnas accepted speaking invitations at MIT, Stanford, and other engineering campuses. He was even a panelist at a forum at Los Alamos Lab, after which he called his wife and exploded, "I have just spent the day inside an insane asylum. These people still have brochures that celebrate the dawn of the atomic age." He contributed articles on problems with ballistic missile defense to major scientific journals. He wondered, for a time, whether he would lose consulting business because of his notoriety. But the opposite proved true, and the substantial fees he sometimes received for speaking helped to compensate for the very real turmoil his life was undergoing.

One element in that turmoil was simple physical stress. But a deeper stress for Parnas came from the changes in his worldview which, rather than ending, really only began when he left the SDI panel. As he sees it, "I'm the same algorithm"—or logical structure for making decisions—"but I'm operating on different data." Not only are the data and the beliefs they inform different from those of a few years back, they are interrelated in complex ways, still changing, and not all consistent.

Not only on the subject of arms control but on human motivation, Parnas sees things very differently since leaving the panel. "I had always fooled myself, thinking that all the people working in the military were doing it because they believed they had to defend their country. Sure, they had to make a living too—we all do—but at least they wouldn't do anything that would harm their country, or that was a waste for their country. In fact, I used to get angry at peace groups for calling themselves that. I thought they should call themselves disarmament groups, because I believed that a properly run armed service can be a peace group too. But what I began to see from all this is that people don't think about that kind of thing at all. It's all to get the next contract, get the next promotion, get some money for the graduate students. Nobody asks, 'Is this really making the country stronger?' " Not once, he notes, did a recipient of his criticism ever contact him to try to understand or to dialogue. "Sometimes," he reflects, "I think the Nuremberg trials apply."

Never before had he doubted, as he does now, that everyone in the military and weapons industries would be happy to un-invent the bomb. In his view, most participants in SDI research think they are involved in basic research or, at worst, in a money-grab for the expansion of human knowledge. Nevertheless, the military potential of Star Wars as a first-strike system has not eluded him. "It might be just a means of getting out of the treaties against testing weapons in space. But then you listen to Edward Teller talking about his nuclear-excited laser, and it sounds for all the world like an offensive weapon."

The deeper Parnas's discomfort with things as they are, the greater is his tendency to shift into a problem-solving mode and the more serious is his interest in alternatives to the policies he is challenging. Every time he spoke in public, someone in the audience would ask,

"Okay, if SDI isn't a good idea, what is?" At first, he had no answer. Wanting one for his own peace of mind as well as to appease his questioners, Parnas at first reminded himself that he was doing a service by blowing the whistle on the problem even if he hadn't found a definitive solution. For a while, he tried to hold off questions with an analogy: "Suppose you discover this tribe of teen-agers in Florida who believe that orange juice is a contraceptive. It keeps failing, so they try new things like adding a little pulp or eating the seeds. So you go tell them, 'No. No way. Citrus won't do it.' Even if you haven't come up with a pill, you've done them a favor."

But that answer was only a palliative. He began reading, and the best answers he found were time-tested ones. In the extensive correspondence between Einstein and Freud, for example, he was moved by passages like this one from Freud:

> Under primitive conditions, it is superior force—brute violence, or violence backed by arms—that lords it everywhere. We know that in the course of evolution, this state of things was modified, a path was traced that led from violence to law. But what was this path? Surely it issued from a single verity: that the superiority of one strong man can be overborne by an alliance of many weaklings, that *l'union fait la force*. Brute force is overcome by union, the allied might of scattered units makes good its right against the isolated giant. Thus we may define "right," (i.e. law) as the might of a community.[13]

The first parallel that struck Parnas while reading this passage was the emerging status of the United States as the kind of intransigent, isolated giant "that lords it everywhere." Disturbing little news items began to take on greater significance. The government of Canada appointed an official ambassador for disarmament, while the government of the United States sacrificed a major arms control agreement at Reykjavik by insisting on continuing SDI as a "bargaining chip." The United Nations held a major conference on disarmament and development which examined the human cost of weapons stockpiling. The United States boycotted it. Amid rapidly shifting questions and rarely satisfactory answers, Parnas began to feel more sure of one thing: Change, when it comes, will probably not be ushered in by the leadership of either superpower, but will emerge from the allied might of the world's majorities whose lives are now shaped by cold war policies.

Fighting fatigue and the nagging suspicion that "my department chairman isn't too happy with all this," Parnas has reluctantly concluded that he will never stop being an activist. He is at times consumed by and at times disgusted with the range of possibilities for changing the world and the ineptitude with which those possibilities are often implemented. "Another invitation to speak at a rally!" he fumes. "Why do these demonstrators insist on talking to each other instead of getting out and talking to the people who aren't convinced yet? Maybe I should go tell them not to demonstrate."

More difficult, he admits, are the questions of what strategies *do* make sense for citizen activists and how the tide will be turned. The only thing of which he is sure is that it's a hard problem: harder than just convincing the US Congress, most of whom pass the buck to the voters who, they claim, will kick them out if they appear skeptical of SDI; harder than convincing the voters, because so many entrenched institutional forces profit from things as they are. He thinks that demystifying science and challenging the cult of the technological wizard would go a long way toward making those forces less entrenched. "Look at the way science is reported," he points out. "All you hear about is the progress, never the failures." He fantasizes about creating an organization, whimsically called PEST, Public Education in Science and Technology.

Watching his activity and seeing both its results and the enormity of the problem, Lillian has been equally unable to remain aloof. She thinks about ways to contribute as a professional through long-term, serious peace education. But contribute what? Methods of teaching conflict resolution? Computer-based tools for teaching global issues? Curriculum development? Consulting? More graduate school? They will figure it out one step at a time. For now, in the moments she captures to enjoy tapes of Chinese music or make cardboard animals with Henrietta, Lillian finds peace in the notion that "even if Dave is out giving speeches and running himself ragged and I'm at home with my career on hold, we're both doing what we're doing for the children."

10 THE FIRST RESISTER
DANIEL COBOS

The RC-135 is a state-of-the-art military aircraft, equipped with three kinds of radar, electronic surveillance equipment, and a fuel system that lets it stay in the air up to ten hours at a stretch. Gray and white, with blackened nose and prominent external antennae, the craft looks a little like a surreal giant insect. A specially outfitted Boeing 707, known as a "Rivet Joint" plane, the RC-135 is a major element in US airborne reconnaissance. Seymour Hersh reports,

> In 1985, the Strategic Air Command's eighteen RC-135s completed a six-year upgrading program that significantly expanded the aircraft's collection and processing capability; Rivet Joint flights are now able to collect short-range tactical signal intelligence on Soviet naval and ground forces. It was this added ability that, presumably, convinced the military to begin flying Rivet Joint missions over Central America in support of government troops in El Salvador and the CIA-sponsored rebel Contras waging war against the Nicaraguan government. By mid-1984, according to an NSA official, there were twelve Rivet Joint flights a month, originating from Howard Air Base in Panama.[1]

As an air force sergeant, Daniel Cobos flew those missions up to three times a week from the headquarters of RC-135 operations, at Offutt Air Force Base in Nebraska. Cobos worked as a Spanish translator on these flights from 1984 to 1987, a period encompassing the two years when Congress, via the Boland amendment, had explicitly prohibited such military aid to the contras.[2] According to a July 1987 press release, Cobos's "duties included monitoring electronic messages from Nicaragua and, after translation, sending them to the Pentagon, CIA, and NSA, any of which may have passed this intelligence to the Contras." He says that those "signals" were sometimes family conversations, sometimes troop movements. Cobos, 31, was the first active-duty military recruit to receive national attention as a resister to US activity in Central America. And when he received an honorable discharge in the fall of 1987, the likelihood increased that he would not be the last.

Dan Cobos is an unassuming guy with slightly punk haircut whose only observable affectation is a habit of wearing one yellow and one turquoise sneaker. He was voted "Most Friendly" in his high school class and nominated for "Airman of the Year" at Offutt in 1985. Even at the height of his battle, he was adamant about not wanting to alienate his colleagues in the military or to ram his values down anyone's throat. When he speaks about his conscientious objection, it is in the style of one not yet used to being interviewed, not entirely comfortable, yet painfully honest, even in admitting his confusion about how much to reveal. He has steadfastly refused to disclose classified information to the press, although he says he will testify before Congress if invited. But even without those details, the broad outlines of his awakening— his discoveries of the human impact of the program he took part in—are as troubling to a listener as they are to him.

"A lot of my attitudes are tied to the fact that I'm a Mexican-American," he speculates. My family always put a lot of emphasis on being proud of who we were, but what we were, above all else, was Americans. It's always been very important for me to assimilate, to please people. I'd much rather walk away from a fight than get into one—this one included."

But even after his victory, controversy continued to surround Cobos, both because his stance had such strong emotional reverberations around the base and because he appears to be sitting on key evidence of an air force reconnaissance program which ran counter to the Boland amendment. A few weeks after he handed in his application for conscientious objector status, he was informed that the air force was conducting an investigation to see whether he had violated his security clearance agreement, a charge which could have led to court-martial. At the same time, his brother, Sergeant Jesus Cobos, was questioned about his own politics and loyalty by superiors at Lackland Air Force Base in Texas. So Cobos, who had intended to go through the CO process as quietly as possible, began to see wisdom in the advice of his attorney, who insisted, "Publicity is your first line of defense." Flanked by two lawyers, he took part in a press conference in Omaha largely to make clear that his brother had nothing to do with, and didn't even endorse, his action. But, as difficult as it was, he also felt it was time to tell his story.

Military life and values were an integral part of Cobos's childhood and youth. His father, a medical corpsman in the army for twenty-eight years, raised his children to obey orders and appreciate the generosity of the military, which had provided the family with a degree of comfort—the first color TV set in the neighborhood, yearly vacations— unknown to most Mexican-Americans in Laredo, Texas. But more than "a way out" of poverty, the military has been so ingrained in his identity that, when asked how his beliefs on national security evolved, he pauses and says, "Hmm. Until about a year ago, I wouldn't even have taken on that question. I would have said, 'You couldn't possibly understand because you're a civilian.' "

Cobos's cold war ideology and political awareness, such as they were, formed early. During a short period when his father was stationed in Alaska in 1962, he remembers "very realistic" bomb drills in which the Soviet Union, just across the Bering Strait, loomed large. His next memory, in third grade in Texas, is of a teacher in Catholic school who pulled down the wall map and explained the domino theory: "Here's Vietnam, and here's where we have to fight the communists, because otherwise they'll come down and cross the ocean and come up through South America, like this, through Central America and Mexico . . . "

Growing up, Cobos never dared question the basic battle lines between "us" and "them." But the Vietnam War, in which his father served, was still "all confusing" to him. Though he always acknowledged the right of those who opposed the war to stay out of it, Cobos was convinced of the war's necessity from the beginning. "I viewed the Vietcong as the enemy. I certainly viewed the demonstrators at Kent State as a bunch of hooligans and troublemakers who got what they deserved. I thought Bob Hope was an absolute saint for going over there; that may sound trivial, but it's important. The man was the most highly decorated civilian I knew of." Yet for all his certainty, he remembers some strongly discordant elements in that worldview. The well-known photograph of a napalmed Vietnamese girl running down a road screaming is burned into his brain. And though he considered the Vietcong to be the enemy, he was confused because "I could never figure out how to distinguish between them and the Vietnamese people. I had real trouble with that."

His high school years were spent in the Philippines, where his father was stationed at Clark Air Force Base. "We were there when martial law was declared by Marcos in 1972," Cobos recalls. "I woke up one Saturday morning and couldn't pull in any of the radio stations or TV. Then we started hearing announcements that Marcos would speak to the nation that afternoon, and that anyone with weapons should turn them in immediately. I remember thinking it was the best thing that could happen to the Philippines because it had seemed like a really lawless place, and I always took it for granted that the law would be on my side."

As he came of age, Cobos learned on a personal level that "when you're overseas, it's a license to do anything you want. Here I was sixteen years old, and I could go off base to bars and drink all night. Everybody had a maid and a yard boy and a tailor, and I remember being told not to overpay these people because it would mess up the economy. Until about a year ago I believed that. But while I was there, I just closed out things like the extreme poverty." He had the best of several worlds, attending an international school with "some of the most liberal teachers I've ever had," relying on the good offices of the military to keep him out of serious trouble, and passing as a Filipino in the streets but identifying as an American when it was helpful.

At high school graduation, "Most Likely to Succeed" was the honor his parents wanted him to receive, but "Most Friendly" was what he got and treasured. He went to junior college in Laredo for two years, ran out of money and spent a few months at odd jobs, then graduated from the University of Texas with a bachelor's in psychology.

During those years he first tasted political activism and met the first serious challenges to his own assimilated identity through friends who were Chicano activists. What they were trying to do was modest enough: provide support services for the then miniscule number of Chicano students at the University of Texas so they would not simply pack it in from a sense of isolation, press for affirmative action recruitment policies, and start some Chicano history and literature courses. Their cultural pride triggered his memory of his mother's voice, filled with sorrow, saying, "The values and traditions of our people will be lost with your generation." He found campus activism exciting but scary, because it meant relating to people on a basis other than his carefully cultivated friendliness and confronting his own lifelong assimilation. It was a season of many changes, from which he finally pulled back when some members of the group started talking about a trip to Cuba.

"At the time, I just wasn't about to be involved with people who would go to Cuba. Their meetings seemed very covert. I saw Cuba as the evil of this hemisphere, a puppet of the Soviet Union. I was also thinking at that time that I could have some sort of political career, and a trip to Cuba might be a skeleton in my closet later. They were nice people, but I saw them as radicals, which to me meant being anti-American, not being part of the mainstream, rejecting traditional values and morals. They weren't, of course. They were respectable people. They went to school and had good grades and part-time jobs and were nice people, but they liked Cuba and I drew the line there."

In college, he recalls having a worldview that was "pretty jingoistic" and taking the 1980 Iranian hostage crisis in particular "real personally." At an Oktoberfest in Texas that fall, when a crowd hopped up on beer began chanting, "Bomb Iran, Bomb Iran," he joined in with gusto.

Because of his family's background, Cobos had always regarded the military as a possible career path. When he finished his bachelor's in psychology, he felt overqualified for half the available jobs and underqualified for the rest. He had a vague idea about using his psychology degree to help people, but he was short on both specialized skills and overall goals. For a time, Cobos lived in a group household of dedicated party-goers and worked by day as a cashier at Lackland Air Force Base. In the air force community were the people he could most identify with. There were also, he realized, no shortage of troubled families, dissatisfied workers, problem drinkers, people adrift from too many moves—people whom he could help.

Cobos went to see the local recruiter, who told him that counseling jobs in the air force were hard to come by. And he found himself listening in rapture to a pitch for an alternative, a career in cryptologic linguistics. The friendly female recruiter reinforced his view of base life as, apart from a degree of regimentation, a big campus scene. Cobos was initially selected to train in Middle Eastern languages, which fit perfectly with his view of renegade nations like Iran as the major threat to US security in the 1980s. But one day he and some friends took a Spanish proficiency test to get out of an afternoon's work, and language school in Monterrey immediately gave way to his assignment at Offutt, following technical training. "I still don't know what the air force means by 'cryptologic linguistics.' I was a translator, that's all," he chuckles.

The first assault on his expectations of comfortable living came after induction and basic training, during survival school in rural Washington state. In the course of a week of winter camping, teams of recruits were required to "adopt" and feed a pet rabbit, and then to kill it for food. Cobos was appointed the rabbit tender for his team. "We were specifically instructed, when the time came, to kill the rabbit in the most humane way possible. But then our instructor took it away from me. 'You didn't see this,' he said to the other instructor. Then he put a noose around the rabbit's neck and tried, literally, to pull its head off. He was yanking and yanking and finally did it. And that was our dinner." All the recruits were horrified, but no one confronted the instructor.

The rabbit incident was archetypal in an air force career that unfolded on two disturbingly separate levels. Work and social life seemed easygoing, fraternal. Working conscientiously was the norm, although militaristic zeal was relatively rare. But woven into an otherwise comfortable daily pattern were images of extraordinary and often gratuitous violence. One was the Catholic chapel at Offutt, where fiercely militant images on the stained glass windows seemed out of place with the motto, "Peace Is Our Profession." In his CO application, Cobos describes the visual impact of that stained glass, "different organizational emblems from the squadrons of Offutt, lightning bolts from the sky, missiles pointing in every direction. A huge window depicted a uniformed man standing under flying fighter jets and an exploding bomb, with his forlorn family behind him. I felt alienated, and I didn't feel the comfort I'd come to associate with being in the Church of my upbringing. I felt like my Church was involving itself in something profane."

Cobos might have held to his pattern of keeping that discomfort to himself, but for a friendship that forced him to find a voice. Ralph Reed, Cobos's next door neighbor and close friend, was a computer operator for space operations for a two-year tour, ending in December 1987. Reed joined the air force as a job, not an adventure. Handsome, gregarious and very young, he cultivated and doubtless earned a "bad boy" image at the base. Reed brags that he is a star graduate of the military's drug rehabilitation program and acquired a reputation for driving to work in a beat-up red Toyota bearing a "Hands Off Central America" bumper sticker. He is a prize-winning distance runner who consumes prodigious quantities of black coffee and lives in an apartment cluttered with reading material. In his living room is a mound of several hundred science fiction novels. On the kitchen table is a two-inch layer of publications: *The Christian Science Monitor, The Economist, The Nation, Monthly Review.* Reed has always been critical of interventionist foreign policy. When Grenada was invaded, he says, "I was so upset I could hardly go to work, couldn't talk to anybody."

Cobos, who was an off-base roommate of Reed's around that time, describes him as "Henry Higgins to my Eliza Doolittle." The two ran long-distance together in the Omaha heat and sat around their unglamorous apartment talking into the night. "When we first met," Reed recalls, "Daniel's worldview might be described as center-rightist. He was more liberal on domestic issues, poverty and civil rights and so forth, than on international ones. He also struck me as someone who had been through a few things, whereas most of the other people in the air force seemed like 'normal kids.' But we would argue endlessly about politics. I remember a long, angry discussion in which Daniel insisted that Castro was as bad as Marcos if not worse, and I argued the opposite."

It was Reed who pushed him to justify his arguments—about Cuba, about the role of the United States abroad, about how much of the cold war might be avoidable—and, increasingly, to justify his work. Reed also introduced him to an off-base social circle which became instrumental in his change of heart. Omaha, perhaps because of its proximity to such a prominent air base, has a small but thriving alternative community centered around peace activism. Cobos's initial feelings about "those people" recalled his reaction to his college friends who had gone to Cuba. They seemed nice. They seemed to be leading full and interesting lives. But they clashed so sharply with every expectation he had been brought up with that, for most of his time at Offutt, he tried to keep his distance.

Cobos tried, but every path for growth open to him seemed to lead him closer to the dreaded counterculture. After a year or so at the base, stomach trouble sent him to the base doctor who said, "You're eating too much red meat, too much junk. You need a simpler diet." He joined a food co-op to find alternatives to scruffy and overpriced supermarket produce. He began reading about vegetarianism, first from a health perspective, and later with an appreciation for the ecological and spiritual arguments behind it. "Living in Omaha and smelling the stockyards every day, once I started to think about it, that wasn't a very good advertisement for eating meat," he says. Deciding what to eat was a highly personal way to draw a line: by becoming a vegetarian, Cobos accepted and reinforced in himself a distaste for killing anything and a commitment to live his life more intentionally. Eating meat became a metaphor for other ways of doing things—from the agribusiness he saw driving out small farms all around him to the war system—which made a certain kind of sense in the abstract but in context were disastrous. The food co-op, which he initially saw as a way to get good vegetables, also served as an alternative distribution system for goods and, inevitably, ideas. Typically Cobos and Reed would help cut the cheese and measure out the lentils each week; Reed would get into a two-hour discussion with somebody about something, and Cobos, waiting for him, would be slowly drawn in.

Tying together many of these issues, and igniting the first spark of interest too strong to deny, was the struggle of the Hopi to resist displacement at Big Mountain, Arizona, their last sacred land, now claimed by mining interests. A Native American woman in the co-op told him about the prophecies that if this sacred land is lost, the earth's final hope will be too. His cultural sensitivity and Catholic conscience were both awakened, and for the first time, Cobos took initiative on an issue all by himself. He set up a showing of *Broken Rainbow*, the award-winning documentary about the conflict. Enlisting Reed as lieutenant, he called film distributors, priced theatres, designed posters, wrote ads, lined up volunteers, and pulled off a benefit which is still a source of pride to him. But when it was over, he thanked everyone who had helped while sidestepping invitations to socialize, and was so wary of being labeled "counterculture" that he threw away their phone numbers.

At the same time, discomfort with the SAC chapel led him to try different kinds of worship in the community. One that attracted him was the Unitarian church where the food co-op happened to meet. He showed up on Sundays a few times, and there he was forced to think about Central America through his first contact with refugees. Urged by Reed and bolstered also by his knowledge of suffering refugees back in Texas, he attended a benefit for a Guatemalan family at the church. He met quite a few Central Americans in 1985 and 1986, including one who was to become a close friend and contribute to his moment of decision, a Salvadoran named Antonio.

Antonio had left his wife and large family behind when he fled El Salvador. Just out of prison, with torture scars on his chest and the sight in one eye severely compromised, Antonio heard that the death squads were looking for him again. Meeting him, Cobos reflects, "I have a hard time believing what any government says, whether it's the Sandinistas or the United States or the government of El Salvador, because governments are bureaucracies and even if they're well-meaning, what they say is a compromise among all the different things the people in them want to say. But when I talk directly to a human being about personal experience, I can pretty much tell when I'm getting the truth. When someone takes off his shirt and shows you his scars, when someone flees and leaves his family behind, you know he's not kidding around."

When he first shook the hands of Central Americans, he could not help but see how much they were like him: in physical features, in cultural warmth, in regarding the comfortable North American middle class with a mix of admiration and servility. He remembers sitting around with a group of young Central American men, chatting about their common military experience, answering their careful questions about pay and training and discipline, and sighing inwardly with relief that they did not ask him more about his job. Then one night, at a presentation by his friend Antonio, Cobos felt an unprecedented aloneness: in just a few days he would leave for Howard Air Force Base in Panama for training. Gazing at the map on the wall at the event forced him for the first time to understand that he was going to be living in the region which until now had been known to him only through Antonio and from the air.

In his CO application, Cobos details the feelings that forced their way to the surface during that "surrealistic nightmare" in Panama.

> Central America was no longer just a place on a map or in the tales of Antonio, and reality seemed twisted and vicious. Whenever I

walked on the flight line, with the jungle surrounding me and camouflaged helicopters flying up above, visions of Vietnam entered my head. On one occasion one of my coworkers looked at me and remarked that now he really felt like he was in the military. It was hard for me to look the Panamanians in the eye, because I began to see myself as a mercenary. The poverty of the people was staggering, and hearing the other Airmen make light of their condition ("How stupid these people are, to be happy to win toilet paper and shampoo on this game show") embarrassed and disgusted me.

Until then, he had managed to filter out any racial innuendos that he might have heard. Now he became hypersensitized, and around him he heard evidence that his colleagues in the military did not hold all human life in equally high esteem. He remembered that after a peace demonstration at Offutt, one friend had mumbled, "We should nuke 'em all." Another sergeant had responded to a report on Central American casualties by laughing at "those Third World idiots." And in Panama, when he made an effort to engage a fellow student in discussion about what they were both up to, he was told, "I don't give a damn. They can all die."

Sometimes he saw the poor of Central America as "them," sometimes as people more similar to him than he was to his air force fellows. On a visit to some Indian villages near the Colombian border, an old man asked, "Where are you from? You look like you belong right here." By that time, Cobos was beginning to wonder. In Panama, for the first time his image of himself as one of the privileged began to wane. He "came back feeling like a hired hand, and feeling that my government was waging war against people I have more in common with than I do with the people running this country." Before the trip and even after he returned, he describes a "pattern of denial" which was possible only as long as he stayed in his adopted Anglo culture and away from Central Americans.

On his return Cobos managed to slip back into Anglo culture, but only briefly. When he spotted Antonio across the room at a party, he knew he was in trouble. "How are you doin', my friend? Where have you been lately?" Antonio quizzed him warmly.

"Panama," he admitted. "Uh, for my job."

Antonio stared at him, stared through him, with something beyond anger: sorrow, a penetrating disappointment. "So you're the one who has been bombing my country."

After that encounter, Cobos began to have such violent and confusing nightmares that he was afraid to go to sleep. He dreamed he was standing on the bank of a surging river of blood. All around him were buckets of blood, and he was pouring them into the river. He woke up another night from flashes, like black-and-white photos, of bombed cities and children's bodies scattered around them everywhere.

To his waking mind, the realities in Omaha and Panama differed like matter and antimatter. When he was wandering the streets of Panama City, speaking Spanish and letting his Chicano identity surface, Cobos could see the United States and even the more visibly racist of his air force buddies as the other, the oppressor, and he could feel moral clarity in his call home to Reed after a week: "I'm getting out. I can't do this any more." Back in Omaha, he saw the situation from the opposite perspective, as a member of the US military who had, by choice, assimilated himself morally as well as culturally. The dissonance between what he was concluding about the air force's overall mission in Central America and what he still experienced in the day-to-day friendliness of his colleagues was too sharp to deal with. The people who shot the breeze and flew missions with him, the people who had nominated him "Airman of the Year," the people whose approbation he had always sought, those people continued to participate in the same missions and activities in support of them. Were they bad people?

Cobos took himself to see the base chaplain, assuming that "you had to be a real Bible beater" to qualify as a conscientious objector, but needing to know if there was any other way out. The chaplain's counsel was balanced. The Catholic church, he began, did not support Cobos's extreme stance; the Catholic church had defended the "just war" concept for centuries. But the chaplain also admitted that Cobos's beliefs sounded sincere and principled enough that they might qualify, and sent him to the library to research the regulations for himself.

At first his research reinforced his skepticism. The language of the regulations refers strongly to the kind of orthodox religious conviction embodied in traditional "peace churches." Cobos, though still nominally a Catholic, had been getting spiritual nourishment everywhere from Unitarian fellowships to Native American spiritual circles. But in the course of his research Cobos heard about and contacted the Central Committee for Conscientious Objection in Philadelphia, a research and advocacy group with roots in Quaker discipline and secular antiwar activism. Through their counsel, he learned that the Supreme Court had indeed ruled that religious orthodoxy alone could not be applied as a test of the validity of a conviction against war. To be a conscientious objector, one must be opposed to war in any form, be sincere, and show evidence that one's beliefs were strong enough to be a foundation for moral choices.[3]

Cobos started writing the application essay as 1986 gave way to 1987, never sure whether he would submit it. Central America was the catalyst, but what he ended up writing was much broader. "I cannot kill. I cannot take a life." He cited experiences from his Catholic upbringing and survival school to seeing the warlike images in the SAC chapel and his encounters with Antonio. He pointed equally to experiences in the air force, such as his time in Panama, and to outside influences, including the holistic worldviews of people he was meeting and books he was reading through the food co-op. He started out objecting to a particular military intervention, but once forced to examine the rest of his beliefs and to imagine concretely participating in war, he began to express a set of beliefs that were clearly at odds with his actions.

Much of the debate around the legal definition of conscientious objection centers on the meaning of "war in any form." An air force lawyer asked him at one point, "What if some dark, evil force was to invade your country and kill your neighbors and your family. Would you take up arms?" Cobos reflexively answered, "That's a ridiculous question. It sounds like it's out of a bad science fiction book. I can't in conscience participate in any war that I can imagine being sent into by this air force, that's all."

He felt too fragile most of the time to read anything about Central America, but he bought a paperback copy of Dr. Charles Clements' *Witness to War* and found it comforting to hold the book in his hands. Clements, he knew, had been a conscientious objector, and had spent six months in an air force psychiatric hospital for refusing to fly more combat missions in Vietnam. "If he could survive that, I can survive this," Cobos reminded himself.

Clements, an outspoken voice against the US role in Central America for the same reasons he came to oppose Vietnam, says he in turn has been inspired by Cobos. "Daniel's case is different from mine because so many pilots were rebelling when I did. He's the first, this time around, and that's much harder. The experience is incredibly isolating, and you quickly notice that the military has power over every aspect of your life. Your colleagues are generally fearful of being too friendly to you once you've been identified as perhaps disloyal. Altogether, those experiences lead to a sense of isolation that's very difficult. You have no frame of reference while you're going through the process."[4]

Ironically, one day as he was almost finished with the application, an administrator stopped him and insisted that he sign a nondisclosure agreement that was supposed to update and tighten an earlier one. "No, I can't sign that. I'm leaving," he said.

Until the moment he handed over the carefully typed, fifteen-page application, he says, he had been operating on autopilot, not consciously deciding but acting anyway. But when the paperwork left his hand, the weight also lifted from his mind. "It was an incredibly heady experience, one of the happiest days of my life."

Following standard procedure, the air force withdrew his security clearance, effectively grounding him, and assigned him to a clerical position while his CO application made its way through the base hierarchy and up to the Pentagon. Initially, his commanders and colleagues were astonished but not particularly disapproving. "People would walk past me as I sat there, with an escort, without my badge, and they'd say, 'What did you do wrong?' and I'd say, 'Nothing. I haven't been driving under the influence. I haven't been beating up on anybody. I just have a disagreement with the air force, and I feel I have to make a statement.' My escort would confirm, 'No, he hasn't done anything wrong.' It was an incredibly affirming experience. But by about two o'clock, I had a blinding headache and was so emotionally drained that they looked at me and said, 'Go home and rest.' "

The weeks that followed were a time of peace and clarity. Cobos planted flowers and caught up on yard work. He took pleasure in the simplicity of his clerical job. He found that while a few of his friends distanced themselves from him, others went out of their way to express understanding. "Several people said, 'Hey, if I didn't have kids to support, I'd do the same thing.' "

But the friendliness and acceptance vanished when the publicity began. In the course of researching his options, he had gotten in touch with the GI rights group Citizen Soldier and had made contact with attorneys Tod Ensign and Louis Font. Font, a celebrated conscientious objector in the Vietnam War, advised, "What got me out of the military, in the end, was publicity." He proposed a similarly high-profile strategy in this case. Cobos said yes much as he had said yes to the military in the first place, understanding its general significance but not comprehending what it would be like for him personally.

The first publicity to hit the stands was Ensign's article in one of the most provocative media possible, the New York-based *Guardian,* a stridently anti-US weekly newspaper. When Reed met him for lunch waving a copy of the article, Cobos was so shaken he was physically unable to drive back to work. Local media coverage soon followed. Many days he sat at his desk too preoccupied to work, having no idea whether his co-workers were oblivious to the situation or were freezing him out. Finally, one friend came up to his desk and said, "Congratulations. I admire your courage. I saw you in the paper."

When he made the decision to become a CO, Cobos was elated, in part because he felt that his life was back under control. When the publicity started, that control disappeared and the good will of many colleagues evaporated. "No one confronted me, but I could feel the hatred and the anger, even from people with whom I really had developed an affinity."

Soon Cobos was standing in front of his commanding officer, receiving a warning that the air force was investigating him for possible security violations.[5] Still, the encounter was "very calm . . . he read me my rights. I told him I wasn't going to say anything without a

lawyer present and he said, 'Okay, I guess I can't ask you anything.' "
Cobos was warned to refer interview requests to the base's public
relations office. He agreed, although he says that he interpreted it as
a requirement for balance, and that the air force later told him it had
been intended as an order not to make public statements himself. He
left in a daze.

But the publicity continued. Howard Silber, the *Omaha World-Herald*
military affairs editor, wrote a piece which captured and even
highlighted the sensation Cobos and the air force each for their own
reasons wanted to avoid. It began, "A Strategic Air Command
intelligence sergeant was stripped of his security clearance after he
claimed. that reconnaissance planes from Offutt Air Force Base
sometimes eavesdropped on radio communications between Nicaraguan
military units fighting contra forces."[6] Apparently unfamiliar with the
published statements of Hersh, Richelson, and others, Silber continued,
"Cobos' statement about the Central America flights is the first public
allegation of electronic intelligence operations conducted by RC-135
reconnaissance planes in or near Nicaraguan airspace."

When he heard that the Silber article was out, Cobos drove tensely
to the local convenience store to buy a newspaper, and nearly lost
control of the car driving home. A hysterical laugh kept erupting from
him as he visited friends far into the night and heard them echo his
suspicion, "Yeah, looks like you're in some trouble." By morning, his
distress was such that Cobos could not remember what he had done
with the car keys. Reed, awakened to help search, said, "Hey, drive
my car. The bumper sticker will be the least of your problems."

"No way!" screamed Cobos. "I'm not into picking fights with these
people!" The keys eventually turned up, but the incident deepened his
sense of panic and vulnerability. Cobos remembers sitting in a stall in
the men's room at work thinking, "This is it. They're going to break
the door down and come take me away." Around the same time, his
mother called from Texas to let him know that the press there was
speculating about whether he would be charged with espionage. She
also reported that his brother was receiving some fallout and was, to
say the least, uncomfortable.

The decision to take the offensive through a press conference was also
uncomfortable, but it seemed imperative to reclaim the high ground after
what his mother had told him. His Omaha press conference was attended
by area newspapers, the wire services, and an air force camera crew which
filmed and taped the proceedings from beginning to end. Cobos sat between
his two attorneys, Ensign and Font, at a long table in the Unitarian church,
read a terse press release, and then opened the floor to questions.

"Were SAC planes from Offutt flying spy missions over Nicaraguan
airspace?" Cobos was asked several times.

"I cannot comment, but if I'm asked to testify before a congressional committee I will do so," he replied carefully.

That evening with a contingent of friends, Cobos faced the television set with a peculiar combination of the giggles and the sweats. "Maybe I won't even be on," he said, and the five o'clock news passed without his appearance. But as the next broadcast began, just as he was starting to relax, Cobos remembers, "I saw this face on the screen that looked familiar, but it didn't quite register that it was me. Then a voice started in, all melodramatic and booming: 'He says he knows, but he isn't telling—' and that was how the TV coverage of my story began."

With the publicity came a flood of phone calls offering moral support and asking, "What can I do to help you?" Cobos soon started to think about taking up some of those offers, since he expected to be unemployed soon and since his legal expenses would be significant and possibly massive. His attorneys advised him that many people in his situation raise those funds by holding some kind of a benefit. When people called with offers of help, Cobos mentioned that idea. With no more leadership from him than that, a Daniel Cobos Defense Committee was born of Omaha folk who knew him from the co-op, his *Broken Rainbow* film showing, and other activities at the Unitarian church. The night of the benefit party, Cobos bounced around the corner to the church in his usual mismatched sneakers and casual garb, and was astonished to discover that people were standing in line to get in. He stood in line too, until a volunteer noticed him and said, "Hey, you don't have to buy a ticket. This party's for you!"

The benefit was a success. His legal fees were raised, and his spirits were more so. Again, the balance shifted. The fear dissipated, and the sense returned that his life was sufficiently in control. Objectively, his future was very much out of his hands, but at least Cobos understood that he wasn't alone. And with that regaining of control came a new sense of legitimacy, an understanding that turning back was not an option and that going forward would be difficult but ultimately manageable. Krissa Lee-Regier, a co-chair of the Daniel Cobos Defense Committee, observes, "The thing that has stood out most strongly about Daniel is that he still wants very much to be a nice guy. But he has learned through this experience that, if you're going to take a stand on principle, you're going to get some hostile responses sometimes, and that doesn't mean you're doing anything wrong."

The hardest thing about the whole experience, Cobos says, is the phones ringing and the strangers asking him to explain, dissect, justify, and interpret his action. In every handful of people who contact him to offer genuine support, he sees one or two who seem to home in on him as a tool to publicize their own agendas. Cobos is widely asked to comment on the significance of his action for US policy, for peace, for the security of the base, for the future of the Western world. He is still trying simply to make sense of it in his own life. But even before his application for discharge was approved, he found himself saying yes to invitations to speak at rallies and forums, and hesitantly identifying as an activist. "I can't say I think my action represents some kind of universal mandate," he says. "I hate having people make moral judgments for me, and I'm not going to do that for other people. But I wish more people would speak out."

In the months while his fate was being deliberated by the air force and he was pondering the simple questions of what to do next for a living, Cobos functioned without a grand plan or ideology, but with the sense that a path was unfolding. During a visit by John Linder, brother of the US engineer murdered by contras while working on a rural electrical project in northern Nicaragua, Cobos happened to read a copy of a letter from a colleague of Ben Linder who remained in the war zone. Her words were the first articulation Cobos found of the combination of fear and confidence, humility and a sense of special destiny, that he had felt in standing up to the military. "There have been no choices for us in this, but I say this to myself and know at the same time that this is not something imposed from outside, either. We have no choice. And we are making our own decisions, as free individuals. Both things are true, completely contradictory, and completely true."[7]

As his story spread, Cobos learned that while he was the first high-profile objector to the airborne reconnaissance program, he was not the first conscientious objector to activities in Central America and the Caribbean. The *Alert,* the national newspaper of the Committee in Solidarity with the People of El Salvador, published a letter by Lieutenant Joseph R. Bongiovi of Fort Lewis, Washington. A Notre Dame graduate who had become concerned about the US role while an ROTC cadet and whose concern had deepened during his basic training at Fort Benning, where he saw "thousands of Latin American officers and troops trained at the School of the Americas there every year." Bongiovi's letter pointed to a handful of kindred spirits, including Dr. David Fletcher, who had refused to run the medical program in support of the Grenada invasion. But Cobos, like most "peacetime" conscientious objectors, was the only airman at his base to take such an action, and he was acutely aware of that fact.

Four months after filing his CO application, Cobos went to Boston to speak on the MIT campus. He ambled onstage in jeans, a silk-screened T-shirt, and a clashing suit jacket. The auditorium was packed and the audience, a mix of students and community residents, rose to welcome him. After a few anecdotes delivered in the terrified breathiness of the inexperienced public speaker, Cobos settled into a conversational style and recounted the history of his turnaround. The path, as he described it, was anything but a straight line. It was made of unwitting leaps, long periods of retrenchment, some directed searching, and much reeling from encounters he never would have sought out.

"What's next for you?" he was asked.

Continuing to speak seemed like an obligation, Cobos said, disruptive though it was to his life. But the strongest activism he felt able to carry out was saying no to the air force. Beyond that, Cobos expressed a deep desire to get his life back into some kind of balance. Approached by a TV producer about the possibility of a docudrama on his experience, he thought, "Maybe I'll take the money I get from that and open a hospice." At any rate, Cobos is sure of one thing. "I want to use my psychology background for real in some kind of counseling role. I want to help people directly. Maybe military families. Maybe people with AIDS. When I went into the military, I didn't admit it, but there was a voice in the back of my mind saying I wasn't quite ready for that responsibility, that I lacked some maturity or strength or insight. Now, thanks to the military, I don't feel that I lack those resources anymore."

11 _____CHANGING LIVES

These lives are a reminder that integrity is possible even when things get messy, and that integrity itself is not a matter of whitewashed innocence, but of owning and trying to correct one's very human errors. They are struggles toward ethical autonomy, defined in a rare study of that even rarer phenomenon as "the willingness to assert one' own principled judgment, even if that entails violating rules, values, or perceptions of the organization, peer group, or team." They show it is possible to pause in one's course, rethink the issues, define a new and more authentic path, fight to bring it into being—and survive. These individuals rode the tides of self-doubt and conflict with others, not in the name of ideological fervor—in spite of their original ideological inclinations, in fact—but in pursuit of freedom and integrity and lives that made sense. They have gone through, or are still going through, extremely rocky times. But it is fair to call these success stories. For every door that has slammed shut, another has opened up which is at least as interesting. These people are all strengthened by their experiences, in shape, assertive, effective in their political work, and living full if not overflowing lives. They are, as Judy Genesio puts it, "younger than before."

The publishing industry cranks out guidebooks by the ton purporting to help readers live more coherent, grounded, satisfying, and effective lives, without addressing the individual's relationship to any social grouping larger than family, workplace, and immediate circle of friends. If global issues are mentioned, it is generally as a nasty environmental problem to be tuned out or better accepted. These stories suggest the opposite: that looking at the connection between one's day-to-day work and its broader significance is essential to a sense of coherence, even in seemingly "apolitical" dimensions of life.

To do so is to go through a radical process, not only in the conclusion one reaches, but in the relationship of those seemingly intellectual convictions to the core of each person's psyche and spirit and patterns of living. They involve the extremes of euphoria and anguish. They are changes not only in career path but in styles of living and thinking about the world: close relationships, spiritual life, ethnic and class background, sexuality, cosmology. These are true crises of identity. They cannot be reduced to or explained by predictable passages such as midlife crisis, no matter how interwoven these may be. But whatever is going on here, it is deeper than any mood swing or experiment in lifestyle. Even if these people were to abandon their new assessment of the role of the weapons labs or the CIA or the military, they would not go back to being the people they were when they served those organizations. They have learned something fundamental and they understand that, in the words of a machinist who quit his job on the B-1 bomber after reading the Catholic bishop's pastoral letter on peace, "wishing you hadn't asked the questions is like wishing you hadn't learned to read or write."

"Most of us greet radical innovation with all the enthusiasm of a baby meeting a new sitter," writes Ellen Goodman in *Turning Points,* her study of changes in people's lives as a result of the feminist movement.[1] That resistance runs deepest when the innovations are in our own system of belief and patterns of living, when they require us to make peace with most of the elements of our familiar environment, and which, once they start, have such a tendency to snowball. But if conservatism were the only dimension of the human personality, we would not be evolving even as tenuously as we are. The standard response to change is not automatic resistance. It is ambivalence, caution, and fascination. Hugh Prather tells the story of a woman who quite consciously and spontaneously decided to turn her life upside down, walking out without notice from what seemed to be a successful career and marriage and roots in her community. After three years of living abroad, she came home—not as a naughty child and not as the adult she had been, but as a continually changing human being who made a home for herself wherever she was and whose behavior, abrupt though it was, was the only honest response she could make to an inner fire. "Even more unexpected than the story," Prather writes, "was the reaction at our table. We were all staring at the woman as if she were a heroine. A time comes when you need to clean house. No, you need to go even further, you need to burn the house down with yourself inside it. Then you must walk from the fire and say, I have no name."[2] The changes documented here differ sharply from hers because they are anchored in the recognition of real-world responsibilities as well as self-discovery for its own sake, but they are met with this same combination of dread and relief.

Relief and satisfaction come in large measure from the fact that, in their own minds at least, these subjects have reclaimed the moral high ground. They have come to understand themselves and their rebellion not as anomalies, but as rational, dignified responses to the circumstances of their lives. They have moved forward, not by forgetting what they have learned, but by integrating it into their lives and reconciling it with their old beliefs.

These changes represent a broadening of vision—not just "getting the right answer" but taking more factors into account. they lead to new vantage points from which the old ones are seen as understandable, but limited, ways of looking at the world. Because they are experienced as growth, even when it brings recognition or error if not evil in one's earlier life, they do not paralyze the individual with guilt but make self-acceptance a natural outcome. This is all the more true because, radical though they are, these journeys are also homecomings to more authentic interpretations of values the individual has held all along.

How people change like this—going along with their peers one day, asking all sorts of uncomfortable questions the next—is an issue whose importance goes beyond wars and weapons. These developments take place as nearly everything does, in complex and contradictory ways. There is no magic key to explain why they happen, or for whom, or how. Each turning point involves long periods of dissatisfaction and muddled feelings, punctuated by breakthroughs that may or may not be recognized, confused by the shadow play of all the other changes and crises that make up a human life. Explanations have a way of raising more questions than they answer. As Arthur Egendorf writes in *Healing from the War,*

> Many vets changed during the war. People ask, "What did it?" and expect to hear a story that explains how it happened. But the expectation is misplaced. The change is never explained by the sequence of events. All you get from a story is that a man [sic] goes into a situation looking at the world one way, and then, after his whole view comes apart for reasons he can never fully explain, he emerges seeing things another way . . . and the times and places we call turning points in our lives can no more be explained or justified than the elements an artist chooses for a work of art.[3]

But there are some common themes, and the search for them is worthwhile and at times fascinating. There is still truth to Robert Jay Lifton's 1971 observation that "depth psychology is impoverished in insights on adult change." In his study of Vietnam veterans who turned against the war during their processes of healing from it, he identifies three overlapping stages in "open personal change," (change due primarily to the individual's autonomous behavior rather than the influence of a controlling environment such as a mental hospital or prison).[4] First, there are moments of some sort of confrontation powerful enough to blow away old assumptions—often, for veterans, a confrontation with death, whether their own or others'. But Lifton notes that this confrontation can also take the form of other powerful lessons about vulnerability or the forced collapse of a belief system. This confrontation activates guilt which, although it has fallen into disrepute in our culture's emotional repertoire, can be animating as well as paralyzing. The second of these phases is "reordering" of beliefs and patterns of living to achieve an animating relationship with that guilt. Finally, alongside the first two phases and building on them, there is renewal, the creation of new forms and styles to go with new values. And the major factor in making that renewal possible is an attitude that Lifton describes as playful, spontaneous, experimental, open, present in the moment. This general outline is born out in the stories in these pages.

These processes of change are so complex that it is almost irresistable to seek models or structures to help explain them. No such structure is a perfect fit, but a few do illuminate important themes. First, it is not entirely whimsical to suggest parallels to the experience of religious conversion. In the words of the spiritual "Amazing Grace"—written by a slave trader turned abolitionist—"I once was lost, but now I'm found / was blind, but now I see."[5] Or, as William James describes it,

> To be converted, to be regenerated, to receive grace, to experience religion, to gain an assurance, are so many phrases which denote the process, gradual or sudden, by which a self hitherto divided, and consciously wrong, inferior, and unhappy, becomes unified and consciously right, superior, and happy, in consequence of its firmer hold upon religious realities . . . whether or not we believe that a direct divine operation is needed to bring such a moral change about.[6]

Subjectively, these journeys are indeed seen as movement from division to wholeness and darkness to light, at least in retrospect. But in spite of their spiritual element, only a few involve divine intervention. Faith, theological understanding, and even charismatic spiritual encounters were significant in many of these experiences. But no amount of religion got even the most faithful off the hook of interpreting their experiences for themselves.

A second model comes from natural science, but has been widely used by social philosophers in analyzing the transformation of groups and cultures. It is the concept of "paradigm shift," which Thomas Kuhn describes as the essence of scientific revolutions—for instance, in the displacement of Newtonian physics by quantum mechanics. His analysis in *The Structure of Scientific Revolutions* provides a vocabulary for examining many kinds of individual and social change which involve rejecting or transcending long-held beliefs.[7] In scientific research, Kuhn says, communities within a discipline are united by their agreement on basic assumptions which together constitute a paradigm—definitions, experimental methods, standards of proof— and which, once agreed upon, don't have to be redefined with every experiment. The same can be said for communities of engineers, soldiers, intelligence agents, or diplomats. What Kuhn calls "normal science" seeks to discover and measure the details of an agreed-upon range of phenomena without explicitly thinking about the paradigm itself. These agreed-upon limits keep scientists from being hamstrung by an overabundance of logical possibilities and perspectives, and so they allow progress to be made. Still, they represent a compromise because they remove from the realm of conscious deliberation many of the limiting assumptions which shape that progress. They obscure the fact that "objective" scientific judgments flow from the highly subjective realm of researchers' personal agendas, biases, loyalties, and intellectual strengths and weaknesses, which all shape the questions they choose to study.

Scientific revolutions take place when normal science unearths phenomena that do not make sense within the accepted paradigm—for instance, when light behaves in ways inconsistent with the assumption that light is a wave. When that happens on a wide enough scale, the orderly and structured world of normal science is replaced by excitement, confusion, the questioning of core assumptions, and the formation of new relationships among thinkers, ideas, and disciplines.

Marilyn Ferguson, applying Kuhn's analysis to social transformation, writes,

> Eventually, too many puzzling observations pile up outside the old framework of explanation and strain it. Usually at the point of crisis, someone has a great heretical idea. A powerful new insight explains the apparent contradictions. It introduces a new principle . . . a new perspective. By forcing a more comprehensive theory, a crisis is not destructive but instructive.[8]

Paradigm shift makes concerns that were once central seem peripheral, and concerns that were once disregarded take on paramount importance. Ferguson compares it to "seeing the hidden pictures" in children's puzzles. It is not just a linear development, but a transformation.

The parallels between the ostensibly objective but actually human world of science and the ostensibly neutral but arguably partisan world of the military-industrial-intelligence complex are greater than they might appear to be. And the journeys recounted in these pages do have that transformational quality. Descriptions of them as linear sequences of events always require arbitrary choices of structure which at best approximate the real journeys. As experienced, they are much more than linear sequences of events because their essence is the interplay among events. The ultimate impact of the lessons learned is a qualitative change in personality and values, in one's way of approaching life.

But besides these grand transformational breakthroughs, these changes involve many small and unglamorous instances when these men discovered that they had been thrown off course by misinformation, propaganda, or ideology. As the poet Wendell Berry remarks, "You can't always outsmart people, but you can just about always out-dumb them." These stories are about people's discoveries that they have been out-dumbed, and this recognition gives rise to a particularly sharp determination to fight back. David MacMichael typifies this when he says, "I was brought up believing in the Democratic ideal, and I still do. But when I look at the propaganda that has been brought forth, especially by the CIA, to subvert that ideal, my response is, 'I fell for that? How bloody crude.' "

These changes, then, are about the cultivation and exercise of critical consciousness, that quality of mind which resists rigidity, experiments freely with new interpretations, keeps asking new questions, and at least tries to live out the answers. A third model for interpreting these processes is what the Brazilian educator and social theorist Paulo Freire calls "conscientization," the gradual awakening of critical consciousness and with it the faculty of conscience, which is capable of knowledge not only in the abstract but as it relates to human well-being.[9] This contrasts with what Freire calls "magical consciousness," the mode of awareness in which things "just happen" and the connections among them are rarely considered. Some of the men in this book realized early in life that they were blessed (or cursed) with critical consciousness, and all of them have cultivated and learned to live with this quality.

But these men, and most North Americans in similar positions, differ markedly in one respect from the Third World populations in which Freire documented the dynamics of consciousness raising. When the poor and oppressed reflect on their situation, it is with the hope of changing it to their advantage. When professionals and even laborers in the United States—a country with 5 percent of the world's population which consumes 60 percent of the world's resources—engage in a similar process, it is not likely to yield results that benefit them materially. It is not surprising that this educational process, in our own culture and context, involves a fair amount of spiritual crisis.

A major barrier to conscientization in Freire's analysis is "massification," the submission of the individual's awareness to the authority of the group. So it should come as no surprise that the men in these pages share qualities and experiences which set them apart from others. They are mavericks: nearly every one describes a sense of apartness, uniqueness, or even alienation, and the ability at times to turn that separateness to advantage. There is a larger-than-life quality to many of their personalities and experiences. They are ordinary people who have pushed themselves into extraordinariness; they are independent-minded and stubborn because they have taught themselves to be.

A second common aspect is a rigorous and early ethical teaching of some kind, either at home or school or church. A disproportionate number of them are or were Catholics. While much of that education may have been cast off years ago, they have hung onto the idea that there is a greater good, that it is meaningful to talk about rights and responsibilities, that dreaming is part of being human. They have never been nihilists.

A third shared feature in these lives is the inclusion of a regular opportunity for self-reflection. That opportunity may come through meditation or prayer, psychotherapy or a support group, reading, mountain climbing, or a close relationship involving especially good communication. Although it may take many forms, there is always space for a critical self-awareness that is not otherwise possible. Along with that self-reflection comes the ability to live with uncertainty, to chew on a question long enough to produce an answer, and in the meantime to admit, "I don't know." They are self-aware, but rarely self-obsessed.

"It is by the goodness of God that in our country we have those three unspeakably precious things: freedom of speech, freedom of conscience, and the prudence never to practice either of them," Mark Twain wrote.[10] Talking about the loss of this prudence requires looking beyond the individual to the institutional environments that shape attitudes and define the range of acceptable dissent.

The plain fact is that most people who are ethically uncomfortable with their work do not directly protest, do not pound desks or even write polite memos, do not consider their objections appropriate topics for discussion in the lunchroom, and certainly do not resign in protest. As Tom Grissom observes, "It's not really remarkable that most people stay in the weapons industries, given the atmosphere. It's remarkable that I left."

Despite the variety of corporate cultures and the opportunities for individual expression and eccentricity within them, some of their institutional characteristics are constant. Even before Eisenhower's warning about the danger of the military-industrial complex, a mystique has always surrounded those guarded realms where armaments are made and troops are trained and secrets are (theoretically) kept. Much popular writing by insiders and journalists investigating weapons factories, the CIA, the foreign service—and to a lesser extent the military, because so many people have been through it—emphasizes the exotic nature of these institutions. They are glamorized in the novels of Robert Ludlum, or dissected in Paul Loeb's *Nuclear Culture* as institutions whose primary ethical standard is "acquiescence to authority." Either way, popular culture sees them as environments like no others.

Foremost among their unique aspects is secrecy, which isolates participants from each other as well as the outside. As Sissela Bok writes in *Secrets: The Ethics of Concealment and Revelation,*

> Secrecy can harm those who make use of it in several ways. It can debilitate judgment, first of all, whenever it shuts out criticism and feedback, leading people to become mired down in stereotyped, unexamined, often erroneous beliefs and ways of thinking. Neither their perception of a problem nor their reasoning about it then receives the benefit of challenge and exposure. Scientists working under conditions of intense secrecy have testified to its stifling effect on their judgment and creativity. And those who have written about their undercover work as journalists, police agents, and spies, or about living incognito for political reasons, have described similar effects of prolonged concealment on their capacity to plan and to choose, at times on their sense of identity.[11]

Besides the secrecy of concealment, other isolating influences come into play: the physical barriers created by fences and security guards, the functional isolation experienced by anyone working on a finite piece of a massive project, and the natural tendency of specialists thrown together in such lines of work to socialize mostly with people who understand them best—each other.

Finally, work in the national security establishment is unique because it is paid for and so legitimated—whether knowingly or by default—by the taxpayers.

Despite such differences, many of the institutional characteristics which shape values and inhibit dissent are not so much unique as they are normal, resembling as they do the workplaces most of us report to every day. In these subcultures as in most others, there are some who believe wholeheartedly in what they do and others who fall into place. There are raises and promotions, friendships and technical challenges, company social functions and benefits, and the certainty of a familiar environment. There is personal loyalty, desire for approval, emphasis on honoring commitments, and the tendency to give one's peers the benefit of the doubt. There are also direct sanctions for failing or refusing to play by the rules, whether explicit or tacitly understood. But the most common reinforcements are the ordinary rewards for ordinary loyalty.

When the stakes are high enough, positive reinforcements can be wielded as cunningly and deliberately as any punishments. For example, in the aftermath of Watergate, Edward Weisband and Thomas M. Franck studied the ethical climate in the federal government through the stories of officials who resigned in protest. Even at the height of that constitutional crisis, only a handful made a clean break. Others, presumably, tried in good faith to keep themselves and their colleagues honest while continuing to do their jobs. And rewards as well as threats were what lured the majority to match their ethical standards with their leaders'. When Attorney General Elliot Richardson resigned to protest the firing of the special prosecutor, Archibald Cox, the Nixon administration's efforts to keep Richardson quiet

> were not crude threats to his political future but much more effective appeals to the very sense of personal ethics which was prompting the resignation. Subtly calling on loyalty and gratitude, the President let Richardson know that he had been on the short list of five persons who would have been acceptable nominees for the Vice-Presidency. Nixon also saw to it that Richardson was shown the ultraconfidential Brezhnev letter that had triggered the world-wide armed forces alert of October 25, 1973. If he felt he must resign, Richardson was admonished, he must do so silently. This was a moment of great peril. [12]

In addition to consciously wielded reinforcements, many others are built into the system. In material terms, the worker is often well treated, and appreciates this fact in light of the perceived shortage of alternatives. Lou Raymond's pay and benefits, and Bill Perry's seemingly infinite resources for doing his job, are not unusual. In addition, the military, the civil service, and government contracting are sectors of the economy where rules and expectations are often clearly spelled out, and where civil rights are directly legislated and meaningfully enforced. And so despite the racism experienced by Vietnam-era combat forces, the image of today's military as an equal opportunity employer—in hiring if not thereafter—has some credibility. [13]

The net result of these incentives is to create, over time, enough identification with the institution that outspoken displays of dissent are hard even to consider. This is nothing extraordinary; it is a basic principle of management science.

Another normal aspect of any social group, whether a bomb factory or a church choir, is a sense of decorum highly offended by public controversy. This perspective is exquisitely illustrated in an article by

Michael May, a director at Lawrence Livermore Laboratory. Likening the frequent demonstrations at the lab to "some movie version of a medieval war," May laments the "narrowing of perspective" on both sides which accompanies the nuclear weapons debate or any other conflict. He speculates that if demonstrator and scientist were to sit down together over a beer, they might get along fine and find numerous areas of common ground in their interests and experiences. It is only when the focus is on "the small picture," the nuclear weapons debate, that these areas of common ground are forgotten. His discomfort with the demonstrators is due not to their outrage at the development of new generations of nuclear weapons, nor even to their implicit assessment of politics-as-usual as ultimately ineffective, but to their disturbance of daily life in its fullness and wonder.

May exhibits a common style of philosophical liberalism: a tolerance for all points of view which acknowledges none of them as sufficiently compelling to change the status quo. He concludes,

> This is not to argue against the peace movement. There are many different evaluations of the situation. History is rich enough to support them all. This is only to point out that in demonstrations as in foreign affairs, there is an inherent conflict between means and ends. The conflict comes about because we are part of the problem as well as the only hope for its solution. The means used in the situation at hand determine whether the effort will count as peacemaking or not, rather than the theories championed.[14]

Even after his departure from Livermore, Bill Perry might have agreed completely with May that the loss of tolerance and breadth is regrettable. But what began Perry's real rift with Livermore was the realization that nuclear weapons are not the small picture or a concern that can be put on the shelf at will, but instead are part of the big picture which threatens all our lives. Once he understood that, the attributes Perry had enjoyed in his co-workers—gentility, detachment, patience, and the ability to see many possible answers to any question— seemed less like virtues. The value placed by the staff at Livermore on loyalty to each other and to the enterprise appeared less benign, and he was forced to understand that work for peace on a global scale may require local confrontation.

Healthy human development can be seen as a journey from preoccupation with the self toward the ability to mesh one's interests with those of the broader community and to act in behalf of those shared interests.[15] Genuine attention to the greater good is not necessarily the same as doing what one is told or emulating what one sees other people doing. It involves assessing competing interests and making subjective judgments. It is always a difficult process. Are the psychological factors that keep people obediently building nuclear weapons, for example, really so different from the ones that make people watch six hours of television a day, smoke cigarettes, or engage in other mundane forms of self-destruction? All these behaviors fall into the category of normal disempowerment Abraham Maslow dubbed "the psychopathology of the average."[16]

This state of consciousness truly inhabits the gray area between craziness and sanity. As Roger Walsh writes in *Staying Alive: The Psychology of Human Survival,*

> Fear, greed, aversion, ignorance, unwillingness to delay gratification, defensiveness, and unconsciousness—these are marks of psychological immaturity. They point to the fact that global crises reflect more than the gross psychopathology of, say, a Hitler. They also reflect the myriad forms of "normal" psychological immaturity, inauthenticity, and failed actualization. This is perhaps most evident in politics, where decisions of enormous impact can be shaped by personal insecurities, personality foibles, and interpersonal jealousies.[17]

In terms of human development, part of the problem may be leftover from childhood, when we bonded to our peer group and never really learned how to loosen those bonds in a situation calling for independent judgment. The developmental studies of Jean Piaget show that children over the age of five or six invariably treat tattling on a peer as worse than the offense which prompted the tattle.[18] Weisband and Franck speculate that

> Children are not alone in deploring the tattler in their ranks. By discouraging an infant's tendency to tattle, we encourage him or her to develop reciprocal relations with the peer group rather than continue infantile dependence on the superior authority of the adult. Reciprocal dependence is the halfway house on the steep road from parent-authority dependence to ethical emancipation, mature individuation, and responsible self-determination . . . But in our society, the opprobrium against speaking out or going public, against telling tales out of school, lingers long after it has ceased to be socially functional.[19]

In addition to the immaturity which discourages "tattling" on peers or challenging the "parental" authority of the boss, and the use of carrots and sticks to reward and punish, many institutional factors hamper those who take an independent ethical stand. They include the diffusion of responsibility which makes it hard even for the willing tattler to figure out where to point the finger, the scientific subculture's professed disregard for politics, the "sophistication" that disdains idealism, and the sheer busyness that relegates issues like the meaning of it all to the back burner. Their common denominator is not a willful rejection of responsibility, but the unwillingness to ask the relevant questions—in James Baldwin's words, "the innocence which constitutes the crime."[20]

In spite of such "innocence," it is impossible to make bombs, direct covert operations, or prepare for warfare without at some level facing the possibility of killing. It is both interesting and dangerous to make the inevitable analogy with the professionals in Nazi Germany who did their jobs and maintained psychic stability by "doubling," or creating two virtually separate selves.[21] The German example is useful because it has been so widely studied, but there is no basis for assuming that other cultures are incapable of similar abominations. While most of those currently employed in the US national security establishment are not directly engaged in genocide, their work, too, involves confronting it as a reality. Interestingly, several of the men in these pages describe their process of maintaining innocence in language that suggests some degree of doubling: Grissom's identification with the "divided self," MacMichael's "moral ambivalence," and Raymond's sensation of standing apart while he told his supervisor of his decision to resign.

Somehow, in the lives of these individuals, a fabric of belief and commitment that once seemed sturdy began to unravel. The more the tapestry came apart, the more other images could be seen through it. An awareness that something was not right led to a greater sensitivity to additional observations that did not fit the accepted worldview, which in turn led to a more active gathering of information and resulted in a deeper and steadier awareness of the issues. For a while, this deterioration felt like a series of bad days—or years—at the office; things didn't go right but there seemed to be no overall pattern to the problems. But the problems didn't go away, and the individuals— all men who say they value a sense of control very highly—eventually began to look for patterns to explain them. Finding the patterns changed not only their views of the situation but their personalities, self-concepts, and spiritual selves.

The transformations experienced by these individuals took place largely without the divine intervention of a religious conversion, the climate of ferment that characterizes a scientific paradigm shift, or the sustained group reflection used by Freire and his followers to cultivate critical consciousness. In many cases, they took place in the least conducive environments imaginable, inside institutions which emphatically were not undergoing revolutions in thought. What made these people ask the next question in the sequence and take their own questions seriously? What were the "hooks" which helped unravel the tapestry of old beliefs? They were moments of confrontation: questions by others which conveyed ethical seriousness without being judgmental, opportunities—or nudges—to speak from the heart and without a script, voices of emotional support which allowed the individual to face doubts instead of pushing them aside, and practical decisions which forced a choice between the old understanding and the new.

What were the sources of the ideas, models, and myths which helped these individuals arrive at alternative interpretations of events instead of being stuck in permanent chaos? Sometimes new views seemed to spring fully formed from their generally inventive minds or through discussion with close friends and loved ones. But often they came from encounters with well-known "great heretics," in person or in print. They included public figures with a strong moral vision and a coherent interpretation of events, such as Martin Luther King, Helen Caldicott, Daniel Berrigan, as well as lesser-known activists in their own communities. Every one of these people was positively and strongly influenced by the peace movement, either directly through personal encounter or indirectly by its contribution to the overall debate. The greatest of these influences came from people who live out the values they profess, who are strong-minded without being judgmental, and who can talk and listen with real caring for the person in crisis.

These "great heretics" provide information, recast the ethical issues, confront the individual, and demonstrate ways that action is both possible and effective. Their impact seems to come from a mixture of passion and groundedness in the vision that motivates them. But to appreciate their examples, the individual must have a key commodity: imagination. Although not all these subjects use that faculty in overtly artistic pursuits, they all exercise it quite naturally. As Mary Watkins writes in a well-known essay, "In Dreams Begin Responsibilities," the imagination is a faculty for survival because it

> brings to life the particular—particular scenes with particular characters. In so doing, it moves the heart. The imagination's way into perceiving nuclear war is not the rhetoric of numbers, technological jargon and probabilities (which numb one), but is of specific images, particular losses.
>
> It is also only through imagination that we can entertain the possibility that these weapons could be dismantled in the name of peace, as it has never happened before that a weapon has been made and not used. It requires a utopic imagination, an imagination which does not simply mirror the world but which can create what the Romantics called a heterocosm, or another world from this one, which once alive imaginally, can inspire action.[22]

To be able to see the whole range of future scenarios, from disastrous to utopian, and to embrace virtually every one as possible, is to exercise what Lifton calls the "apocalyptic imagination." He writes,

> The technological dimensions of contemporary atrocity seem to me
> to require that we attune our imaginations to processes that are
> apocalyptic in the full dictionary meaning of the word—processes
> that are "wildly unrestrained" and "ultimately decisive," that involve
> "forecasting or predicting the ultimate destiny of the world in the
> shape of future events" and "foreboding imminent disaster of final
> doom."[23]

Imagination cannot be awakened selectively. Once it begins to function,
the process tends to be self-perpetuating. The conscious self sometimes
preserves a sense of control by making the "right" decisions, but other
times can only float on a current of deeper change and wrestle for
survival amid a deepening awareness of crisis.

Whatever its influences and however long its gestation—sometimes
years, sometimes a weekend—this crisis eventually bursts from the
realm of the abstract and demands practical decisions. Old assumptions
no longer work, and old patterns of living become harder, then
impossible. The denouement often unfolds in high Shakespearean
fashion, characterized by feelings of chaos and the loss of an ability to
express, rationalize, and feel in control. The symptoms vary in relation
to the individual's inner resources, support system, external
circumstances, and luck. Often, the crisis which precipitates a decision
appears on the surface to have little to do with the issues at hand. Yet
it brings them into focus and, to the individual in his sensitized state,
seems to touch every aspect of his life and values and to demand
resolution, in Perry's words, "like when you have a toothache and you
just want it to stop."

A key element in the resolution of the crisis seems to be the acceptance
that what is happening is real, legitimate, lasting, and related to
something other than personal idiosyncrasies. When doubts begin, it
is common to say, "I just don't get it. Something must be wrong with
me." The problem is often compounded by the solitary nature of any
ethical struggle and the particular secrecy in these environments. As
Joanna Macy points out,

> If our deepest concerns for our worlds are unmentionable, if we hide
> them like a secret shame, they alienate us from other people. Although
> these concerns may seem valid, on the cognitive level, their distance
> from the tenor of life around us makes us question them on the feeling
> level. A psychic dissonance is produced that can lead us to question
> not society's sanity, but our own.[24]

To break through this debilitating perception means directing one's
attention outward, fitting personal discoveries into a larger context,
comparing observations with other people to find patterns, and testing

new ideas in action as well as in the abstract. To speak and act on the truth is to fight back by building a new vision in place of the old, and by finding a new confidence. When one hears one's own voice and begins to believe it, one can then say, "I'm not crazy; maybe *they* are." What once looked like an end becomes a beginning.

Slowly and awkwardly, these people come to see themselves less in harmony with the institutions which once defined them. The more they understand themselves as outsiders—different, independent—the less inclined they are to accept the received wisdom or to assume that their interests and the institution's coincide.

A decision to resign, go public, and burn bridges involves more than developing dissident views. It involves deciding that acting on one's views is meaningful and worth the price. In other words, it means reckoning anew the degree of power one has to affect matters and where it lies. Often these awakenings involve discovering limits to the power one seemed to have on the inside, and a sobering recognition that the insider's "power" was dependent on being "with the program." Such recognition nevertheless affirms that the actions of individuals have significance. It is the discovery of a hard-to-measure but real efficacy that comes from believing one is right. And it is a rejection of the claim, "I'm just one person. My work is inconsequential. And besides, if I don't do it, somebody else will."

Why do these insights about power come so decisively for some and not at all for others? Some of these men point to key experiences which they alone had and which, like lightning bolts of information and insight, struck them but missed their colleagues. Beyond such coincidences, Bill Perry has a theory: "When you really have power, you don't have to think about it. You just use the power." Many of these men began thinking strategically about the ways power is exercised within institutions early in their careers and out of pure ambition. The times they thought most urgently about it have been when they felt their own power threatened—when their effectiveness on the job was sabotaged, when their managerial philosophies were called into question, when they seemed to be getting screwed—or when they experienced discomfort in their power over other people, as Cobos did when he landed in Panama.

In all these ways, they were forced to ask coldly realistic, unsettling questions about who had power in their institution and what it was being used for. In fact, much of their bitterness is connected to the realization, "I've been had!" It is hard to learn that lesson without becoming cynical. But to emerge with an answer about where real power lies, to put that answer into practice, and to see worthwhile results, is to come out newly empowered.

These changes involve radical reassessments not only of where power lies, but in many cases of what personal power is. From the traditional, muscle-bound view, which identifies power with status, public visibility, and the ability to hire, fire, and allocate resources, they are coming to see other sources of power: organizing of the disenfranchized, strategic thinking, noncooperation, wit, truth telling. This "new" view (actually a longstanding cultural undercurrent) is populist: people hold power through their participation or refusal, their words and influence. It is also spiritual: extraordinary power can be called forth in ordinary people when they respond with their whole being to an imperative. This is the power Gandhi saw in allying oneself with truth, the power of inner conviction gained by taking a stand and breaking with the tribe. Various writers have named this phenomenon "power-with" or "power-from-within," in contrast with patriarchal "power-over" others.[25]

Other themes turn up repeatedly in these stories. Cross-cultural experiences loosened rigid ways of thinking for many of these men. So did exposure to liberation theology, reading the Scriptures through the eyes of the poor and oppressed. Many of these subjects point to occasions when they were helped or forced to look at events from a radically different vantage point. For Tom Grissom the new vantage point was that of future generations, when he asked how he and his colleagues would be judged in a future war-crimes trial. For others, it was the perspective of "the other"—Vietnamese peasants, Salvadoran refugees, Nicaraguan villagers, Soviet diplomats. A key element for many was awakening to the simple fact that the enemy is a human being—a process Einstein termed "widening our circles of compassion." Some call this breadth of caring "global consciousness." Of course, there is the pitfall of failing to distinguish true global consciousness—awareness and feelings about grand themes coupled with personal humility and acknowledgment of the complexity of issues—from plain old hubris. But awakening genuine compassion for the enemy, the victim, and the planet involves a new and humble sense of one's own fallibility and one's responsibility as two inseparable sides of the same coin.

In *Faces of the Enemy*, Sam Keen argues that dehumanization of the adversary is a cornerstone of the psychological processes that make war possible.[26] As evidence, he cites a stunning collection of war propaganda—images ranging from voracious Nazis and a demented ayatollah to a leering, red-eyed Richard Nixon with fields of slaughtered peasants where his brain should be. These images are similar across cultures and through history. Some are of enemy nations, others of enemy groups within a nation. Keen makes the case that any war-making society or hostile group dehumanizes the enemy for not only pragmatic reasons—to make possible the otherwise repugnant act of killing—but also for psychological ones, to project onto "the other" unacknowledged darker elements of its own personality or culture. For example, widespread images of Soviet society as coldhearted and conformist may reflect a refusal to see the same qualities in our own culture. Soviet stereotypes of self-serving, ambitious Americans may play a similar role. Whether a result of war or a root of war, this process keeps "us" locked into a permanent state of enmity with "them." If this thesis is true, coming to terms with the humanity of the enemy is difficult and complex because it requires dealing with not just the realities of a particular war, but whatever pain, angst, and emptiness such projections serve to keep at bay. Keen describes the process of reintegration or "metanoia" (the opposite of paranoia) as "repentance, reowning the shadow, turning around, having the flexibility to adopt many different perspectives" which often requires "a long process of purification . . . a season in purgatory." It is feeling long-denied pain, but also coming home to oneself.[27]

In addition to seeing through the eyes of "the other," these awakenings often involve the realization that one is "the other" in someone else's frame of reference. Participating in the war-making enterprise means fitting into a larger scheme defined by others, leaving little room for clearheaded evaluation of the ethical and practical issues at hand. This is the common price for a sense of belonging, a group identity more parochial than commitment to the greater good. John Mack, a leading researcher in psycho-social questions of the nuclear age, argues that the crux of any meaningful "nuclear age psychology"—addressing why we build bombs and engage in other acts of organized violence, and how we might wean ourselves away from these practices—is our uncritical bonding to the tribe, letting our ideas and values be shaped by its lowest common denominator.[28]

So it is not surprising that in almost every story of "breaking ranks" there is a dissimilation from the dominant culture and a reassertion of individuality and uniqueness. It is not a wholesale rejection of the dominant culture, but a process of making peace with one's differences. With a new affirmation of oneself as black, Hispanic, working class, or Catholic often comes the awareness that one has been working against the interests of one's own group.

On all these levels, such awakenings are emotional, uncontrollable, rough. They repeatedly violate the taboo against losing one's cool. They require living with questions and not jumping for the first available answers. They require self-reflection and self-awareness, learning to feel the twentieth-century terror of planetary annihilation, and overcoming everyday uptightness in order to confront authority, withstand peer pressure, or say "ouch" when something hurts.

To the extent that they involve confronting the dreaded "v-word"— vulnerability—these processes in men also lead to a new definition of masculinity. The military, the foreign service, the CIA, scientific institutions, and the weapons industries remain fundamentally brotherhoods, despite the slow integration of women. In many respects, traditional male expectations played a role in attracting these men, and others like them, to their initial professions: combat as a male rite of passage, scientific achievement as a historically masculine ground for excellence, the linear career path as a breadwinner's cross to bear. Each story of separation from old roles involves new self-acceptance independent of them.

These men did not allow their masculine side—strengths or flaws—to wither. They are aggressive, feisty, strong, and stubborn. But their emotional and expressive options have expanded as they navigated the waters of change, were compelled over and over to admit confusion, leaned on friends and loved ones, and were sometimes swamped by emotions too strong and surprising to control. Jerry Genesio is not alone in having "learned from Nicaragua that it's okay for a man to cry in public." In their relationships, too, they have discovered that the road does not have to be so narrow. Those who stayed in relationships generally became less role-oriented. On a pragmatic level, a number of them are now able to be full-time peace activists only because their wives are the primary wage earners.

But the most interesting changes are more subtle and are related to new understandings of personal power as well as male options. Now these men are less boxed-in by the myth of the heroic loner and more comfortable with working relationships that are cooperative rather than hierarchical. They are more concerned with the quality of their work than how much it pays, more interested in long-term sustainability than short-term effect. They see their efforts to change the world as inseparable from their efforts to be better and more satisfied people.

Their new images resemble what Mark Gerzon describes in *A Choice of Heroes*:

> Healer, Companion, Mediator, Colleague, Nurturer . . . The human qualities they symbolize transcend sexual identity. They reflect awareness of the earth, of work and family, and of the human body, mind and soul, an awareness that any man or woman can develop . . . These traits are based on values; they are not sexual, but ethical . . . Unlike the old archetypes, which were for men only, the emerging masculinities are not. They are, in fact, emerging humanities.[29]

Connected to this broadening is a new outlook on ethical standards— just as demanding, but without the comforting certainty of rules. These and other life crises have taught these men not to expect hard and fast answers or universal standards of morality, and have left them relying less on rules and more on the dictates of compassion. Their most difficult decisions have been delayed and complicated by questions like, "What about all the people who aren't taking this stand? If I'm right, am I condemning my friends and colleagues as wrong?" What finally allowed many of them to take a stand is an ethics based on situational judgments rather than universal principles.

Based on his study of human beings' mechanisms of moral reasoning, Lawrence Kohlberg created his well-known scale of moral evolution. At its pinnacle, he placed people whose moral reasoning is based on an immutable, universal standard of behavior.[30] But most of these men find it impossible to claim that their choices are right for everybody. They know only what is right for them. These critics speak out with urgency, sorrow, outrage, and strong visions about how the world could be different. They are deeply concerned with questions of responsibility. But they don't in general point fingers at others. They struggle to balance their anger with a firsthand understanding of the complexity of problems, to reconcile the awareness of particular abuses of power with the knowledge that we all share some responsibility. Perhaps they can be dismissed as insufficiently moral according to Kohlberg's standards. But then we must pass a similar judgment on one of the greatest philosophers of the twentieth century, Bertrand Russell, who wrote from prison as a conscientious objector during World War I, "Don't judge people morally: however just one's judgment, that is a barren attitude. Most people have a key, fairly simple; if you find it, you can unlock their hearts."[31]

These dissenters force us to look beyond all the elegantly derived moral principles in the world and consider the necessity to disregard them and face the consequences when the complexity of a situation demands it. How this ability relates to a less rigid male socialization is a rich and thorny topic. Researchers on the psychology of women point out that classic studies of moral reasoning such as Kohlberg's focused on men. Some commentators have tried to distinguish two ethical outlooks on the basis of gender ("men are linear; women are contextual"). As Nel Noddings writes in *Caring: A Feminine Approach to Ethics and Moral Education,*

> One is tempted to say that ethics has so far been guided by Logos, the masculine spirit, whereas the more natural and, perhaps, stronger approach would be through Eros, the feminine spirit . . . It is feminine in the deep classical sense—rooted in receptivity, relatedness, and responsiveness. It represents an alternative to currently popular views, for it begins not with moral reasoning but with the moral attitude—that is, with the longing for goodness.[32]

But Russell, the conscientious objectors in these pages, and other men experimenting with new ways of living suggest that the difference is one of not gender but group identity. To have a moral attitude in an essentially amoral culture is to be on some level an outsider.

These awakenings are not sudden steps into enlightenment or discoveries of a channel to guaranteed truths. They are processes of growth and learning, intermixed with struggles for psychic survival, efforts to hang on to an eroding sense of self, find acceptance, solve mysteries, anesthetize pain, test limits. These men see themselves as having been used and in some cases burned. They want vindication, even revenge. Their activism, inspiring though it may be, reinforces the positions on which they have staked a great deal. But this personal dimension does not invalidate their message or negate the importance of their public statements. Few of the visionaries of this or any age would be called well adjusted. What sets these apart from average human beings is not freedom from conflict or purity of motive, but the ability to transcend the parochial aspects of whatever conflict they may be muddling through and to apply its lessons to global issues—however haltingly, to follow the example of Gandhi, who in Erik Erikson's words could "lift his private patienthood to the level of the universal one, and try to solve for all what he could not solve for himself alone."[33] These journeys may begin as reactions to a series of insults or compromising situations. But they end up as more because they force the individual to come to terms with some aspects of the global situation, and his role in it, for his own peace of mind. They may begin as reaction, but they become movements toward integrity. "Anger is a great driving force for a few years," says Ralph McGehee. "But eventually it dissipitates. You can't run on it forever." Yet he still runs on powerful fuel, and he does it because, in reaching the point within the CIA when he could say, "The emperor is naked," he also had to say, "This emperor is dangerous."

To have lived through such enormous changes and come out stronger is to experience the world as a place of open-ended possibilities, no matter how much turbulence some of them may bring. It is to know from experience that people can change radically, can take risks and live through them, can be better than they thought they could. Often to their great surprise, these people have discovered a freshness and optimism not from denying the facts but from facing them. This deserves emphasis. Confronting reality, whatever it may hold for them individually, is the source of much of their wholeness, sense of purpose, self-knowledge. They do not deny the difficulty of their choices, or the sometimes brutal nature of the balancing act they must perform between addressing global problems and looking after their own needs. But it is that realism, even the struggle of it all, which illuminates and transforms their lives.

12 *WAGING PEACE*

Never doubt that a small group of thoughtful, committed citizens can change the world. Indeed, it's the only thing that ever has.
—Margaret Mead

Sin bravely.

—Martin Luther

Veterans through the ages have come home saying that war is hell. The veterans in these pages—veterans of active duty, science and industry, the intelligence agencies, and the foreign service—are saying more: that war is preventable. Not just war in the abstract, but real wars in progress and the larger one that always looms. Their stories illustrate how personal motives of a not very grand nature influence national security decisions. They illustrate the ways in which dissident voices are silenced, ignored, co-opted, or heard too faintly. But they also show uncannily how truth, once spoken, can transform both the situation and the speaker.

The stories in these pages are not just about isolated individuals, but about the slow and ambiguous progress of a movement. The leaps of faith and commitment represented by these individual stands radically transform both the actor and the situation. While most of us, most of the time, err on the side of caution, these people help shift the moral balance toward risk taking and new vision. They are mavericks, as are most of the brave souls who lead in historic change, and this fact does not make them easy role models. But their lives illustrate that it is possible to challenge authority and grow stronger in the process. They hold out the possibility of changes big enough to be worth working for, both in national priorities and in the way we live our lives. They redefine what is possible, what we we can ask of each other, what we can call forth in ourselves. They invite us to cut through our own limiting expectations and consider that, as George Leonard wrote in his study of human transformation, "Not to dream more boldly may be, in view of present realities, simply irresponsible."[1]

There have always been dissidents like these. Their presence, by itself, is no guarantee that their words have begun to be heeded. But their impact is obvious; each one has been a catalyst for increased awareness, activity, commitment, morale. Whether the issue is a campaign against reopening a nuclear reactor or a lawsuit against illegal contra supporters, a freeze referendum or a fast, these men have followed the dictates of conscience into a position of high visibility, and have been rewarded with unexpected opportunities to stick their necks out even farther. They have found themselves in these positions in part because so many people seem hungry for leadership toward a less indiscriminately violent and more reliable approach to security. That hunger is for heroes, public figures who do not negate the people but instead encourage each of us to "be all that we can be."

The problems these dissidents identify are broader than a single policy or a single administration. The issue is not simply nuclear arms, interventionist strategies, or covert operations, but the institutional and psychological factors that breed these. Some trace their beginnings to the National Security Act of 1947, some to the Monroe Doctrine, some to the mysterious roots of human aggression. But they point out specific ways in which the problems have been exacerbated during the 1980s: the huge increases in military spending; the "privatizing" of foreign policy activities and, with it, a reliance on executive orders rather than votes of Congress to establish foreign policy; and the vastly expanded control of information by the executive branch of government, including the sweeping use of secrecy agreements to censor the nonclassified public statements of former federal employees and the exponential growth of the "black" or secret military budget.[2]

These critiques are radical in that they address root cause and structural concerns rather than try to "cure" symptoms. They are radical, but on the commonly understood political spectrum, they speak to the values of the right as well as the left. They underscore that lasting peace requires economic justice and relations among nations based on the same values that we say we stand for at home. But they also affirm that war and peace issues in the late twentieth century are profoundly related to constitutional rights and the rule of law. James Madison's warning that tyranny at home will be justified by a threat from abroad has been sounded more and more frequently in recent years. And its converse is also worth noting: Irresponsible foreign policies are countered only by a revitalized democracy at home.

Among the recent reminders of these relationships—if the Iran-contra and Pentagon procurement scandals are not sufficient reminders—are the FBI's infiltration of churches providing sanctuary to Central American refugees; efforts by the Immigration and Naturalization Service to refuse citizenship to US-born expatriate writer Margaret Randall for her political views; the denial of visas to Tomás Borge and other high-ranking Sandinistas; the confiscation by US customs officials of notebooks from journalists returning from Nicaragua; the exposure of a national effort by the FBI to infiltrate the Committee in Solidarity with the People of El Salvador in order to pass intelligence about Salvadoran dissidents and refugees back to that country's police; and the 1987 firing of career FBI agent John C. Ryan for refusing to investigate two nonviolent peace groups—the Veterans Fast for Life and a midwestern Plowshares group—as possible terrorist organizations.

Even before the judgment of the International Court of Justice, the US government had long disregarded domestic law—the War Powers Act, the Neutrality Act, and the Boland amendment—as well as international law, including the UN and OAS charters and the Nuremberg accords. Wrestling with these issues is in the interest of everyone who expects a system to function by agreed-upon rules.

The testimonies in these pages warn us about a peculiarly American militarism—friendly, flexible within its limits, generous in its incentives for participation, and able to maintain loyal followers less by violent threats than by attempting to make itself the only game in town. Its features include an overreliance on weaponry, intrigue, the inability to understand power as anything but domination, obsession with ends, and obsessive disregard for means, leading to what Adrienne Rich calls "the contempt inherent in the political lie."[3] Their warnings echo the one sounded by two former marines, Commandant David Shoup and Colonel James Donovan, in *Militarism, USA*. Shoup and Donovan place some of the blame on bureaucratic imperatives and structures which diffuse accountability and government agencies "which, together with defense industry, academic research groups, and Congressmen with vested interests, bolster each other and receive such a disproportionate amount of Federal funds that there is no effective counterbalance or means of changing their momentum and direction." But their deeper explanation, backed up by the testimonies in these pages, has less to do with rigid institutional barriers than with the psychology that makes them effective. They go on, "The principal instrument of the power of this bureaucracy is fear, fear of the hazards and disruption which is claimed will result if the defense establishment is not provided with all it demands."[4]

Fear is the deeper problem: insiders' fear of invisible enemies, of being blamed for "losing" some strategic spot to communism, of threats to their power; and the public's fear of a faceless enemy and of stepping out of line. A decorated and proven soldier who tried to challenge the escalation of the Vietnam War from within the Pentagon, David Shoup concluded flatly that there was no way to counter the momentum toward war once it is driven by sufficient hysteria. The critics in these pages are more optimistic—at least on their good days—maintaining that the one force capable of halting that momentum is a sufficiently aroused public. Based on their firsthand knowledge that human beings can change, they hold out some hope that this immense power can be ignited.

Do their stories shed any light on ways this miracle can be achieved? They suggest a formula of equal parts evolution and revolution—a revolution not built on chaos in the streets but on ideas, visions, and confrontation that is nonviolent, focused, disciplined, and sustained. They are a reminder that public questioning of foreign policy and national security is intimately tied up with questioning about how we live our lives and who is running things. Abstract arguments about nuclear weapons or foreign wars have little power to capture the imagination and inspire ongoing commitment unless they are related to the particulars of our lives: family or friends in the military who are suddenly faced with a tour of duty in Honduras, teenagers who decide not to go to college because the future is so uncertain, refugees knocking on the church door and FBI agents following close behind, protesters at the factory gate, jobs in the United States being exported to Third World countries. These personal connections are catalysts for questioning, choices, action. So is the perception that the answers to our questions matter, that the problems are not superficial but systemic, that the range of possible futures which can be influenced by our choices is wide.

Signs of the time for a change of direction are never as clear as we would like. Strategists of the Reagan revolution did not succeed by waiting for guarantees, but by articulating a vision and taking advantage of the available indications that it ws attainable with hard work. Today, there is no shortage of indications that a new approach to peace—based on common security rather than "us-versus-them"—is struggling to be born. The United States and the Soviet Union have each, with elegant symmetry, lost major interventionist wars in Nicaragua and Afghanistan, wars that had been the obsession of each set of leaders but had received less than the full support of either public. Yet in the face of these losses the superpowers remain territorially secure and relatively at peace with each other. Tension between them showed signs of moderation at the end of the Reagan era, thanks to mutual efforts at summitry, the INF treaty, the unilateral

Soviet testing moratorium, new agreements for crisis communication, plus the proposed joint Mars flight and other visions of peaceful collaboration—all arguably hastened by the rise in citizen diplomacy and other forms of grassroots pressure. Aided in part by the jumpiness of Wall Street, both sides seem simultaneously willing to acknowledge the economic ravages of arms racing. And, as the two great global paternalists face this reassessment of their role, they are helped along by the emergence of a mature and capable Third World statesmanship, as illustrated by the Arias peace plan in Central America.

After a decade devoted to giving the cold war paradigm one more try, it is not surprising that calls for a new vision have been sounded more broadly and eloquently every year, and from sources more and more solidly established in the political mainstream. In *Tales of a New America,* Robert Reich of Harvard's Kennedy School of Government argues that our old cultural myths—liberal and conservative alike—have reinforced the notion of a benevolent, responsible "us" and a threatening, self-serving "them."[5] Reich warns that debates about every issue from defense to social welfare are based on "morality tales" so entrenched that we rarely ask whether they are still meaningful. He christens them the Mob at the Gates, the Triumphant Individual, the Benevolent Community, and the Rot at the Top. These myths, while they may simplify and console, always reinforce the idea that the world is broken down into "us" and "them" without letting us assess the issues afresh in each new situation. "When we become so enchanted with our morality tales that we wall them off from the pressures for adaptation, the stories may begin to mask reality rather than illuminating it," Reich warns. "In the years ahead, the stories Americans tell one another will haltingly, gropingly, continue to change. Current liberal and conservative variants of our core mythologies, both of them accepting the conventional borders between 'us' and 'them,' will gradually give way to a subtler assumption of interdependence. These new stories will speak less of triumph, conquest, or magnanimity, and more of the intricate tasks of forging mutual responsibility and enforcing mutual obligation."

The stories of dissidents like the ones in these pages—who are breaking ranks not just with a particular administration's policies but with a whole framework of belief—help sketch out the details of a possible new paradigm. It would be built on recognition that hostile relationships have roots—political, economic, and cultural—and that some of those roots are found in our own behavior. It would be built on a vision of security as participation in a community of nations with laws and conventions, rather than trying to survive as a renegade and a law unto ourselves.

This search for a new paradigm of security—the replacement of the notion of win-lose with one of common security—is a realignment of the relationship between "us" and "them." To do this—between nations just as much as between individuals—requires removing from real-world conflicts the added baggage of projections, stereotypes, and irrational fears to enable a clearer look at the ways "we" may resemble "them," not only in our common humanity but also in our shared human imperfections. To counteract the politics of paranoia, we will need a politics of "metanoia"—an owning of our collective shadow—so that enemies, when they do arise, can be dealt with pragmatically rather than taking on larger-than-life status as the imagined source of all evil.

With this development could come a realistic possibility of enhanced openness, a return to the idea of secrecy as a last resort rather than the norm. With this openness would come a new strength and resilience in institutions, new ability to incorporate criticism in the development of policies rather than having to deflect it later, and less vulnerability to embarrassing and costly mistakes. We could serve our own interest as well as that of justice by recognizing that dissent is by its nature responsible.

With that greater openness and recognition of legitimate differences would come compassion for the stress that intrudes in the lives of human beings when they are not allowed to shape the world they live in. A compelling vision of peace is one which starts with the individual, celebrates each person's uniqueness, and honors each person's conscience rather than treating it as a necessary inconvenience. With that honoring of the individual comes a recognition of work as more than a means to a paycheck, an acknowledgment that very few jobs are ethically neutral, and a climate of support for the individual in thinking choices through as consciously as possible. In the same breath of fresh air would come a broader and more resilient understanding of patriotism: not xenophobic, fearful chauvinism of the nation, but the pride that comes with self-knowledge, self-acceptance, and accountability—as Charlie Liteky said in giving up his Congressional Medal of Honor, "love of country strong enough to right the wrongs."

"The peace movement can write a very good protest letter, but that is not enough," said the Buddhist monk and activist Thich Nhat Hanh during the Vietnam years. In order to realize its potential, "the peace movement must learn how to write a love letter."[6]

To whatever extent "the peace movement" has helped in the transformation of the dissidents in these pages, it has been by offering them "love letters": support for open-ended questioning, nonjudgmental moral witness, ideas and information offered without investment in their immediate payoff. And the peace movement's failures and moments of self-sabotage—also amply documented here, as in the inability of the "angry peace people" to communicate with

John Graham—have often been tied to lack of will or skill in the writing of love letters.

The 1980s have illustrated on a grand scale the bankruptcy of "us-versus-them"—not only internationally, but in domestic politics as well. The nuclear disarmament movement, relying heavily on a Reagan-bashing strategy, may have contributed to consciousness raising and debate, but failed in every case to stop particular weapons systems from being developed or deployed. The New Right and Moral Majority, which marched onto the political scene with such optimism and epitomize this polarizing tendency, are in disarray. Both movements operated by standard political wisdom: accenting divisions between their followers and the perceived mainstream, simplifying the issues, blaming each other and sometimes the current administration for the world's problems, and defining themselves substantially in terms of what they were against.

The grassroots peace initiatives which have influenced the cold warriors in these pages—and show promise in reaching others like them—have emerged from a different vision. Instead of trying to mobilize only "our side," they attempt to satisfy both the desire for social justice and the need for security. Rather than seeking to simplify the issues for quick, dramatic political mobilizations, the post-Vietnam peace movement—at least at its best—has acknowledged and dealt with complexity, even when it has meant raising more questions than it could immediately answer.

It has also worked on being a movement that serves and empowers more than the small percentage of the public which finds political participation easy. In *Habits of the Heart,* a study of individualism and commitment in the United States, a team of sociologists led by Robert Bellah ask the fundamental questions, "What motivates people to play more than a minimal role in public life? What do we mean by citizenship?"[7] They find that there are two working definitions of "politics" that make the term come alive and inspire wide participation. One is local, "a matter of making operative the moral consensus of the community . . . one of the central meanings of the word 'democratic' in America." The other is "the high affairs of national life which transcend particular interests." Both of these contrast with the "politics" that deadens the imagination and feeds cynicism: that of the party, the machine, and the special interest. The peace movement, despite attempts to label it a special interest, has made headway in influencing public sentiment because it has defined issues in terms of the well-being of our communities, the vitality of our political culture, the credibility of our nation, and the relationship of these to the policies we pursue abroad.

The peace movement's achievement in bringing politics home to people is due to more than hard work. One contribution has been the incorporation of nonviolence theory, and continued efforts to understand more deeply what it means in the US context, because it engages the issues emotionally and not just cerebrally. A second contribution has been the unprecedented rise in citizen diplomacy, whether to the Soviet Union or Central America. This makes possible grassroots education with a new sophistication and depth, creates people-to-people links and alternative institutions, and affects relationships between countries directly, in ways governements have little choice but to acknowledge.

A third contribution has been the growing psychological sophistication, and particularly use of the insights of the human potential movement, in activist work. Resisting the norms of one's peer group and working for social change requires great inner resources: independent judgment, the ability to think on one's feet, strong vision, physical and emotional stamina. As Carl Rogers wrote in 1972,

> Politically, then, if we are in search of a trustworthy base to operate from, our major aim would be to discover and possibly to increase the number of individuals who are coming closer to being whole persons—who are moving toward a knowledge of, and harmony with, their innermost experience, and who sense, with an equal lack of defensiveness, all the data from the persons and objects in their external environment. These persons would constitute an increasing flow of wisdom in action . . . They might become the vitalizing stream of a constructive future.[8]

This provides tools for understanding organizational development, communication skills, conflict resolution, and burnout prevention. The insights of the human potential movement do more than help activists and potential activists to cultivate their inner resources. They also transform the relationships underlying their work from imbalanced, potentially manipulative, or at least mistrustful ones into reciprocal, respectful ones in which the activist's role is not to propagandize but to encourage questioning and growth. This, in turn, creates the possibility for communication between the movement and the many people who have a healthy distaste for ideological extremes.

The movement against military intervention in Central America illustrates what is possible, and how difficult the possible can be. Since the downfall of the Somoza dynasty in Nicaragua and the outbreak of El Salvador's civil war, public pressure has mounted on Washington to stop favoring military solutions and to deal with the region's revolutionary movements in their historical contexts rather than as de facto threats. Nicaragua's state of emergency from 1982 to 1987, the Miskito Indian question, and the FMLN's tactics of sabotage and conscription in El Salvador have forced conscientious activists to deal with complexity, challenge their own ideological rigidity, and understand the issues in their historical contexts, much as they would have the government do. The very accessibility of Central America has forced and helped peace activists to grow up politically. Tens of thousands of US citizens have visited the region. They have come home to their communities and talked with adversaries, refining their truths and dealing, however hesitantly, with the errors committed by the side they have chosen to support.

At the same time, there has been an honest groping on the left for principled ways of dealing with the Soviet Union's transgressions as well as its newly discovered humanity. One illustration of this is an article in *Sojourners* magazine, often an opinion leader in the Christian peace movement.

> If we want to end the Cold War, we should recognize that there must be changes in the economic status quo and political balance of power within both the Soviet Union and the United States . . . One way for the American peace movement to do that is to take every opportunity, including official contacts where they exist, to publicize and support the struggles of those in the East who are our allies in the struggle against both oppression and war. We can also avoid the asymmetrical alliances that lend an unearned legitimacy to undemocratic Soviet institutions.[9]

A great deal has been written on the potential of a marriage between 1960s activism and 1970s personal development. *Utne Reader,* a quarterly digest of progressive media, devoted an entire issue in 1987 to the theme, "New Left Meets New Age."[10] While this gives rise to some amusing images—troops of demonstrators eating tofu ice cream and listening to meditation tapes on headsets—it also suggests a necessary synthesis of the visionary and the pragmatic among critics of the cold war paradigm. As this process continues, it brings enormous new potential for mainstream Americans to become effective peace activists in their own communities, and creative new ways to do so. Conventional activities within the movement—putting out newsletters, visiting legislators, organizing street demonstrations— have been supplemented by a range of new efforts which articulate a positive vision as well as oppose abuses. They include a growing citizen diplomacy movement which uses both informal delegations and formal "sister city" agreements to create people-to-people relationships outside established channels, campaigns to raise material aid—from artificial limbs to school texts—for victims of war, volunteer watchdog groups which plant themselves in the war zones of Central America and accompany refugees seeking to return to their contested lands, the movement to provide sanctuary and legal aid to refugees in the United States and to help them tell their stories, and exposure tours to Central America, the Caribbean, and the Soviet Union, where US visitors in

1988 were expected to total over eighty thousand. And travel is only one of many organized opportunities for dialogue and exploration across once-forbidden boundaries, both international and psychological. Others are the "Congressbridge," a series of cable TV meetings between the US Congress and the Soviet Politburo; the Nuclear Dialogue Project, a network of citizen groups developing personal relationships with decision makers for mutual understanding; Search for Common Ground, Project Victory, and other training projects in mediation and conflict resolution skills; Interhelp, a network of psychologically oriented peace activists who use counseling methods, spirituality, and even humor to help people overcome their paralysis about the global situation; the Citizens Network, a grassroots campaign helping people think about the arms race as a human problem rather than a technological one; and Peacework Alternatives, a Catholic network devoted to providing resources and counseling on the ethical struggles of weapons workers themselves. These are powerful because they do not deal in neatly packaged answers but in helping people live out the questions. They encourage the risk taking that is necessary for real transformation.

The vast majority of these projects were created not by professional activists or well-funded organizations, but by people who until recently did not see themselves as political—who needed to redefine the term for themselves and to think long and hard about how to integrate such work into already full lives. They came to recognize that while activism may be a short-term drain, it is a long-term gain in self-esteem, skills, and fulfillment.

Robert Jay Lifton, one of the earliest observers of "psychic numbing," writes,

> Something in terms of feeling is happening that's important—after the decades of numbing that followed the Second World War, the numbing is beginning to break down . . . It's a breakdown of the kind of collective arrangement, collusion, and "not-feeling"— especially not feeling what happens at the other end of the weapon, and especially what might happen to us. People are afraid. When I talk to audiences now, kids at colleges are frightened, sometimes at secondary schools, and ordinary audiences. The polls show that most Americans fear and even expect a nuclear war in the not too distant future. That's new. There's a movement now toward awareness or a shift in consciousness, which is quite hopeful.[11]

To observe that "people are not numb" does not automatically imply that they are entering the peace movement in droves or engaging in a mass exodus from weapons work. Some people are newly empowered, but others are newly overwhelmed by the awareness of a level of danger which is no longer deniable. These efforts to serve as midwives for a fundamental shift in consciousness and to aid in the cultivation of resources for dealing with despair are crucial ingredients in whatever positive future we eventually create.

Taken out of context, such emphasis on collective angst might seem a bit morbid. But these approaches to peace work do not invent a threat; they remind us of those which already exist. They reflect a deep confidence that people, once awakened and drawn out of their isolation, will reclaim their inner power and will know what to do with it. They seek to bring about positive change not by convincing or coercing but by helping more people to look around themselves and to make peace on a deeper level with their situations. They are based on building consensus and individual transformation, not as an escape from practical politics but as the basis for it. Their political savvy comes from an underlying vision informed by the psychological and spiritual insight that human beings, even in the most stressful situations, have a built-in actualizing tendency, a will to survive and grow.

We are not numb anymore. Thanks to the last few years of progress in genuine consciousness raising, the peace movement may now be capable of leaps in power and credibility which had been previously impossible. Even the failures of grassroots activism in the early 1980s, such as the derailing of the nuclear freeze movement, might better be looked at as premature but necessary efforts. The groundwork has been laid by more than a decade's education in the issues, the growth of conflict resolution skills, the development of strategy, and the time for personal healing. The signs that this work has begun to bear fruit are in emerging activism within a number of groups not usually known for opposing military policies in peacetime.

Probably the largest of these groups, veterans have always been a good deal more active in community leadership and politics than the general population. In his 1944 study, *The Veteran Comes Home,* Willard Waller noted, "Many times has their blind fury changed the course of history."[12] Of course, much veteran activism has centered on direct concerns such as benefits and on military policy in general. In the past, apart from the extreme circumstance of mass carnage and social deterioration during the Vietnam era, veterans have been a reliable force in support of military campaigns. But since Vietnam, that loyalty is not so easily won.

A distinct veterans peace movement is emerging. It brings together veterans of "the good war" and "the bad war" and the period in between, who talk to each other about how wars get started and how peace opportunities are missed. It is distinguished by its timing: too long after the Vietnam War to be simply reactive to it, but soon enough to take into account the lessons of Vietnam veterans—from Agent Orange and post-traumatic stress to the politics of the Veterans Administration—and to help a forgetful public remember.

This is not to say that all veterans oppose intervention or nuclear deterrence or, for that matter, repudiate the Vietnam War. A telling sign that old battle lines still exist is the controversy over the filming of Jane Fonda's *Union Street,* which the actress tried to bring to Holyoke, Massachusetts in early 1988. One James H. Denver, a former state commander of the American Legion, led a rebellion against the presence of "Hanoi Jane," claiming that Fonda's visit to North Vietnam in 1972 condemned her to "live in the history of the country alongside two other charmers, Axis Sally and Tokyo Rose, who were tried and imprisoned for their acts."[13]

But in standing up to the Pentagon on its present policies, few groups have more personal motivation, earned credibility, or factual ammunition from their own experience than veterans. Veterans are in a unique position to counter the glamorization of war with reminders of its tedium and ugliness. They know better than the average reporter how to read between the lines of a Pentagon press release, or what really happens when legislators come to a war zone for a briefing. As they travel the college-and-church-basement speaking circuit, activist veterans are a long-overdue counterpoint to Rambo, role models whose appeal is based on real-life stories rather than myth. They talk about ways their efforts were used to promote ends they would never have chosen. They remind listeners how oversimplified a dispute can get when both sides are armed. They invite an open-minded exploration of the roots of organized violence through the best available entry point, their own lives.

This rootedness in personal experience—the understanding that "the personal is political"—is a common ingredient in powerful social movements. It was the explicit slogan of the current wave of feminism, as well as a spark igniting organized labor, environmentalism, and the struggle for civil rights. And in fact, with its passion, rootedness in individual experience, and relationship between political activism and personal healing, this young veterans movement displays the vigor, growth potential, bonding, and life-changing ability of the women's movement of two decades ago.

On the surface this parallel is puzzling, since the women's movement stemmed from a drive for personal liberation, while the veterans peace movement seems to be an ethical response on the part of people who have nothing concrete to gain by taking a stand. But as they continue to meet in "rap groups"—which often parallel feminist consciousness-raising groups—many veterans find that they still have not finished addressing the emotional fallout from their combat experience. Years later, it is not unusual for Vietnam veterans to admit that they identify with victims of rape. The fifty thousand who have committed suicide since the end of the Vietnam War and the countless others who wrestle with substance abuse or populate the prison system are eloquently documented in Arthur Egendorf's *Healing from the War* and Joe Klein's *Payback*.

Finally though, the emergence of a veterans peace movement signals a shift in the balance because it shows that veterans see themselves less as victims and more as an active force in shaping their future. Just as Lifton observed two decades ago in *Home from the War,* many veterans are concluding that the only way to truly pull themselves together psychologically and spiritually is to tell their stories, make peace with their histories, and use their mounting influence against a repetition of the mistakes they saw in their wars. For veterans who never stopped believing in the justice of the US role in Vietnam, healing may take the form of searching for buddies they believe are missing in action. For veterans who see that war as an error if not a travesty, the path to healing is through trying to prevent the repetition of that mistake.

Representing complementary outlooks in this many-faceted movement are two veterans we have seen before: Jerry Genesio and Charlie Liteky. Genesio is a mainstream, working-class activist who has gone to great lengths to make Veterans for Peace accessible to vets who never considered themselves part of a peace group. He has built a traditionally structured organization, run on parliamentary procedure and meat-and-potatoes banquets, honoring the symbols and images and folklore of every war in living memory even as it criticizes official policies. VFP's leadership tirelessly demystifies the issues, cheers on local chapters, and makes activist work as easy as it can ever be.

Liteky, Brian Willson, and kindred spirits represent an opposite extreme, although their roots are in the same working-class values. They galvanize small numbers who are willing if not driven to face greater physical risks and the disruption of their lives in order to sound an alarm that rings strident with their own despair. Because of their war experiences or particular life histories, they offer themselves as a bridge between the US public, which has the luxury of keeping its contact with Central America indirect, and the victims of war who have no such luxury.

In their unique form of nonviolent hardball, veterans who engage in long fasts and high-risk civil disobediences have forced an essential debate—in the peace movement as well as in the military, foreign policy, and law enforcement circles—about nonviolence in the US context, what forms are effective, and what cultural barriers get in the way. They compel those who are used to regarding nonviolence as the prayerful detachment of a St. Francis to acknowledge its active nature, its need for strategic thinking, and the real risks it involves. And among many who share their passion but are troubled by their tactics, they raise the question, "How shall we confront the entrenched power structures in this country in ways that are effective but not self-punishing?"

But these veterans are not only—and maybe not primarily—symbols of sacrifice. The supreme illustration of this point is Willson who, propped up by two canes and standing on his artificial legs on the Capitol steps during a 1988 fast against contra aid, broke into a spontaneous jig and recited Emma Goldman's "If I can't dance in it, it's not my revolution."[14] More difficult than their risk taking is the challenge they present as role models of ongoing commitment, not just in response to crises. They are full-time, hard-working, self-employed activists. They have found alternative sources of material as well as emotional support, from speech honoraria to spouses' paychecks. They have burned the bridges from their earlier lives and taken up a share of the burden as they see it. This, more than any physical act of daring, is their essential challenge.

Among activist veterans regardless of their public impact, there is a culture of a renaissance. Permeating the writings and speeches of this movement are images of a transformed warrior—the one who keeps, even deepens, the traits of valor, discipline, service, and vision, but carries them to a deeper level in the service of nonviolence instead of violence, and universal rather than parochial interests. Floating on seemingly no resources yet magically supported, differing wildly as to political strategy yet somehow working together, these veterans inspire others in spite of—or because of—their sometimes ragged images, urgent language, and "prophetic disequilibrium." At the opposite end of the spectrum of emotional energy in these struggles are many of the scientists who have taken stands against weapons development and the militarization of their profession. Their stories convey the same sense of personal reawakening, and in their words the same moral struggle is heard. But there is, for the most part, an absence of hope that their stands will be more than isolated witnesses. Even when a respectable number of scientists become fired up, as they have over SDI, the flame seems less able to spread than it does among veterans. There are obvious reasons for this in the self-reinforcing nature of the cultures of industry and academia. It is more risky and emotionally charged to try to counter the policies of institutions on which one still relies for income and self-definition. Besides, most weapons researchers do not see the fruits of their labors tested under realistic conditions, unlike veterans whose military experience seems to provide a natural aversion therapy.

Members of the scientific community hold some of the most concentrated power to stop the arms race and to challenge the militarization of the economy by "just saying no" or by bringing their considerable influence to bear on public policy and the directions taken by industry. Scientists were a major force in ending atmospheric nuclear testing in the 1960s and in creating momentum for the antiballistic missile treaty of 1972. And through the pledge to decline research money and voluminous public testimony, they have been a major force in raising such critical questions about the logic of SDI that, by 1986, former Undersecretary of Defense Richard Perle was forced to admit the program was "in real trouble."[15]

The SDI debate arguably polarized science more than any military development since the bomb itself. By 1986, a staggering majority of researchers were convinced that the program would not provide an effective defense—98 percent of National Academy of Science members in the most relevant fields. The really bitter aspect of the debate has been about not the program's viability but the ethics of accepting funding given the doubts.

While SDI has forced debate among scientists, in the process it has allowed other, formerly controversial scientific developments—from new generations of nuclear weapons to binary nerve gas—to be tacitly redefined as "conventional," almost benign. A cynic could suggest that the flap over SDI, rather than being based on conscience, has grown from concern that excessive greed would cause the collapse of an otherwise comfortable relationship with the Pentagon. Indeed, a resolution before the 1986 annual board meeting of the American Association for the Advancement of Science, modestly calling for greater effort to seek out nonmilitary funding sources, was rejected by almost two to one.[16]

Yet the long silence about ethics in the scientific profession shows signs of breaking. The epic disasters of the 1980s—Challenger, Bhopal, Chernobyl—must play some role. "Alarmed by the quickening pace of the arms race, and particularly by President Reagan's Strategic Defense Initiative, scientists, engineers, and others in defense-related work are wrestling as perhaps never before with the ethical implications of what they do," the *Wall Street Journal* said in 1986. And much of that wrestling seems to be deepening, not resolving, the doubts of these professionals. A survey by the Institute of Electrical and Electronics Engineers found that, for over one third of its ten thousand members, a major factor in considering job changes was the availability of nonmilitary work.[17]

But the availability of nonmilitary work—to say nothing of nonmilitary work offering comparable pay and stimulation—is limited in the US economy, and especially at the cutting edges of science, where the Department of Defense has for the last decade been the primary funding source. The flow of funds from the Pentagon to academic institutions between 1960 and 1986 totalled $20 billion in constant 1987 dollars.[18] The Department of Energy (DOE), the National Aeronautics and Space Administration, and the National Science Foundation have also gone into the weapons business on a massive scale in the 1980s, with DOE's 1988 budget request for weapons programs standing at $8.1 billion, or 65 percent of the department's spending.[19] Noting the sharp shift toward military applications in the Reagan administration's space policy, giving the Defense Department priority access to the space shuttle, the *Wall Street Journal* notes that "military men . . . are increasingly calling the shots in the U.S. space program."[20]

Among researchers and other professionals who become concerned about the impact of their work, there is a genuine dilemma: Can more good be done by staying inside and using the resources of one's position to influence policy, or by making a public break? Early in his career, Albert Einstein argued vehemently that scientists should isolate themselves from weapons-related work. Later he changed and held that if everyone with ethical sensitivity were to pull out of the military research sector, it would go forward with no internal voices of restraint at all.

That dilemma is just as vexing today for scientists, as well as soldiers, tradespeople, diplomats, or intelligence professionals. Those who make a public break with their institutions gain credibility in their ethical stands and the freedom to express them. A full break is also a clear if expensive way to be noticed by former colleagues and shatter the silence surrounding the issues. Such a stance is a singularly dramatic statement against business as usual and an implicit warning that the established channels of protest are inadequate.

Staying inside means hanging on to those channels, struggling to believe in them and the individuals who personify them, searching for creative ways to make them work. Staying inside means income and the access to current technical developments which a scientist's sense of credibility and legitimacy demands. The seductiveness of inside power is well known, as is the temptation to rationalize one's presence as making a difference. But examples exist of researchers who are truly having an impact on the policy debate from within.

Lawrence Livermore Lab, for example, has been the scene of several long and dramatic battles over scientists turned dissidents. One revolves around Dr. Roy Woodruff, the prestigious director of the weapons program and a chief designer of the neutron bomb, who had become increasingly vocal in his criticism of SDI. After a history of behind-the-scenes protest, Woodruff went public in 1987 with the claim that Edward Teller had given misleading technical information to the Reagan administration about essential aspects of the X-ray laser, a cornerstone of the SDI concept. Soon afterward, Woodruff was "reassigned" to an entry-level analyst's position in a windowless cubicle so isolated that his colleagues dubbed it "Gorky West." But he was finally reassigned—significantly, right after the signing of the INF treaty—to the post of director of verification, responsible not for developing weapons but for helping treaties to work.[21]

Another, more sustained controversy at Livermore surrounds Hugh DeWitt, head of a group which works in the theoretical area of strongly coupled plasma physics. DeWitt's public visibility began after his career as a physicist at Livermore had been established for twenty-one years. The occasion was the 1979 effort by the government to suppress the publication of Howard Morland's article on the H-bomb secret by *The Progressive,* which was an effort to challenge the cult of secrecy surrounding nuclear weapons. DeWitt wrote the key affidavit demonstrating that Morland's material came from unclassified sources, including an encyclopedia article written by Edward Teller. The lab responded to DeWitt with a letter of reprimand—the first step in firing—followed by formal charges of mishandling classified information, which were only dropped after a large-scale public outcry.[22]

Sobered but not silenced, DeWitt decided at that point to keep the highest possible profile. His motives ranged from professional self-preservation and anger at his treatment to mounting concern about new arms developments. Since then, he has been a strong advocate of a comprehensive test ban and a reliable voice of testimony against lab management in congressional debates over the necessity of new weapons systems. While Livermore's directors have been strong opponents of a nuclear test ban treaty, DeWitt's has been among the most persuasive public voices arguing on technical grounds that the US nuclear arsenal can be well maintained without any further testing.

Starting in late 1987, DeWitt began to worry again about job security when he received a sharply lowered performance review with the warning that he had not been doing enough "programmatic" or weapons-related work. And with scientists less prominent than Woodruff and DeWitt, the Department of Defense and its supporters have shown no lack of creativity in keeping dissidents within bounds. In 1986, Representative Dan Burton of Indiana proposed legislation that would have defunded entire universities where faculty members refused to do SDI research. In the newsletter of Accuracy in Academia, a right-wing watchdog organization, Burton explained, "If they're not willing to do their part to help defend America, I don't see why they should receive our tax money." Undersecretary of Defense Donald Hicks, an administrator of Pentagon research contracts, said in 1986 that if scientists "want to get out and use their roles as professors to make statements, that's fine, it's a free country . . . [but] I'm also free not to give the money."[23]

Many creative efforts have been made by researchers to steer a middle ground between lockstep loyalty and a complete break with their institutions. Growing numbers of scientists and engineers in national labs and weapons industries sign monthly donation checks to their local peace groups. Student groups have organized, as part of graduation ceremonies, an optional pledge to think seriously about the ethical ramifications of any job offer. Some university faculty have refused to accept military funding, while others have formed committees to study the military influence on their campuses and seek out alternative sources of funding, with varying degrees of success. Still others, frustrated by their colleagues' reluctance to discuss the military dependence of their research, have succeeded in passing campus-wide bans on accepting funds for such controversial programs as SDI, chemical weapons, and genetic engineering. Though none of these have survived a vote of university trustees, the threat was sufficient that Nobel laureate David Baltimore devoted his keynote address at the 1988 conference of the American Association for the Advancement of Science to an impassioned plea against them.

But protest on a significant scale among scientists will not take place without a more powerful stimulus; every reminder of the human costs of ethical passivity has helped. Even more powerful—and parallel to the healing process experienced by veterans through peace activism—would be a rediscovery of the human values which science at its best serves. A large-scale movement of scientists toward reformulating their profession's priorities will depend on a similarly large-scale movement toward economic—and academic—conversion. This in turn requires a strong positive vision of a demilitarized science.

Such a vision will give scientists the strength to say no to weapons work and the impetus to find or create other sources of funding. A vision of the power of science in the service of humanity might encompass simple technology for developing countries, low-pollution transportation, safe energy sources, nonpoisonous pest control, reversal of acid rain, restoration of rain forests, cure and prevention of the epidemics that ravage us. The power of that vision as an alternative to weapons work is illustrated by the story of a foremost weapons pioneer of an earlier era, Ted Taylor, the Los Alamos scientist chiefly responsible for miniaturizing nuclear weapons. Taylor left the weapons lab to work on civilian nuclear power and left that to develop solar energy when he concluded that nuclear power and weapons were inevitably connected. He describes his former self as "an addict" to the lure of cutting-edge physics. Today, though he could retire comfortably, Taylor works nonstop in research areas like water purification and creation of hydrogen fuel from water by solar-powered electrolysis. "I have become as fascinated with this work as with anything I've ever done, including nuclear weapons," he maintains. "Working on these technologies is exciting to just about anybody because they combine high tech and low tech, they create something new and different, and they produce things that people really want."

The ability to appreciate many of these civilian applications, and the hybrids of "high" and "low" technology they involve, seesm to require a qualitatively different imagination than the one that motivates many researchers on weapons. It is holistic, not fragmented. It may be related to what Lifton calls the "apocalyptic imagination," the imagination without limits, the imagination that cannot separate action from consequence or parts from wholes, the imagination that can envision both the dimensions of possible doom and the aliveness of an equally possible healed world.

Because of their experience, credibility, inside knowledge, and strategic positions, the present and former employees of the military-industrial-intelligence complex are destined to influence the national security debate far out of proportion to their numbers. The elite among them—the scientists and officers and diplomats and members of the intelligence community—have the expertise and visibility to help set the terms of debate. Others, and particularly the laborers who assemble the submarines and missiles, are most significant as barometers of social change. They are likely to vote for the continued funding of their employers until the question of economic conversion is seriously dealt with—as some state governments are beginning to do—and until the other institutions which play a role in their lives, such as churches and unions, find ways to translate rhetoric into the concrete support these populations need.

In the meantime, these stories offer examples of a resistance which grows not from any enjoyment of confrontation or from lack of anything better to do, but from a sense of responsibility and commitment to the truth even at its most inconvenient. These are citizens who came to challenge the prevailing wisdom out of the same love of country and ethic of service that drew them into their initial careers. Given the drama of their experiences, it is tempting to suggest that only that profound a love could keep them on track and effective through so much. For all that they have gone through, they are still not nihilists. They model on an individual level many of the values we would benefit from cultivating as a nation.

To address the problems at their core requires admitting how entrenched they are, and how entrenched the taboos are against the public's conceiving them as "our business." This is the first of many taboos which must be broken. We must find some language for talking about group and class interests, wealth and human needs, without getting stuck in the dogma of either Marxism or capitalism. We must reaffirm the value of human labor as more than a means to a paycheck. We must deal with revolutions and revolutionary societies in their full complexity, instead of presupposing that anything which unsettles the status quo should be opposed. We must provide for our own security more creatively than by assuming that more arms or more activity mean more security. We must find ways to talk about right and wrong without descending into self-righteousness. In all these efforts, we will try and fail and try again. But the commitment to try may be the spark of success, because it can call forth a new and transforming quality: the kind of deep, thoughtful, ongoing capacity for self-criticism that is a foundation of real self-love.

Introduction

1. Jessie Wallace Hughan's full statement is, "A war is not like an earthquake or a tornado—it is an act of men and women. Wars will cease when men refuse to fight and women refuse to approve. Do not allow people to lead you to think for a moment that war is a necessary institution." *There Is No Way to Peace, Peace Is the Way: The 1983 War Resisters League Calendar* (New York: War Resisters League, 1982).

2. Jules Archer, *The Plot to Seize the White House* (New York: Hawthorne Books, 1973), pp. 118–119.

3. Smedley D. Butler, quoted in *Point*, newsletter of the Smedley Butler Brigade (Boston).

4. Clyde H. Farnsworth, "Survey of Whistle Blowers Finds Retaliation But Few Regrets," *New York Times*, 21 February 1987. The practice of whistleblowing has been extensively praised, condemned, analyzed and strategized since the early 1970s. See Charles Peters and Taylor Branch, *Blowing the Whistle: Dissent in the Public Interest* (New York: Praeger, 1972) and William McGowan, "The Whistleblowing Game: Truth and Consequences," *New Age Journal*, September 1984, p. 37.

5. Gelya Frank, "Becoming the Other," *Biography* 8, no. 3, Summer 1985.

6. Robert Jay Lifton, "The Postwar War," in *The Future of Immortality* (New York: Basic Books, 1987), p. 64.

7. *Carry It On*, documentary of Harris's draft resistance, trial, and three-year jail term during the Vietnam War. New Film Company and Folklore Productions. Distributed by Vanguard Recording Society, New York.

8. Paul Loeb, *Hope in Hard Times: The Peace Movement in the Reagan Era* (Lexington, MA: Lexington Books, 1986), p. 303.

The Blood of the Poor: Jerry Genesio

1. Jerry Genesio, "The Sweden Heritage," *BitterSweet*, February 1978, p. 18.

2. Jerry Genesio, "A Bad Drop," *Yankee*, April 1979, p. 82.

3. Eduardo Crawley, *Nicaragua in Perspective* (New York: St. Martin's Press, 1984), p. 138.

4. Piet J. Hagen, *Blood: Gift or Merchandise? Toward an International Blood Policy* (New York: Liss, 1982), pp. 168–170.

5. Paul Kulak (producer), "Soldiers of Peace," (Sepulveda, CA: Ashley Productions, 1988). Video.

The Tin Man: Charlie Liteky

1. Paul Hendrickson, "Brothers: Charlie and Pat," in *Seminary: A Search* (New York: Summit Books, 1983), pp. 181–217.

2. Paul Kulak (producer), "Soldiers of Peace," (Sepulveda, CA: Ashley Productions, 1988). Video.
3. *Congressional Record*, 7 May 1970, p. 14,614.
4. For additional evidence see Alexander Cockburn, "Torture: Are U.S. Servicemen Involved?" *The Nation*, 21 February 1987, p. 206.
5. Stanley Keleman, *The Human Ground: Sexuality, Self and Survival* (Palo Alto: Science and Behavior Books, 1975), p. 35.
6. Paul Hendrickson, "The Calling of Charlie Liteky," *Washington Post*, 3 October 1986, p. D1.
7. *Above and Beyond: A History of the Congressional Medal of Honor* (New York: Time-Life Books, 1985).

The White Man's Burden: Ralph McGehee

1. Ralph McGehee, *Deadly Deceits: My Twenty-Five Years in the CIA* (New York: Sheridan Square, 1983), p. 192.
2. McGehee, p. 3.
3. McGehee, p. 82.
4. McGehee, p. 109.
5. McGehee, p. 114.
6. Victor Marchetti and John D. Marks, *The CIA and the Cult of Intelligence* (New York: Dell, 1975).
7. See *The Pentagon Papers* (New York: Quadrangle Books, 1971).
8. William Colby's version of events is quite different. In his memoir, *Honorable Men* (New York: Simon & Schuster, 1978), he expresses high concern for the quality of intelligence reporting throughout the Far East division and takes credit for implementing a quality control system for reports. He downplays Thailand as an arena of struggle, but alludes to it as one of the "spluttering insurgencies" where the "CIA was able to launch some low-key village-level counterinsurgency programs."

In Vietnam, Colby writes, "the station worked hard to improve intelligence on the enemy in the countryside, giving priority to the Viet Cong political apparatus rather than the communist military units, which the American and Vietnamese army commands concentrated on. We coined the word infrastructure to describe the secret communist political network in South Vietnam and its 'political order of battle'—the provincial committees and subcommittees, the organizers and activists and the local guerilla and terrorist squads who acted as the 'enforcers' of communist authority in the local communities, executing village chiefs, conscripting young men for training and assignment to main force units, mining roads, and dropping grenades in the morning markets to demonstrate their power and the inability of the government to protect the people. With this phrase to identify its target, the station began to work to get the various American and Vietnamese intelligence agencies, civilian and military, to cooperate and exchange information about the 'command and control structure' of the people's war enemy.

"CIA sponsored and built a national interrogation center in Saigon under the auspices of the Vietnamese Central Intelligence Organization to conduct proper and professional interrogations of communist captives and defectors, and trained Vietnamese in the right techniques to use in it. This training certainly did not include torture, which is morally impermissible and produces bad intelligence . . . "

Colby portrays the agency as hamstrung by many constraints but still the most realistic purveyor of intelligence and analysis on the scene, an assessment which does not necessarily contradict McGehee's. He writes, "the good sense of the CIA officers in Vietnam, their greater familiarity with the country and its people, because of their longer tours of duty there, and their professional tendency to penetrate behind the facades of the situations they faced, all made them valuable contributors in Country team discussions, and they provided a useful counterpoint to the optimism of the proponents of the panacea programs. And the Agency's analysts in Washington served in a similar way, their estimates on events in Vietnam being by far the most realistic, as shown in the Pentagon Papers, although their conclusions were in great part neither welcomed nor adopted by the policymakers" (pp. 191–193).

9. McGehee, p. 114.

10. Transcript. Available from CIA on Trial Project, PO Box 43, Amherst, MA 01004.

In Some Other World: David MacMichael

1. Philip Taubman, "In from the Cold and Hot for Truth," *New York Times*, 11 June 1984.

2. "Challenging the CIA's Evidence," *Time*, 25 June 1984, p. 19.

3. Taubman.

4. For a concise summary of US policy decisions shaping the Nicaraguan counterrevolution, see Peter Dale Scott, Jonathan Marshall, and Jane Hunter, *The Iran-Contra Connection: Secret Teams & Covert Operations in the Reagan Era* (Boston: South End Press, 1987). For a detailed investigation of the La Penca bombing and contra-drug connections, see Leslie Cockburn, *Out of Control* (New York: Atlantic Monthly Press, 1987).

5. "Calling the Bluff," *Sojourners*, August 1984, p. 19.

6. Taubman.

7. "World Court Says U.S. Violated International Law by Aiding Contras," *Washington Post*, 28 June 1986, p. A1. "The Court rejected U.S. arguments that there was substantial proof of Nicaraguan arms smuggling to El Salvador to indicate that Nicaragua had a major role in El Salvador's guerrilla war." In votes of 12–3 on nine points and 14–1 on the remaining four, the judges found the United States at fault for "training, arming, equipping, financing and supplying the contra forces," the mining of three harbors, a series of armed attacks on these harbors and adjacent oil storage facilities, and ongoing intelligence overflights of Nicaraguan airspace.

For two sides of the international law questions about Court jurisdiction, see Moore, "The Secret War in Central America and the Future of World Order," *American Journal of International Law* 80, no. 43 (1986), and James P. Rowles, " 'Secret Wars,' Self-Defense and the Charter—A Reply to Professor Moore," *American Journal of International Law* 80, no. 44 (1986).

8. Letters to the editor, *New York Times*, 2 July 1986 and 23 August 1986.

9. Stephen Kinzer, "Sandinista Asserts War Has Taken 12,000 Lives," *New York Times*, 18 July 1985.

10. David C. MacMichael, "Democrats Can Seize Central America Issue," *New York Times*, 17 July 1984.

11. "Calling the Bluff," p. 20.

12. Stephen Kinzer, "Aide to Nicaraguan Defense Chief Is Reported to Defect to U.S.," *New York Times*, 3 November 1987, p. 1.

13. In June of 1988 the lawsuit was dismissed by a federal district court for "lack of evidence" connecting the La Penca bombing and the secret team. As the Christic Institute vowed to appeal and many defendants threatened to sue for malicious prosecution, the battle showed signs of continuing. Many commentators considered the dismissal an effort to delay any trial until after the 1988 election.

14. James Traub, "The Law and the Prophet," *Mother Jones*, February/March 1988, p. 21.

A Soldier of Fortune: John Graham

1. Joseph P. Blank, "The Last Cruise of the Prinsendam," *Reader's Digest*, November 1983, pp. 238–264.

Solving Puzzles in the Dark: Thomas Grissom

1. Robert Jungk, *Brighter Than a Thousand Suns* (New York: Harcourt Brace Jovanovich, 1985).

2. Debra Rosenthal, "Weapons Work: A Study of the Moral Reasoning of Scientists and Technicians in America's Nuclear Weapons Design Facilities," unpublished manuscript, 1987.

3. Joanna Macy, *Despair and Personal Power in the Nuclear Age* (Philadelphia: New Society, 1983), p. 13.

4. Thomas Grissom, *One Spring More* (Francestown, NH: Golden Quill Press, 1986), p. 61.

5. Thomas Grissom, *Other Truths* (Francestown, NH: Golden Quill Press, 1984), p. 97.

6. *Other Truths*, p. 27.

7. Gordon McClure, "An Open Letter to Sandia," *Coatimundi*, Fall 1986.
8. *Other Truths*, p. 45.
9. Edward Abbey, *Desert Solitaire* (New York: McGraw-Hill, 1968), p. xiv.
10. "Plutonium Not Needed, Scientist Says," *Seattle Times*, 13 November 1986, p. H12.
11. *One Spring More*, p. 51.

A Dyed-in-the-Wool Democrat: Bill Perry

1. William Broad, *Star Warriors* (New York: Simon & Schuster, 1986), p. 14.
2. The question of the percentage of Livermore's work that is nuclear is intrinsically imprecise, since it requires fixing a constantly shifting line between theoretical physics— much of it broadly applicable—and the projects that in fact stem from it. But the purposeful emphasis on weaponry at Livermore is reflected in Broad's unabashed description of the complex as "Teller's nuclear laboratory" (p. 20). He notes, "In a glossy brochure issued during its silver anniversary, Livermore claimed to have designed nine out of ten of the strategic warheads in the nation's nuclear stockpile" (p. 15).
3. King's writings on the war include "Proposed Vietnam Form Letter" and "The Domestic Impact of the War on America," speech delivered in Chicago on 11 November 1967 (Records of the Southern Christian Leadership Conference, Martin Luther King Center for Nonviolent Social Change, Atlanta, GA).

King's evolving position on Vietnam and on the relationship between warfare and racism are discussed in Stephen B. Oates' biography, *Let the Trumpet Sound* (New York: New American Library, 1982).
4. *The Last Epidemic* is available from Physicians for Social Responsibility, 1701 Q Street NW, Washington, DC 20009.

To Take a Chance: Lou Raymond

1. Reverend Kevin Bean, co-chair of the Connecticut State Senate's Task Force on Manufacturing, interview with author.
2. Lou Buttino, interview with author.
3. General Dynamics 1987 Annual Report (San Diego, CA).
4. Joanne Sheehan, "Opposing Trident," *The Mobilizer*, Spring 1986, p. 15.
5. Robert C. Aldridge, *First Strike!* (Boston: South End Press, 1983), pp. 73–74.
6. Howard Morland, Coalition for a New Foreign and Military Policy, interview with author.
7. Sheehan, p. 15.
8. Karol Wojtyla (Pope John Paul II), "The Armaments Factory Worker," in *Easter Morning and Other Poems* (New York: Random House).
9. Patience Stoddard, "Plowshares into Swords: Thoughts on the Balance Between Prophetic and Pastoral Ministry and the Dilemma of the Defense Worker," doctoral dissertation, Harvard Divinity School, 1986.

The Bigger Fleece: David Parnas

1. U.S. Senate, Committee on Governmental Affairs, Hearings on Department of Defense/ Strategic Defense Initiative Organization Compliance with Federal Advisory Committee Act, 19 April 1988.
2. Anne C. Roark, "Military Influence Stirs Campus Debate: 'Star Wars' Politicizing Science in U.S.," *Los Angeles Times*, 13 April 1987.
3. Two recent studies echo this criticism on technical and strategic grounds. "Star Wars at the Crossroads: The Strategic Defense Initiative After Five Years," a June 1988 staff report prepared for Senators Bennett Johnston of Louisiana, Dale Bumpers of Arkansas, and William Proxmire of Wisconsin, calls the program "a financial and military disaster." A study released by the Office of Technology Assessment, the scientific arm of Congress, emphasizes the ease with which Soviet countermeasures could destroy any system. See "SDI: Technology, Survivability and Software," US Congress, Office of Technology Assessment, 6 June 1988.
4. McGeorge Bundy, George F. Kennan, Robert S. McNamara, and Gerard Smith, "The President's Choice," *Foreign Affairs*, Winter 1984. Reprinted in Don Carlson and Craig Comstock (eds.), *Securing the Planet* (Los Angeles: Tarcher, 1986), pp. 194–209.
5. Robert M. Bowman, "Star Wars: Sure, It Will Work," *Baltimore Sun*, 4 April 1986.

6. Greg Fossedal, "Exploring the High Frontier: New Defense Option Would Stifle Soviets, Help Chances for Peace," *Conservative Digest,* June 1982.

7. For a reader-friendly explanation of Parnas' contribution to software engineering and other computer phenomena, see John Shore's *The Sachertorte Algorithm and Other Antidotes to Computer Anxiety* (New York: Viking, 1985).

8. Shore, p. 218.

9. Richard Lau responds, "I have only vague memories of my conversation with Parnas. I do not believe he has lied about my statements, but I do think he has viewed the entire episode through a funny filter. I believe he expected to come to the Eastport panel and find all kinds of abuses. In terms of the conflict-of-interest question, we naturally wanted people who had experience in SDI work, and in that sense, in seeking people who had experience in relevant areas, you inevitably get people who might compete for a contract, who in that broad sense have a conflict of interest."

10. Danny Cohen and David L. Parnas, "SDI: Two Views of Professional Responsibility," Institute on Global Conflict and Cooperation, Policy Paper No.5, University of California, San Diego. Cohen did not return the author's phone calls.

11. Again, Lau has "no vivid recollection," but does remember a lunch at which Parnas asked, "Suppose we can't do it, will they kill the program?" and to which he responded, in essence, "Of course not, that isn't the way it works."

12. David Parnas, "Software Aspects of Strategic Defense Systems," *American Scientist,* September/October 1985, pp. 432–440.

13. Bertrand Russell (ed.), *Einstein on Peace* (New York: Schocken Books, 1968), p. 193.

The First Resister: Daniel Cobos

1. Seymour Hersh, *The Target Is Destroyed* (New York: Random House, 1986), pp. 8–9. Intelligence expert Jeffrey Richelson also refers to these flights over Nicaragua as routine. In *American Espionage and the Soviet Target* (New York: Morrow, 1987) he writes, "While aerial overflights of Soviet territory have ceased, the United States—and specifically the Strategic Air Command's 9th Strategic Reconnaissance Wing at Beale AFB, California—still does a brisk business in aerial reconnaissance. With U-2's, SR-71's, and RC-135's and other airplanes, the 9th SRW operates what is known as the Peacetime Aerial Reconnaissance Program, or PARPRO for short. Actual tasking is the responsibility of SAC's Strategic Reconnaissance Center at Offutt AFB in Nebraska. PARPRO involves overflights of North Korea, Cuba, Nicaragua, and other 'troublesome' countries in the Middle East and Asia" (p. 205).

2. The Boland amendment of 1984, expanding on the 1982 ban on covert operations "for the purpose of overthrowing Nicaragua's government," explicitly prohibits any administration agency involved in "intelligence activities" from "supporting, directly or indirectly, military or paramilitary operations in Nicaragua by any nation, group, organization or individual."

3. Robert A. Seeley, "Advice for Conscientious Objectors in the Armed Forces," (Philadelphia: Central Committee for Conscientious Objectors, 1984). Pamphlet.

4. Dr. Charles Clements, interview with author.

5. According to Offutt Air Force Base spokesman Lieutenant Colonel Ralph Tosti, no official investigation was ever initiated, although the air force did look into the case informally before deciding a formal investigation was not warranted.

6. Howard Silber, "SAC Man Protests Spying on Nicaragua, Case Pending," *Omaha World-Herald,* 17 June 1987. Silber writes, "The Offutt-based RC-135's frequently fly near areas from which information is sought by the National Security Agency and other U.S. intelligence organizations. Radio messages and other electronic emissions are recorded. Foreign language specialists aboard often provide simultaneous translations of messages for immediate evaluation. Among the members of the Offutt squadron to which Cobos is assigned are Air Force personnel who are fluent in Russian, Spanish, Chinese and other languages."

7. Mira M. Brown, "Letters from Nicaragua," unpublished collection.

Changing Lives

1. Ellen Goodman, *Turning Points* (New York: Fawcett Crest, 1979).
2. Hugh Prather, *Notes on Love and Courage* (Garden City, NY: Doubleday, 1977).
3. Arthur Egendorf, *Healing from the War* (Boston: Shambhala, 1986), p. 89.
4. Robert Jay Lifton, *Home from the War* (New York: Simon & Schuster, 1971).
5. John Newton (1725–1807), composer of "Amazing Grace," had his own religious conversion experience during a storm at sea and turned around from a profitable life as captain of a slave ship to become a Christian missionary and committed abolitionist. See John Pollock, *Amazing Grace: The Dramatic Life Story of John Newton* (New York: Harper & Row).
6. William James, *The Varieties of Religious Experience* (New York: Modern Library, 1929), p. 186.
7. Thomas Kuhn, *The Structure of Scientific Revolutions* (Chicago: University of Chicago Press, 1970).
8. Marilyn Ferguson, *The Aquarian Conspiracy: Personal and Social Transformation in the Eighties* (Los Angeles: Tarcher, 1980), pp. 26–33.
9. Paolo Freire, *Education for Critical Consciousness* (New York: Continuum, 1973).
10. Mark Twain, *Following the Equator* (New York: Greystone Press, 1899).
11. Sissela Bok, *Secrets: On the Ethics of Concealment and Revelation* (New York: Pantheon, 1982), p. 25.
12. Edward Weisband and Thomas M. Franck, *Resignation in Protest* (New York: Viking, 1975), pp. 3–4.
13. Cynthia Enlow, *Does Khaki Become You?* (Boston: South End Press, 1982).
14. Michael May, "Demonstrations: A Moral Equivalent of War," *Christian Science Monitor*, 29 December 1986.
15. Robert Kegan, *The Evolving Self* (Cambridge: Harvard University Press, 1982).
16. Abraham Maslow, *Toward a Psychology of Being* (Princeton: Van Nostrand, 1968), p. 16.
17. Roger Walsh, *Staying Alive: The Psychology of Human Survival* (Boston: New Science Library, 1984), p. 41.
18. Jean Piaget, *The Moral Judgment of the Child* (New York: Free Press, 1965), p. 290.
19. Weisband and Franck.
20. James Baldwin, *The Fire Next Time* (New York: Dell, 1968), p. 18.
21. Robert Jay Lifton, *The Nazi Doctors* (New York: Basic Books, 1986).
22. Mary Watkins, "In Dreams Begin Responsibilities: Moral Imagination and Peace Action," in Valerie Andrews, Robert Barnak, and Karen Walter Goodwin (eds.), *Facing Apocalypse* (Dallas, TX: Spring, 1987), pp. 70–95.
23. Robert Jay Lifton, *The Future of Immortality* (New York: Basic Books, 1987), p. 259.
24. Joanna Macy, *Despair and Personal Power in the Nuclear Age* (Philadelphia: New Society, 1983).
25. Macy uses the terms "power-with" versus "power-over." Starhawk, in *Dreaming the Dark* (Boston: Beacon Press, 1982), prefers "power-from-within" and "power-over." Marilyn French, in *Beyond Power*, a recent and scholarly discussion, calls the life-affirming form "power-to" (accomplish, generate, create) and the oppressive form "power-over."
26. Sam Keen, *Faces of the Enemy: Reflections of the Hostile Imagination* (New York: Harper and Row, 1986).
27. Sam Keen, *The Passionate Life: Stages of Loving* (New York: Harper and Row, 1983).
28. John Mack, interview with author.
29. Mark Gerzon, *A Choice of Heroes: The Changing Faces of American Manhood* (Boston: Houghton Mifflin, 1982), p. 262.
30. Lawrence Kohlberg, "Development of Moral Character and Moral Ideology," in M. L. and L. W. Hoffman (eds.), *Review of Child Development Research* (New York: Russell Sage Foundation, 1964).
31. Bertrand Russell, *The Autobiography of Bertrand Russell*, Vol. 2, *The Middle Years, 1914–1944* (New York: Bantam, 1969), p. 121.
32. Nel Noddings, *Caring: A Feminine Approach to Ethics and Moral Education*, (Berkeley:

University of California Press, 1984). Two other versions of this discussion are found in Carol Gilligan, *In a Different Voice: Psychological Theory and Women's Development* (Cambridge: Harvard University Press, 1982) and Jean Baker Miller, *Toward a New Psychology of Women* (Boston: Beacon Press, 1976).

33. Erik Erikson, *Young Man Luther* (New York: Norton, 1958), p. 7.

Waging Peace

1. George Leonard, *The Transformation: A Guide to the Inevitable Changes in Humankind* (New York: Delacorte, 1972).

2. For discussion of the trend toward "privatization," see Peter Dale Scott, Jonathan Marshall, and Jane Hunter, *The Iran-Contra Connection: Secret Teams and Covert Operations in the Reagan Era* (Boston: South End Press, 1987), pp. 7–18. On the growth of the "black" budget, see Jeffrey Richelson, " 'Invisible' Air Force Eludes Taxpayer: Big Budget, No Oversight for Stealth Warplane," *Boston Globe,* 27 March 1988, p. A27.

3. Adrienne Rich, "Women and Honor: Some Notes on Lying," in *On Lies, Secrets and Silence* (New York: Norton, 1979), p. 186.

4. Colonel James A. Donovan, *Militarism U.S.A.* (New York: Scribner's, 1970). Foreword by General David Shoup.

5. Robert Reich, *Tales of a New America* (New York: Times Books, 1987).

6. Thich Nhat Hanh, *Being Peace* (Berkeley, CA: Parallax Press, 1987), p. 79.

7. Robert Bellah, Richard Madsen, William M. Sullivan, Ann Swidler, and Steven M. Tipton, *Habits of the Heart: Individualism and Commitment in American Life* (Berkeley: University of California Press, 1985), pp. 200–203.

8. Carl Rogers, *On Personal Power: Inner Strength and Its Revolutionary Impact* (New York: Delacorte, 1977), p. 250.

9. Danny Duncan Collum, "New Thinking for the Peace Movement," *Sojourners,* March 1988, pp. 5–6.

10. *Utne Reader,* March/April 1988.

11. Robert Jay Lifton, "Art and the Imagery of Extinction," in *The Future of Immortality: Essays for a Nuclear Age* (New York: Basic Books), p. 259.

12. Willard Waller, *The Veteran Comes Back* (New York: Dryden Press, 1944), p. 5.

13. Don Aucoin, "Fonda Furor," *Boston Globe,* 3 February 1988, p. 2.

14. Vicki Kemper, "The Power Within," *Sojourners,* April 1988, pp. 24–29.

15. Steve Nadis, "After the Boycott," *Science for the People,* January/February 1988.

16. Vera Kistiakowsky, interview with author.

17. Anne C. Roark, "Military Influence Stirs Campus Debate: 'Star Wars' Politicizing Science in U.S.," *Los Angeles Times,* 13 April 1987.

18. Greg LeRoy, "War U: High-Tech Battlegrounds on Campus," *Science for the People,* January/February 1988, p. 11.

19. Edward Markey, "Markey releases analysis of Reagan Energy Budget," press release from office of Representative Edward J. Markey, 12 January 1987.

20. Mark Zieman, "Growing Militarization of the Space Program Worries U.S. Scientists," *Wall St. Journal,* 15 January 1986, p. 1.

21. I. F. Stone, "Star Wars Block," *Nation,* 7 November 1987.

22. Gary Marchant, "Scapegoating the Scientist," *Science for the People,* January/February 1988, p. 39.

23. Gary Marchant, "Political Constraints: Military Funding and Academic Freedom," *Science for the People,* pp. 27–33.

RESOURCES FOR
EDUCATION AND ACTION

Association for Responsible Dissent (ARDIS), PO Box 1030, Elgin, TX 78621, (512) 285-5190 (membership); 422 Arkansas Avenue, Herndon, VA 22070, (703) 437-8487 (research and reference). Organization led by former members of the US national security apparatus, opposing covert operations as a basis of foreign policy.

Bulletin of Atomic Scientists, 5801 S. Kenwood Avenue, Chicago, IL 60637, (312) 363-5225. Magazine of debate and analysis on paths and obstacles to disarmament.

Business Executives for National Security, 21 DuPont Circle, Suite 401, Washington, DC 20009, (202) 429-0600. Nonpartisan group open to active or retired business people, addressing cost-effective defense and creative approaches to peace keeping.

Center for Defense Information, 1500 Massachusetts Avenue NW, Washington, DC 20005, (202) 862-0700. Research and advocacy organization of retired military officers advocating a strong defense without nuclear weapons. Publishes high-quality newsletter, *Defense Monitor*.

Center for Economic Conversion, 222-C View Street, Mountain View, CA 94041, (415) 968-8798. Clearinghouse for research and support for local projects on conversion of industries from military to peacetime applications.

Center for Innovative Diplomacy, 17931 Sky Park Circle-F, Irvine, CA 92714, (714) 250-1296. Resource center for citizen initiatives and creative conflict resolution.

Christic Institute, 1324 North Capitol Street, Washington, DC 20002, (202) 797-8106. Nonprofit interfaith center on law and public policy, currently spearheading the major civil suit against alleged principals in the contra arms-supply network.

Committee in Solidarity with the People of El Salvador (CISPES), 930 F Street NW, Room 720, Washington, DC 20004, (202) 265-0890.

Coalition for a New Foreign and Military Policy, 712 G Street SE, Washington, DC 20003, (202) 546-8400. National lobbying organization which coordinates and provides resources for local efforts against intervention and for nuclear disarmament.

Computer Professionals for Social Responsibility, PO Box 717, Palo Alto, CA 94301, (415) 322-3778. Education on costs and benefits of work in the military sector, support for professionals seeking civilian employment, lobbying for arms control.

Defense Executives for Human Success, c/o Les Arnold, Arnold Magnetics, 4000 Via Pescador, Camarillo, CA 93010, (805) 484-4221. Works for peace through education, citizen diplomacy, and efforts toward realistic economic conversion.

Federation of American Scientists, 307 Massachusetts Avenue NE, Washington, DC 20002, (202) 546-3300. Longstanding organization of scientists supporting arms control and safe energy.

Giraffe Project, Box 759, Langley, Whidbey Island, WA 98260, (800) 344-TALL. Encourages and honors those who stick their necks out for the common good.

Government Accountability Project, 1555 Connecticut Avenue NW, Washington, DC 20036, (202) 232-8550. Advises potential whistleblowers on practical and ethical concerns.

Guatemala News and Information Bureau, PO Box 28594, Oakland, CA 94604, (415) 835-0810.

High Technology Professionals for Peace, 637 Massachusetts Avenue, Room 316, Cambridge, MA 02139, (617) 497-0605. National group for education, lobbying, and support for members seeking nonmilitary work.

Honduras Information Center, 1 Summer Street, Somerville, MA 02143, (617) 625-7220.

Interhelp, PO Box 8895, Madison, WI 53708, (608) 321-1219. International network encouraging people to experience and share their deepest responses to the dangers of nuclear holocaust, environmental deterioration, and human oppression, in order to move beyond powerlessness into constructive action.

Jobs with Peace, 76 Summer Street, Boston, MA 02110, (617) 338-5783. Ongoing campaign for economic revitalization through decreased military spending and greater commitment to human needs.

National Action and Research on the Military-Industrial Complex (NARMIC), 1501 Cherry Street, Philadelphia, PA 19102, (215) 241-7175. Research center and clearinghouse of the American Friends Service Committee.

National Association of Atomic Veterans, PO Box 707, 707 S. Aurora, Eldon, MO 65026, (314) 392-3361. Education, advocacy, and support network.

National Interreligious Service Board for Conscientious Objection (NISBCO), 800 18th Street NW, Suite 600, Washington, DC 20006, (202) 293-5962. Maintains information on selective service regulations and draft counseling resources.

National Network in Solidarity with the Nicaraguan People, 2025 I Street NW, No. 1117, Washington, DC 20006.

Neighbor to Neighbor, 2940 16th Street, Suite 2000, San Francisco, CA 94103, (415) 648-6230. National education and lobbying organization concerned with the US military presence in Central America and the role of our foreign policy in Third World development crises.

Nerve Center, 1917 E. 29th Street, Oakland, CA 94606, (415) 534-6904. Education and lobbying on chemical and biological weapons.

Nuclear Dialogue Project, 106 FitzRandolph Road, Princeton, NJ 08540, (609) 924-1015. Creates and trains citizen groups who "adopt" a policy maker for dialogue and mutual education.

Nuclear Free America, 325 E. 25th Street, Baltimore, MD 21218, (301) 235-3575. Clearinghouse and educational effort supporting local initiatives to establish nuclear-free zones.

Pax Christi Center on Conscience and War, PO Box 726, Cambridge, MA 02139, (617) 354-4354. Historical and political resource center on conscientious objection and the ethical questions posed by war.

Peacework Alternatives, 3940 Poplar Level Road, Louisville, KY 40213, (502) 451-8537. Interfaith project providing education and support on the ethical struggles of armaments workers.

Search for Common Ground, 1701 K Street NW, Suite 403, Washington, DC 20006, (202) 835-0777. Advocacy and training for mediation, citizen diplomacy, and creative conflict resolution.

TECNICA, 3254 Adeline Street, Berkeley, CA, (415) 655-3838. Network of scientists, engineers, economists, and computer professionals who support and organize development projects in Nicaragua.

Union of Concerned Scientists, 26 Church Street, Cambridge, MA 02238, (617) 547-5552. Education and lobbying organization of professionals concerned with arms control and safe energy.

Veterans for Peace, PO Box 3881, Portland, ME 04104, (207) 797-2770. Public education, lobbying, demonstrations, and citizen diplomacy in support of nuclear disarmament and anti-intervention work.

Witness for Peace, PO Box 567, Durham, NC 27702, (919) 688-5055. Interfaith organization which maintains a permanent presence of religious North Americans in the war zones of Central America, by recruiting and training short- and long-term delegations.

It is a rare thing for US citizens to ask, to really ask, how we might best serve our professed beliefs in democracy, freedom, and peace. This is not so surprising. Every day of our lives, we hear that the only road to peace is through preparation for war. Every day, we learn that freedom has more to do with what we can buy than how we might live. Every day, we see that democracy means staged elections rather than the power to set policy. We are offered an awfully narrow mold for our thoughts.

Perhaps more importantly, or at least more powerfully, many of us live quite comfortably. There are problems and stresses, to be sure, and many of us are not entirely satisfied, but we do eat well and we can afford to worry about which model car, what sort of boom box, or which new shoes we might buy. It is easy to settle deep into such outwardly comfortable lives, not wanting to move, not wanting to risk discomfort.

The men interviewed in *Breaking Ranks* have made the seemingly strange choice to slip out of their comfortable, socially approved lives, to take on the uncomfortable, often frightening, but tremendously stimulating task of sorting out just how they might best serve the values they profess. Each has concluded that the work they knew in the military, the intelligence or foreign policy community, or the weapons industry (at least in their current guises) does *not* effectively promote democracy, freedom, or peace, either at home or abroad.

Their dissent is all the more amazing and inspiring because it grows from their experience in some of the most comfortable and controlled segments of our society. Similarly, their insider credentials make their critiques all the more compelling and complex.

Yet as I read and reread the stories in *Breaking Ranks,* what struck me most was not so much these men's courage and heroism—though their journeys are truly inspiring—but their *familiarity.* The more I edit books like this one, the more people I learn about or meet who are asking similar questions and embarking on similarly impressive and even revolutionary journeys. The possibilities of dissent, of asking uncomfortable questions—*and of creating new, more peaceful, just, and democratic ways of thinking and acting*—are remarkably widespread and vibrant.

We here at New Society Publishers are proud to bring you *Breaking Ranks* because it shares some of the more dramatic stories of people taking responsibility for their lives, for our lives, in this troubled world. But it is knowing how many more similar stories you could tell us that gives us hope that the hard work of social transformation is happening.

T.L. Hill
New Society Publishers